Mythology & Belief
A Humanities Reader

CANDACE P. COOPER
Collin College

Ruby Tree Publishing
Dallas, Texas

Copyright © 2014 by Ruby Tree Publishing

All rights reserved. No part of this publication may reproduced in any form whatsoever, by photograph xerography or by any other means , by broadcast or transmission, by translation into any kind of language, nor my recording electronically or otherwise, without written permission from the publisher, except by a reviewer who may quote brief passages in critical articles or reviews.

Ruby Tree Publishing
PO BOX 50051
Dallas, TX 75250
www.rubytreepublishing.com

Printed in the United States of America

ISBN 978-0-692-30830-1

Table of Contents

PREFACE

Mythology & Belief explores ideas, stories and speeches that have been discussed and even debated for decades in American culture. Although the list of stories and speeches included in this book are not exhaustive, many of those represented in *Mythology & Belief* are staples in the historic conversation of social responsibility and social justice in the eyes of Americans.

The culmination of some of the ancient ideas, particularly in Christianity, have set the course for American law not only in the United States, but in many parts of the western world, and more recently, the world at large. There have been many wars fought based upon the ideas of freedom and democracy, and there have been many personal and global relationships shattered over the role of religion, politics and gender. Dismantling the dogma of religious righteousness and opening the minds of new scholars to original ideas regarding social thought, allows students of higher learning to become more critical in their thinking and assessment of human issues.

Students are likely to find that their world and point of view is similar to their fellow human, who may fundamentally disagree with their belief system. Nevertheless, as students venture further into a pluralistic society beyond the confines of their homes and families to engage a diverse world, they will be well served to find common ground in what they consider foreign. This text starts the journey toward critical thinking and common ground.

Mythology and Belief

Introduction

How to Use This Book

Study Skills

HOW THIS BOOK WORKS

Each section of Mythology & Belief requires student engagement. It is intended to be read with a pen and highlighter, so that students not only read for general meaning, but they also read deeply for understanding. Each text offers subheadings so that students may practice and execute the SQ3R method throughout.

- The margins are also optimized for note taking and implementation of the SQ3R method.

- KWL charts are used in place of chapter introductions to allow students assess their own prior knowledge and provide them with an impetus to research and explore a topic on their own.

- Students write their own introduction to the chapter based upon the KWL chart after researching and reading the selection(s).

- Vocabulary words are bolded to draw student attention during the SQ3R process.

- Short answer questions and essay topics follow many of the readings so that students can critically engage the ideas represented in the narratives, sacred writings and speeches.

- All chapters provide space for the SQ3R notes at the end of each section.

SQ3R

SQ3R is common method used by college students to study for exams.

Survey – The first step is to survey, or scan, the information in the chapter.

- The chapter's title, major headings and subheadings will provide clues needed help you have a clear idea of what is in the chapter and what you will need to know in the end.

- Bolded or italicized vocabulary terms will also help you develop a strong idea of the terms and definitions affiliated with the chapter. The charts, graphs and pictures, may also provide clues about the chapter.

- Considering the information included in the chapter preview, located at the beginning of the chapter, and chapter review at the end of the chapter, will also be helpful in assessing what is included in the chapter.

Question – Next, ask questions about the title, major headings, subheadings, vocabulary terms, charts, graphs and pictures.

- Starting with the basic journalist's questions, who, what, when, where why or how, will help you ask meaning question.

- The answer to the questions will shape your understanding of each of the subsections. Make sure you ask a question you truly want a response to. If you find after reading the text your question has not been answered, then ask another question.

Read – Then, read one section at time to find the answer to your questions. By reading one section at time you will understand and retain information more effectively.

- Be sure to annotate the text by making notes in the margins to help you remember what you read.

- If you find the answer to your question stated explicitly, underline it. If you do not see the answer to your question, ask another question and start the reading process again.

Recite – After reading, write the answer to your question in addition to anything else you learned in the section.

- Use your own words to recite what you learned. *Do not write down the words used in the textbook verbatim.* You only know that you've learned when you are able to explain things in your own words.

- Include information from charts, pictures and vocabulary in the summary.

Review – Finally, review the notes you have taken for each section in the chapter and prepare for your exam.

- Study your notes to see if you can explain the chapter preview and review to a friend or study partner.

- Write a summary of everything you can remember from the chapter. This should be a free writing exercise to test what you have learned so far. Compare the summary to your notes or the chapter review to see if you need to review a section again. Wait at least an hour, then, write the summary again. Continue this process until you feel confident you know the information in the chapter.

You will find SQ3R Analysis forms for each of the selections in the Addendum in the back of the book.

Creating a Summary from Outlining

Outlining a chapter, or a single reading selection, is another valuable study skill. Similar to the SQ3R method, Outlining is most effective when it done one section at a time.

To outline a chapter complete the following steps:

- First identify the main idea of the reading selection or chapter.

- Next, find the main idea of subheadings if there are subheadings.

- Afterwards, identify the major details. They are usually the main ideas of the body paragraphs.

- After writing the major details, then write the minor details.

- Write your notes in paragraph form to create a summary from the information gathered in the outlining process

KWL – Assessing and Accessing Knowledge

K - What I Know
At the beginning of each major section for each chapter, you will have the opportunity to assess your prior **knowledge** topic by writing what you already know about the subject for that section.

W - What I Want to Know
After assessing your prior knowledge to determine what you already know, you will then write questions so that you can ascertain **what you want to know** about the chapter topic.

L – What I Learned
Finally, after assessing your prior knowledge and exploring questions about the subject, you will then begin the process of answering the questions posed in the "W" section. This is also where you can write information you **learn** from your personal research, class discussions and group discussions.

CREATION MYTHS

Beginnings of our World

Chapter 1

Creation Myths

Reading Narratives

Narratives are created based upon creative ideas or real events. Creative texts, based on fantasy, or imagined ideas, are called fiction. Stories based upon real life, or true events, are called nonfiction. A more recent genre of fiction blends both fact and fiction to produce realistic fiction. When it comes to ancient texts, it is sometimes difficult to determine facts because no one from antiquity is still alive to validate the truth of what was said or written.

Oral histories are those that have been passed down through several generations. In West African culture, the griot is a tribal historian and is considered one of the most powerful people in the tribe. The griot's position is important because he is the keeper of the literature and the tribal history. There are novel length stories passed down from the griot to the people of the tribe. Then, in time, another griot will be born and trained, and then they will be the keeper of the stories. One of the most notable texts in West African oral tradition and literature is the Epic of Sundiata which began orally in the 13th century AD. This Malian epic is the story of a king, the famous founder of the Mali Empire, and his adventure to capture his prophesied crown. This story was passed down to the people of Mali through griots, and it was eventually recorded in written form.

Like the Sundiata, the Epic of Gilgamesh is a narrative where Gilgamesh, the mythical King of Uruk, is on a quest, but in contrast to the Sundiata, Gilgamesh is a demigod, where he is part God and part man. The ancient Sumerians recorded his story in written form on stone tablets, and it is available to us today in many forms. The Epic of Gilgamesh includes fantastic adventures and interesting creatures such as talking trees and animals, in addition to gods and goddesses. In many ways it is similar to Greek mythology in its structure.

It is additive in substance, because oral literature tends to build in structure by adding new events. This is often called parataxis, where the author builds up idea after idea with and between them. It is also agnostic because warfare and boasting are at the heart of

Gilgamesh's experience and in the agnostic combative tradition, oral literature tends to be performed in a more combative style. Oral performers are contestants, so they must compete for their audiences.

Greek mythology and many religious stories are also a manifestation of the oral tradition. In Greek mythology, through the transmission of Homer's epics, which were written around 8 B.C., serve not only as a mark of Hellenistic heroism, but also as an agent of understanding for people who wanted make sense of life in the ancient world. There are gods and goddesses who have human forms and even human emotions and personalities. They interact with humans and even involve themselves in their daily lives. We see this in the creation stories affiliated with Prometheus though his interactions with Jupiter.

Unlike Greek mythology, the Torah, or the Hebrew Bible, does not accept man made images of God. Therefore, in the creationist story of Noah's Ark, for instance, God is heard but not seen. Unlike In the Epic of Gilgamesh and "Prometheus", there is no council of gods to determine how mankind should carryout their tasks. Instead, in the Jewish or Hebraic faith there is one triune God who is omniscient, omnipotent, and omnipresent.

In this chapter, you will explore varying mythical and religious accounts of what happened to the world when it was destroyed by water.

As you read, compare and contrast the creation narratives and their structures.
- Determine how the main characters' personalities and impact their decisions.
- Discover how the protagonists respond to instructions from their deities and the moral lessons learn.
- Identify the structure of the narratives to be able to assess them critically.

    Regarding structure, ask yourself:
    - Where is the setting?
    - Who are the main characters?
    - Does it follow a plot structure where everything takes place in one location or do the scenes move forward into several locations?
    - Does the story have a climax and unfolding events that lead to a resolution?

These are the questions to explore as you read the next chapter.

INSTRUCTIONS

1. Complete the KWL chart to see what information you already know about the stories you are about to read.

2. After completing the KWL chart, and conducting research about the story you about to read, write an introduction to introduce this text.

3. At the end of each section, you will complete an SQ3R exercise to study the texts in this chapter.

C H A R T

KNOW • WANT • LEARN

KWL

ALREADY KNOW	WANT TO KNOW	WHAT I LEARNED

The Epic of Gilgamesh

Prologue

Gilgamesh King in Uruk

I will proclaim to the world the deeds of Gilgamesh. This was the man to whom all things were known; this was the king who knew the countries of the world. He was wise, he saw mysteries and knew secret things, he brought us a tale of the days before the flood. He went on a long journey, was weary, worn-out with labor, returning he rested, he engraved on a stone the whole story.

When the gods created Gilgamesh they gave him a perfect body. Shamash the glorious sun endowed him with beauty, Adad the god of the storm endowed him with courage, the great gods made his beauty perfect, surpassing all others, terrifying like a great wild bull. Two thirds they made him god and one third man.

In Uruk he built walls, a great rampart, and the temple of blessed Eanna for the god of the firmament Anu, and for Ishtar the goddess of love. Look at it still today: the outer wall where the cornice runs, it shines with the brilliance of copper; and the inner wall, it has no equal. Touch the threshold, it is ancient. Approach Eanna the dwelling of Ishtar, our lady of love and war, the like of which no latter-day king, no man alive can equal. Climb upon the wall of Uruk; walk along it, I say; regard the foundation terrace and examine the. masonry: is it not burnt brick and good? The seven sages laid the foundations

1

The Coming of Enkidu

Description of Gilgamesh

GILGAMESH went abroad in the world, but he met with none who could withstand his arms till be came to Uruk. But the men of Uruk muttered in their houses, 'Gilgamesh sounds the tocsin for his amusement, his arrogance has no bounds by day or night. No son is left with his father, for Gilgamesh takes them all, even the children; yet the king should be a shepherd to his people. His lust leaves no virgin to her lover, neither the warrior's daughter nor the wife of the noble; yet this is the shepherd of the city, wise, comely, and resolute.'

The gods heard their lament, the gods of heaven cried to the Lord of Uruk, to Anu the god of Uruk: 'A goddess made him, strong as a savage bull, none can withstand his arms. No son is left with his father, for Gilgamesh takes them all; and is this the king, the shepherd of his people? His lust leaves no virgin to her lover, neither the warrior's daughter nor the wife of the noble. When Anu had heard their lamentation the gods cried to Aruru, the goddess of creation, 'You made him, O Aruru; now create his equal; let it be as like him as his own reflection, his second self; stormy heart for stormy heart. Let them contend together and leave Uruk in quiet.'

Description of Enkidu

So the goddess conceived an image in her mind, and it was of the stuff of Anu of the firmament. She dipped her hands in water and pinched off clay, she let it fall in the wilderness, and noble Enkidu was created. There was virtue in him of the god of war, of Ninurta himself. His body was rough, he had long hair like a woman's; it waved like the hair of Nisaba, the goddess of corn. His body was covered with matted hair like Samugan's, the god of cattle. He was innocent of mankind; he knew nothing of the cultivated land.

Enkidu ate grass in the hills with the gazelle and lurked with wild beasts at the water-holes; he had joy of the water with the herds of wild game. But there was a trapper who met him one day face to face at the drinking-hole, for the wild game had entered his territory. On three days he met him face to face, and the trapper was frozen with fear. He went back to his house with the game that he had caught, and he was dumb, benumbed with terror. His face was altered like that of one who has made a long journey. With awe in his heart he spoke to his father:

The Trappers Lament

'Father, there is a man, unlike any other, who comes down from the hills. He is the strongest in the world. he is like an **immortal** from heaven. He ranges over the hills with wild beasts and eats grass; the ranges through your land and comes down to the wells. I am afraid and dare not go near him. He fills in the pits which I dig and tears up-my traps set for the game; he helps the beasts to escape and now they slip through my fingers.'

His father opened his mouth and said to the trapper, 'My son, in Uruk lives Gilgamesh; no one has ever prevailed against him, he is strong as a star from heaven. Go to Uruk, find Gilgamesh, extol the strength of this wild man. Ask him to give you a harlot, a wanton from the temple of love; return with her, and let her woman's power overpower this man. When next he comes down to drink at the wells she will be there, stripped naked; and when he sees her beckoning he will embrace her, and then the wild beasts will reject him.' So the trapper set out on his journey to Uruk and addressed himself to Gilgamesh saying, 'A man unlike any other is roaming now in the pastures; he is as strong as a star from heaven and I am afraid to approach him. He helps the wild game to escape; he fills in my pits and pulls up my traps.' Gilgamesh said, 'Trapper, go back, take with you a **harlot**, a child of pleasure. At the drinking hole she will strip, and when, he sees her **beckoning** he will embrace her and the game of the wilderness will. surely reject him.'

Now the trapper returned, taking the harlot with him. After a three days' journey they came to the drinking hole, and there they sat down; the harlot and the trapper sat facing one another and waited for the game to come. For the first day and for the second day the two sat waiting, but on the third day the herds came; they came down to drink and Enkidu was with them. The small wild creatures of the plains were glad of the water, and Enkidu with them, who ate grass with the gazelle and was born in the hills; and she saw him, the savage man, come from far-off in the hills. The trapper spoke toher: 'There he is. Now, woman, make your breasts bare, have no shame, do not delay but welcome his love. Let him see you naked, let him possess your body. When he comes near uncover yourself and lie with him; teach him, the savage man, your woman's art, for when he murmurs love to you the wild' beasts that shared his life in the hills will reject him.'

Enkidu's Lust

She was not ashamed to take him, she made herself naked and welcomed his eagerness; as he lay on her murmuring love she taught him the woman's art. For six days and seven nights they lay together, for Enkidu had forgotten his home in the hills; but when he was satisfied he went back to the wild beasts. Then, when the gazelle saw him, they bolted away; when the wild creatures saw him they fled. Enkidu would have followed, but his body was bound as though with a cord, his knees gave way when he started to run, his swiftness was gone. And now the wild creatures had all fled away;

Enkidu was grown weak, for wisdom was in him, and the thoughts of a man were in his heart. So he returned and sat down at the woman's feet, and listened intently to what she said. 'You are wise, Enkidu, and now you have become like a god. Why do you want to run wild with the beasts in the hills? Come with me. I will take you to strong-walled Uruk, to the blessed temple of Ishtar and of Anu, of love and of heaven there Gilgamesh lives, who is very strong, and like a wild bull he lords it over men.'

When she had spoken Enkidu was pleased; he longed for a comrade, for one who would understand his heart. 'Come, woman, and take me to that holy temple, to the house of Anu and of Ishtar, and to the place where Gilgamesh lords it over the people. I will challenge him boldly, I will cry out aloud in Uruk, "I am the strongest here, I have come to change the old order, I am he who was born in the hills, I am he who is strongest of all."'

She said, 'Let us go, and let him see your face. I know very well where Gilgamesh is in great Uruk. O Enkidu, there all the people are dressed in their gorgeous robes, every day is holiday, the young men and the girls are wonderful to see. How sweet they smell! All the great ones are roused from their beds. O Enkidu, you who love life, I will show you Gilgamesh, a man of many moods; you shall look at him well in his radiant manhood. His body is perfect in strength and maturity; he never rests by night or day. He is stronger than you, so leave your boasting. Shamash the glorious sun has given favors to Gilgamesh, and Anu of the heavens, and Enlil, and Ea the wise has given him deep understanding. f tell you, even before you have left the wilderness, Gilgamesh will know in his dreams that you are coming.'

Gilgamesh's Dream

Now Gilgamesh got up to tell his dream to his mother; Ninsun, one of the wise gods. 'Mother, last night I had a dream. I was full of joy, the young heroes were round me and I walked through the night under the stars of the **firmament**, and one, a meteor of the stuff of Anu, fell down from heaven. I tried to lift it but it proved too heavy. All the people of Uruk came round to see it, the common people jostled and the nobles thronged to kiss its feet; and to me its attraction was like the love of woman. They helped me, I braced my forehead and I raised it with thongs and brought it to you, and you yourself pronounced it my brother.'

Then Ninsun, who is well-beloved and wise, said to Gilgamesh, 'This star of heaven which descended like a **meteor** from the sky; which you tried to lift,- but found too heavy, when you tried to move it it would not budge, and so you brought it to my feet; I made it for you, a goad and spur, and you were drawn as though to a woman. This is the strong comrade, the one who brings help to his friend in his need. He is the strongest of wild creatures, the stuff of Anu; born in the grass-lands and the wild hills reared him; when you see him you will be glad; you will love him as a woman and he will never forsake you. This is the meaning of the dream.'

Gilgamesh said, 'Mother, I dreamed a second dream. In the streets of strong-walled Uruk there lay an axe; the shape of it was strange and the people thronged round. I saw it and was glad. I bent down, deeply drawn towards it; I loved it like a woman and wore it at my side.' Ninsun answered, 'That axe, which you saw, which drew you so powerfully like love of a woman, that is the comrade whom I give you, and he will come in his strength like one of the host of heaven. He is the brave companion who rescues his friend in necessity.' Gilgamesh said to his mother, 'A friend, a counselor has come to me from Enlil, and now I shall befriend and counsel him.' So Gilgamesh told his dreams; and the harlot retold them to Enkidu.

Enkindu's Transformation

And now she said to Enkidu, 'When I look at you you have become like a god. Why do you yearn to run with the beasts in the hills? Get up from the ground, the bed of a shepherd.' He listened to her words with care. It was good advice that she gave. She divided her clothing in two and with the one half she clothed him and with the other herself, and holding his hand she led him like a child to the sheepfolds, into the shepherds' tents. There all the shepherds crowded round to see him, they put down bread in front of him, but Enkidu could only suck the milk of wild animals. He fumbled and gaped, at a loss what to do or how he should eat the bread and drink the strong wine. Then the woman said, 'Enkidu, eat bread, it is the staff of life; drink the wine, it is the custom of the land.' So he ate till he was full and drank strong wine, seven goblets. He became merry, his heart exulted and his face shone. He rubbed down the matted hair of his body and anointed himself with oil. Enkidu had become a man; but when he had put on man's clothing he appeared like a bridegroom. He took arms to hunt the lion so that the shepherds could rest at night. He caught wolves and lions and the herdsmen lay down in peace; for Enkidu was their watchman, that strong man who had no rival.

He was merry living with the shepherds, till one day lifting his eyes he saw a man approaching. He said to the harlot, 'Woman, fetch that man here. Why has he come? I wish to know his name.' She went and called the man saying, 'Sir, where are you going on this weary journey?' The man answered, saying to Enkidu, 'Gilgamesh has gone into the marriage-house and shut out the people. He does strange things in Uruk, the city of great streets. At the roll of the drum work begins for the men, and work for the women. Gilgamesh the king is about to celebrate marriage with the Queen of Love, and he still demands to be first with the bride, the king to be first and the husband to follow, for that was ordained by the gods from his birth, from the time the umbilical cord was cut. But now the drums roll for the choice of the bride and the city groans.' At these words Enkidu turned white in the face. 'I will go to the place where Gilgamesh lords it over the people, I will challenge him boldly, and I will cry aloud in Uruk, "I have come to change the old order, for I am the strongest here."

Now Enkidu strode in front and the woman followed behind. He entered Uruk, that great market, and all the folk thronged round him where he stood in the street in strong-walled Uruk. The people jostled; speaking of him they said, 'He is the spit of Gilgamesh. 'He is shorter.' 'He is bigger of bone.' This is the one who was reared on the milk of wild beasts. His is the greatest strength.' The men rejoiced: 'Now Gilgamesh has met his match. This great one, this hero whose beauty is like a god, he is a match even for Gilgamesh.'

In Uruk the bridal bed was made, fit for the goddess of love. The bride waited for the bridegroom, but in the night Gilgamesh got up and came to the house. Then Enkidu stepped out, he stood in the street and blocked the way. Mighty Gilgamesh came on and Enkidu met him at the gate. He put out his foot and prevented Gilgamesh from entering the house, so they grappled, holding each other like bulls. They broke the doorposts and the walls shook, they snorted like bulls locked together. They shattered the doorposts and the walls shook. Gilgamesh bent his knee with his foot planted on the ground and with a turn Enkidu was thrown. Then immediately his fury died. When Enkidu was thrown he said to Gilgamesh, 'There is not another like you in the world. Ninsun, who is as strong as a wild ox in the byre, she was the mother who bore you, and now you are raised above all men, and Enlil has given you the kingship, for your strength surpasses the strength of men.' So Enkidu and Gilgamesh embraced and their friendship was sealed.

Complete the SQ3R Analysis. See Appendix.

Short Answer Questions – Gilgamesh - Prologue and Chapter 1

1. According to the prologue, who is Gilgamesh?

2. Where is the setting for this narrative?

3. Who are the main characters?

4. How does Gilgamesh become involved with Enkindu?

5. How does the trapper "trap" Enkindu"?

6. What is the definition of a harlot?

7. Describe how lust plays a key role in Enkindu's pathway to Gilgamesh?

2

The Forest Journey

ENLIL of the mountain, the father of the gods, had decreed the destiny of Gilgamesh. So Gilgamesh dreamed and Enkidu said, 'The meaning of the dream is this. The father of the gods has given you kingship, such is your destiny, everlasting life is not your destiny. Because of this do not be sad at heart, do not be grieved or oppressed. He has given you power to bind and to loose, to be the darkness and the light of mankind. He has given you unexampled supremacy over the people, victory in battle from which no fugitive returns, in forays and assaults from which there is no going back. But do not abuse this power, deal justly with your servants in the palace, deal justly before Shamash.'

The eyes of Enkidu were full of tears and his heart was sick. He sighed bitterly and Gilgamesh met his eye and said,' My friend, why do you sigh so bitterly? But Enkidu opened his mouth and said, 'I am weak, my arms have lost their strength, the cry of sorrow sticks in my throat, I am oppressed by idleness.' It was then that the lord Gilgamesh turned his thoughts to the Country of the Living; on the Land of Cedars the lord Gilgamesh reflected. He said to his servant Enkidu, 'I have not established my name stamped on bricks as my destiny decreed; therefore I will go to the country where the cedar is felled. I will set up my name in the place where the names of famous men are written, and where- no man's name is written yet I will wise a monument to the gods. Because o£ the evil that is in the land, we will go to the forest and destroy the evil; for in the forest lives Humbaba whose name is "Hugeness", a ferocious giant. But Enkidu sighed bitterly and said, 'When I went with the wild beasts ranging through the wilderness I discovered the forest; its length is ten thousand leagues in every direction. Enlil has appointed Humbaba to guard it and armed him iii sevenfold terrors, terrible to all flesh is Humbaba. When he roars it is like the torrent of the storm, his breath is like fire, and his jaws are death itself. He guards the cedars so well that when the wild heifer stirs in the forest, though she is sixty leagues distant, he hears her. What man would willingly walk into that country and explore its depths? I tell you, weakness overpowers whoever goes near it: it is not an equal struggle when one fights with Humbaba; he is a great warrior, a battering-ram. Gilgamesh, the watchman of the forest never sleeps.'

Gilgamesh replied: 'Where is the man who can clamber to heaven? Only the gods live forever with glorious Shamash, but as for us men, our days are numbered, our occupations are a breath of wind. How is this, already you are afraid! I will go first although I am your lord, an4.youmay safely call out, "Forward, there is nothing to fear!" Then if I fall I leave behind me a name that endures; men - will say of me, "Gilgamesh has fallen in fight with ferocious Humbaba." Long after the child has been bony in my house, they will say it, and remember.' Enkidu spoke again to Gilgamesh, 'O my lord, if you will enter that country, go first to the hero Shamash, tell the Sun God, for the land is his. The country where the cedar is cut belongs to Shamash.'

Gilgamesh and Shamash

Gilgamesh took up a kid, white without spot, and a brown one with it; he held them

Notes

against his breast, and he carried them into the presence of the sun. He took in his hand his silver sceptre and he said to glorious Shamash, 'I am going to that country, O Shamash, I am going; my hands supplicate, so let it be well with my soul and bring me back to The Epic Of Gilgamesh the quay of Uruk. Grant, I beseech, your protection, and let the omen be good.' Glorious Shamash answered, 'Gilgamesh, you are strong, but what is the Country of the Living to you?

'O Shamash, hear me, hear me, Shamash, let my voice be heard. Here in the city man dies oppressed at heart, man perishes with despair in his heart. I have looked over the wall and I see the bodies floating on the river, and that will be my lot also. Indeed I know it is so, for whoever is tallest among men cannot reach the heavens, and the greatest cannot encompass the earth. Therefore I would enter that country: because I have not established my name stamped on brick as my destiny decreed, I will go to the country where the cedar is cut. I will set up my name where the names of famous men are written; and where no man's name is written I will raise a monument to the gods.' The tears, ran down his face and he said, 'Alas, it is a lo ng journey that I must take to the Land of Humbaba. If this enterprise is not to be accomplished, why did you move me, Shamash, with the restless desire to perform it? How can I succeed if you w ill not succor me? If I die in that country I will die without rancour, but if I return I will make a glorious offering of gifts and of praise to Shamash.'

So Shamash accepted the sacrifice of his tears; like the compassionate man he showed him mercy. He appointed strong allies for Gilgamesh, sons of one mother, and stationed them in the mountain caves. The great winds he appointed: the north wind, the whirlwind, the stone and the icy wind, the tempest and the scorching wind. Like ' vipers, like dragons, like a scorching fire, like a serpent that freezes the heart, a destroying flood and the lightning's fork, such were they and
Gilgamesh rejoiced. He went to the forge and said, ..'I will give orders to the armourers; they shall cast us our weapons while we watch them.' So they gave orders to the armourers and the craftsmen sat down in conference. They went into the groves of the plain and cut willow and box-wood; they cast for them axes of nine score pounds, and great swords they cast with blades of six score pounds each one, with pommels and hilts of thirty pounds. They cast for Gilgamesh the axe 'Might of Heroes' and the bow of Anshan; and Gilgamesh was armed and Enkidu; and the weight of the arms they carried was thirty score pounds.

The people collected and the counselors in the streets and in the market-place of Uruk; they came through the gate of seven bolts and Gilgamesh spoke to them in the market-place: 'I, Gilgamesh, go to see that creature of whom such things are spoken, the rumor of whose name fills the world. I will conquer him in his cedar wood and show the strength of the sons of Uruk, all the world shall. know of it. I am committed to this enterprise: to climb the mountain, to cut down the cedar, and leave behind me an enduring name.' The counselors of Uruk; the great market, answered him, 'Gilgamesh, you are young, your courage carries you too far, you cannot know what this enterprise means which you plan. We have heard that Hurnbaba is not like men who die, his weapons are such that none can stand against them; the forest stretches for ten thousand leagues in every direction; who would willingly go down to explore its depths? As for Humbaba, when he roars it is like the torrent of the storm, his breath is like fire and his jaws are death itself. Why do you crave to do this thing, Gilgamesh? It is no equal struggle when one fights with Humbaba, that battering-ram:

When he heard these words of the counselors Gilgamesh looked at his friend and laughed, 'How shall I answer them; shall I say I am afraid of Humbaba, I will sit at home all the rest of my days?' Then Gilgamesh opened his mouth again and said to Enkidu, 'My friend, let us go to the Great Palace, to Egalmah, and stand before Ninsun the queen. Ninsun is wise with deep knowledge, she will give us counsel for the road we must go.' They took each other by the hand as they went to Egalmah, and they went to Ninsun the great queen. Gilgamesh approached, he entered the palace and spoke to Ninsun. 'Ninsun, will you listen to me; I have a long journey to go, to the Land of Humbaba, I must travel an unknown road and fight a strange battle. From the day I go until I return, till I reach the cedar forest and destroy the evil which Shamash abhors, pray for me to Shamash.'

Ninsun and Ekindu

Ninsun went into her room, she put on a dress becoming to her body, she put on jewels to make her breast beautiful, she placed a tiara on her head and her skirts swept the ground. Then she went up to the altar of the Sun, standing upon the roof of the palace; she burnt incense and lifted her arms to Shamash as the smoke ascended: 'O Shamash, why did you give this restless heart to Gilgamesh, my son; why did you give it? You have moved him and now he sets out on a long journey to the Land of Humbaba, to travel an unknown road and fight a strange battle. Therefore from the day that he goes till the day he returns, until he reaches the cedar forest, until he kills Humbaba and destroys the evil thing which you, Shamash, abhor, do not forget him; but let the dawn, Aya, your dear bride, remind you always, and when day is done give him to the watchman of the night to keep him from harm.' Then Ninsun the mother of Gilgamesh extinguished the incense, and she called to Enkidu with this exhortation: 'Strong Enkidu, you are not the child of my body, but I will receive you as my adopted son; you are my other child like the foundlings they bring to the temple. Serve Gilgamesh as a foundling serves the temple and the priestess who reared him. In the presence of my women, any votaries and hierophants, I declare it.' Then she placed - the amulet for a pledge round his neck, and she said to him, 'I entrust my son to you; bring him back to me safely.'

And now they brought to them the weapons, they put in their hands the great swords in their golden scabbards, and the bow and the quiver. Gilgamesh took the ax, he slung the quiver from his -shoulder, and the bow of Anshan, The Epic Of Gilgamesh and buckled the sword to his belt; and so they were armed and ready for the journey. Now all the people came and pressed on them and said, 'When will you return to the city? The counselors blessed Gilgamesh and warned him, 'Do not trust too much in your own strength, be watchful, restrain your blows at first. The one who goes in front protects his companion; the good guide who knows the way guards his friend. Let Enkidu lead the way. He knows the road to the forest, he has seen Humbaba and is experienced in battles; let him press first into the passes, let him be watchful and look to himself. Let-Enkidu protect his friend, and guard his companion, and bring him safe through the pitfalls of the road. We, the counselors of Uruk entrust our king to you, O Enkidu; bring him back safely to us.'

Again to Gilgamesh, they said, 'May Shamash give you your heart's desire, may he let you see with your eyes the thing accomplished which your lips have spoken; may he open a path for you where it is blocked, and a road for your feet to tread. May he open the mountains for your crossing, and may the nighttime bring you the blessings of night, and Lugulbanda, your guardian god, stand beside you for victory. May you have victory in the battle as though you fought with a child. Wash your feet in the river of Humbaba to which you are journeying; in the evening dig a well, and let there always be pure water in your water-skin. Offer cold water to Shamash and do not forget Lugulbanda.' Then Enkidu opened his mouth and said, 'Forward, there is nothing to

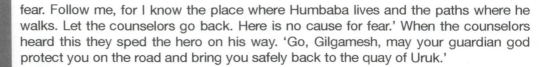

Notes

fear. Follow me, for I know the place where Humbaba lives and the paths where he walks. Let the counselors go back. Here is no cause for fear.' When the counselors heard this they sped the hero on his way. 'Go, Gilgamesh, may your guardian god protect you on the road and bring you safely back to the quay of Uruk.'

Gilgamesh and Enkindu Start Their Journey

After twenty leagues they broke their fast; after another thirty leagues they stopped for the night. Fifty leagues they walked in one day; in three days they had walked as much as a journey of a month and two weeks. They crossed seven mountains before they came to the gate of the forest. Then Enkidu called out to Gilgamesh, 'Do not go down into the forest; when I opened the gate my hand lost its strength.' Gilgamesh answered him, 'Dear friend, do not speak like a coward. Have we got the better of so many dangers and travelled so far, to turn back at last? You, who are tried in wars and battles, hold dose to me now and you will feel no fear of death; keep beside me and your weakness will pass, the trembling will leave your hand. Would my friend rather stay behind? No, we will, go down together into the heart of the forest. Let your courage be roused by the battle to come; forget death and follow me, a man resolute in action, but one who is not foolhardy. When two go together each will protect himself and shield his companion, and if they fall they leave an enduring name.'

Together they went down into the forest and they came to the green mountain. There they stood still, they were struck dumb; they stood still and gazed at the forest. They saw the height of the cedar, they saw the way into the forest and the track where Humbaba was used to walk. The way was broad and the going was good. They gazed at the mountain of cedars, the dwelling-place of the gods and the throne of Ishtar. The hugeness of the cedar rose in front of the mountain, its shade was beautiful, full of comfort; mountain and glade were green with brushwood:

There Gilgamesh dug a well before the setting sun. He went up the mountain and poured out fine meal on the ground and said, 'O mountain, dwelling of the gods, bring me a favorable dream.' Then they took each other' by the hand and lay down to sleep; and sleep that flows from the night lapped over them. Gilgamesh dreamed, and at midnight sleep left him, and he told his dream to his friend. 'Enkidu, what was it that woke me if you did not? My friend, I have dreamed a dream. Get up, and look at the mountain **precipice**. The sleep that the gods sent me is broken. Ah, my friend, what a dream I have had! Terror and confusion; I seized hold of a wild bull in the wilderness. It bellowed and beat up the dust till the whole sky was dark, my arm was seized and my tongue bitten. I fell back on' my knee; then someone refreshed me with water from his water-skin.'

Enkidu said, 'Dear friend, the god to whom we are travelling is no wild bull, though his form is mysterious. That wild bull which you saw is Shamash the Protector; in our moment of peril he will take our hands. The one who gave water from his water-skin, that is your own god who cares for your good name, your Lugulbanda. United with him, together we will accomplish a work the fame of which will never die.' Gilgamesh said, 'I dreamed again. We stood in a deep gorge of the mountain, and beside it we two were like
the smallest of swamp flies; and suddenly the mountain fell, it struck me and caught my feet from under me. Then came an intolerable light blazing out, and in it was one whose grace and whose beauty were greater than the beauty of this world. He pulled me out from under the mountain, he gave me water to drink and my heart was comforted, and he set my feet on the ground.'

Then Enkidu the child of the plains said, 'Let us go down from the mountain and talk this thing over together.' He said to Gilgamesh the young god, 'Your dream is good, your dream is excellent, the mountain which you saw is Humbaba. Now, surely, we will seize and kill him, and throw his body down as the mountain fell on the plain.'

The next day after twenty leagues they broke their fast, and after another thirty they stopped for the night. They dug a well before the sun had set and Gilgamesh ascended the mountain. He poured out fine meal on the ground and said, 'O mountain, dwelling of the gods, send a dream for Enkidu, make him a favourable dream.' The mountain fashioned a dream for Enkidu; it came, an ominous dream; a cold shower passed over him. It caused him to cower like the mountain barley under a storm of rain. But Gilgamesh sat with his chin on his knees till the sleep which flows over all mankind lapped over him. Then, at midnight, sleep left him; he got up and said to his friend, 'Did you call me, or why did I wake? Did you touch me, or why am I terrified? Did not some god pass by, for my limbs are numb with fear? My friend, I saw a third dream and this dream was altogether frightful. The heavens roared and the earth roared again, daylight failed and darkness fell, lightening flashed, fire blazed out, the clouds lowered, they rained down death. Then the brightness departed, the fire went out, and all was turned to ashes fallen about us. Let us go down from the mountain and talk this over, and consider what we should do.'

When they had come down from the mountain Gilgamesh seized the axe in his hand: he felled the cedar. When Humbaba heard the noise far off he was enraged; he cried out, 'Who is this that has violated my woods and cut down my cedar?' But glorious Shamash called to them out of heaven, 'Go forward, do not be afraid.' But now' Gilgamesh was overcome by weakness, for sleep had seized him suddenly, a profound sleep held him; he lay on the ground, stretched out speechless, as though in a dream. When Enkidu touched him he did not rise, when he spoke to him he did not reply. 'O Gilgamesh, Lord of the plain of Kullab, the world grows dark, the shadows have spread over it, now is the glimmer of dusk. When Shamash has departed, his bright head is quenched in the bosom of his mother Ningal. O Gilgamesh, how long will you lie like this, asleep? Never let the mother who gave you birth be forced in mourning into the city square.'

At length Gilgamesh heard him; lie put on his breastplate, 'The Voice of Heroes', of thirty shekels' weight; he put it on as though it had been a light garment that he carried, and it covered him altogether. He straddled the earth like a bull that snuff's the ground and his teeth were clenched. 'By the life of my mother Ninsun who gave me birth, and by the life of my father, divine Lugulbanda, let me live to be the wonder of my mother, - as when she nursed me on her lap.' A second time he said to him, 'By the life of Ninsun my mother who gave me birth, and by the life of my father, divine Lugulbanda, until we have fought thus man, if man he is, this god, if god he is, the way that I took to the Country of the Living will not turn back to the city.'

Then Enkidu, the faithful companion, pleaded, answering him, 'O my lord, you do not know this monster and that is the reason you are not afraid. I who know him, I am terrified. His teeth are dragon's fangs, his countenance is like a lion, his charge is the rushing of the flood, with his look he crushes alike the trees of the forest and reeds in the swamp. O my Lord, you may go on if you choose into thus land, but I will go back to the city. I will tell the lady your mother all your glorious' deeds till she shouts for joy: and then I will tell the death that followed till she weeps for bitterness.' But Gilgamesh said, 'Immolation and sacrifice are not yet for me, the boat of the dead shall not go down, nor the three-ply cloth be cut for my shrouding. Not yet will my

Notes

people be desolate, nor the pyre be lit in my house and my dwelling burnton the fire. Today, give me your aid and you shall have mine: what then can go amiss with us two? All living creatures born of the flesh shall sit at last in the boat of the West, and when it sinks, when the boat of Magilum sinks, they are gone; but we shall go forward and fix our eyes on this monster. If your heart is fearful throw away fear; if there is terror in it throw away terror. Take your axe in your hand and attack. He who leaves the fight unfinished is not at peace.'

Gilgamesh Attacks

Humbaba came out from his strong house of cedar. Then Enkidu called out, 'O Gilgamesh, remember now your boasts in Uruk. Forward, attack, son of Uruk, there is nothing to fear.' When he heard these words his courage rallied; he answered, 'Make haste, close in, if the watchman is there do not let him escape to the woods where he will vanish. He has put on the first of his seven splendours but not yet the other six, let us trap him before he is armed.' Like a raging wild bull he snuffed the ground; the watchman of the woods turned full of threatenings, he cried out. Humbaba came from his strong house of cedar. He nodded his head and shook it, menacing Gilgamesh; and on him he fastened his eye, the eye of death. Then Gilgamesh called to Shamash and his tears were flowing, 'O glorious Shamash, I have followed the road you commanded but now if you send no succour how shall I escape? Glorious Shamash heard his prayer and he summoned the great wind, the north wind, the whirlwind, the storm and the icy wind, the tempest and the scorching wind; they came like dragons, like a scorching fire, like a serpent that freezes the heart, a destroying flood and the lightning's fork. The eight winds rose up against Humbaba, they beat against his eyes; he was gripped, unable to go forward or back. Gilgamesh shouted, 'By the life of Ninsun my mother and divine Lugulbanda my father, in the Country of the Living, in this Land I have discovered your dwelling; my weak arms and my small weapons I have brought to this Land against you, and now I will enter your house'.

So he felled the first cedar and they cut the branches and laid them at the foot of the mountain. At the first stroke Humbaba blazed out, but still they advanced. They felled seven cedars and cut and bound the branches and laid them at the foot of the mountain, and seven times Humbaba loosed his g l o r y on them. As the seventh blaze died out they reached his lair. He slapped his thigh in scorn. He approached like a noble wild bull roped on the mountain, a warrior whose elbows are bound together. The tears started to his eyes and he was pale, 'Gilgamesh, let me speak. I have never known a mother, no, nor a father who reared me. I was born of the mountain, he reared me, and Enlil made me the keeper of this forest. Let me go free, Gilgamesh, and I will be your servant, you shall be my lord; all the trees of the forest that I tended on the mountain shall be yours. I will cut them down and build you a palace.' He took him by the hand and led him to his house, so that the heart of Gilgamesh was moved with compassion. He swore by the heavenly life, by the earthly life, by the underworld itself: 'O Enkidu, should not the snared, bird return to its nest and the captive man return to his mother's arms?' Enkidu answered, 'The strongest of men will fall to fate if he has no judgement. Namtar, the evil fate that knows no distinction between men, will devour him. If the snared bird returns to its nest, if the captive man returns to his mother's arms, then you my friend will never return to the city where the mother is waiting who gave you birth. He will bar the mountain road against you, and make the pathways impassable.'

Humbaba said, 'Enkidu, what you have spoken is evil: you, a hireling, dependent for your bread! In envy and for fear of a rival you have spoken evil words.' Enkidu said,

'Do not listen, Gilgamesh: this Humbaba must die. Kill Humbaba first and his servants after.' But Gilgamesh said, 'If we touch him the blaze and the glory of light will be put out in confusion, the glory and glamour will vanish, its rays will be quenched.' Enkidu said to Gilgamesh, 'Not so, my friend. First entrap the bird, and where shall the chicks run then? Afterwards we can search out the glory and the glamour, when the chicks run distracted through the grass.'

Gilgamesh listened to the word of his companion, he took the axe in his hand, he drew the sword from his belt, and he struck Humbaba with a thrust of the sword to the neck, and Enkidu his comrade struck the second blow. At the third blow Humbaba fell. Then there followed confusion for this was the guardian of the forest whom they had felled to the ground. For as far as two leagues the cedars shivered when Enkidu felled the watcher of the forest, he at whose voice Hermon and Lebanon used to tremble. Now the mountains were moved and all the hills, for the guardian of the forest was killed. They attacked the cedars, the seven splendors of Humbaba were extinguished. So they pressed on into the forest bearing the sword of eight talents. They uncovered the sacred dwellings of the Anunnaki and while Gilgamesh felled the first of the trees of the forest Enkidu cleared their roots as far as the banks of Euphrates. They set Humbaba before the gods, before Enlil; they kissed the ground and dropped the shroud and set the head before him. When he saw the head of Humbaba, Enlil raged at them. 'Why did you do this thing? From henceforth may the fire be on your faces, may it eat the bread that you eat, may it drink where you drink.' Then Enlil took again the blaze and the seven splendors that had been Humbaba's: he gave the first to the river, and he gave to the lion, to the stone of execration, to the mountain and to the dreaded daughter of the Queen of Hell.

O Gilgamesh, king and conqueror of the dreadful blaze; wild bull who plunders the mountain, who crosses the sea, glory to him, and from the brave the greater glory is Enki's!

Complete the SQ3R Analysis. See Appendix.

Short Answer Questions – Gilgamesh – Chapter 2

1. When does the rising action in this section begin?

2. How does Ninsun make Ekindu her son?

3. When does Enkindu earn Gilgamesh's respect?

4. Who is Humbaba and what does he represent? How does he manifest as a foe?

_____

_____

_____

_____

_____

_____

_____

_____

_____

_____

_____

_____

_____

_____

_____

_____

_____

_____

3

Ishtar and Gilgamesh, and The Death of Enkidu

Ishatar and Gilgamesh

GILGAMESH washed out his long locks and cleaned his weapons; he flung back his hair from his shoulders; he threw off his stained clothes and changed them for new. He put on his royal robes and made them fast. When Gilgamesh had put on the crown, glorious Ishtar lifted her eyes, seeing the beauty of Gilgamesh. She said, 'Come to me Gilgamesh, and be my bridegroom; grant me seed of your body, let me be your bride and you shall be my husband. I will harness for you a chariot of lapis lazuli and of gold, with wheels of gold and horns of copper; and you shall have mighty demons of the storm for draft mules. When you enter our house in the fragrance of cedar-wood, threshold and throne will kiss your feet. Kings, rulers, and princes will bow down before you; they shall bring you tribute from the mountains and the plain. Your ewes shall drop twins and your goats triplets; your pack-ass shall outrun mules; your oxen shall have no rivals, and your chariot horses shall be famous far-off for their swiftness.'

Gilgamesh opened his mouth and answered glorious Ishtar, 'If I take you in marriage, what gifts can I give in return? What ointments and clothing for your body? I would gladly give you bread and all sorts of food fit for a god. I would give you wine to drink fit for a queen. I would pour out barley to stuff your granary; but as for making you my wife - that I will not. How would it go with me? Your lovers have found you like a brazier which smolders in the cold, a backdoor which keeps out neither squall of wind nor storm, a castle which crushes the garrison, pitch that blackens the bearer, a water-skin that chafes the carrier, a stone which falls from the parapet, a battering-ram turned back from the enemy, a sandal that trips the wearer. Which of your lovers did you ever love for ever? What shepherd of yours has pleased you for all time? Listen to me while I tell the tale of your lovers. There was Tammuz, the lover of your youth, for him you decreed wailing, year after year. You loved the many colored roller, but still you struck and broke his wing; now in the grove he sits and cries, "kappi, kappi, my wing, my wing." You have loved the lion tremendous in strength: seven pits you dug for him, and seven. You have loved the stallion magnificent in battle, and for him you decreed whip and spur and a thong, to gallop seven leagues by force and to muddy the water before he drinks; and for his mother Silili lamentations. You have loved the shepherd of the flock; he made meal-cake for you day after day, he killed kids for your sake. You struck and turned him into a wolf, now his own herd-boys chase him away, his own hounds worry his flanks. And did you not love Ishullanu, the gardener of your father's palm grove? He brought you baskets filled with dates without end; every day he loaded your table. Then you turned your eyes on him and said, "Dearest Ishullanu, come here to me, let us enjoy your manhood, come forward and take me, I am yours.' Ishullanu answered, "What are you asking from me? My mother has baked and I have

Notes

eaten; why should I come to such as you for food that is tainted and rotten? For when was a screen of rushes sufficient protection from frosts?" But when you had beard his answer you struck him. He was changed to a blind mole deep in the earth, one whose desire is always beyond his reach. And if you and I should be lovers, should not I be served in the same fashion as all these others whom you loved once?'

Ishatar and Anu

When Ishtar heard this she fell into a bitter rage, she went up to high heaven. Her tears poured down in front of her father Anu, and Antum her mother. She said, 'My father, Gilgamesh has heaped insults on me, he has told over all my abominable behavior, my foul and hideous acts.' Anu opened his mouth and said, 'Are you a father of gods? Did not you quarrel with Gilgamesh the king, so now he has related your abominable behavior, your foul and hideous acts.' Ishtar opened her mouth and said again, 'My father, give me the Bull of Heaven to destroy Gilgamesh. Fill Gilgamesh, I say, with arrogance to his destruction; but if you refuse to give me the Bull of Heaven I will break in the doors of hell and smash the bolts; there will be confusion of people, those above with those from the lower depths. I shall bring up the dead to eat food like the living; and the hosts of dead will outnumber the living.' Anu said to great Ishtar, 'If I do what you desire there will be seven years of drought throughout Uruk when corn will be seedless husks. Have you saved grain enough for the people and grass for the cattle? Ishtar replied. 'I have saved grain for the people, grass for the cattle; for seven years of seedless husks, there is grain and there is grass enough.'

When Anu heard what Ishtar had said he gave her the Bull of Heaven to lead by the halter down to Uruk: When they reached the gates of Uruk the Bull went to the river; with his first snort cracks opened in the earth and, a hundred young men fell down to death. With his second snort cracks opened and two hundred fell down to death. With his third snort cracks opened, Enkidu doubled over but instantly recovered, he dodged aside and leapt on the Bull and seized it by the horns. The Bull of Heaven foamed in his face, it brushed him with the thick of its tail. Enkidu cried to Gilgamesh, 'my friend, we boasted that we would leave enduring names behind us. Now thrust in your sword between the nape and the horns.' So Gilgamesh followed the Bull, he seized the thick of its tail. he thrust the sword between the nape and the horns and slew the Bull. When they had killed the Bull of Heaven they cut out its heart and gave it to Shamash, and the brothers rested.

But Ishtar rose tip and mounted the great wall of Uruk; she sprang on to the tower and uttered a curse: 'Woe toGilgamesh, for he has scorned me in killing the Bull of Heaven.' When Enkidu heard these words he tore out the Bull's right thigh and tossed it in her face saying, 'If I could lay my hands on you, it is this I should do to you, and lash the entrails to your side.' Then Ishtar called together her people, the dancing and singing girls, the prostitutes of the temple, the courtesans. Over the thigh of the Bull of Heaven she set up lamentation.

But Gilgamesh called the smiths and the armorers, all of them together. They admired the immensity of the horns. They were plated with lapis lazuli two fingers thick. They were thirty pounds each in weight, and their capacity in oil was six measures, which he gave to his guardian god, Lugulbanda. But he carried the horns into the palace and hung them on the wall. Then they washed their hands in Euphrates, they embraced each other and went away. They drove through the streets of Uruk where the heroes were gathered to see them, and Gilgamesh called to the singing girls, 'Who is most glorious of the heroes, who is most eminent among men?' 'Gilgamesh is the most glorious of heroes, Gilgamesh is most eminent among men.' And now there was feasting, and celebrations and joy in the palace, till the heroes lay down saying, 'Now we will rest for the night.'

Enkindu's Dream

When the daylight came Enkidu got up and cried to Gilgamesh, 'O my brother, such a dream I had last night. Anu, Enlil, Ea and heavenly Shamash took counsel together, and Anu said to Enlil, "Because they have killed the Bull of Heaven, and because they have killed Humbaba who guarded the Cedar Mountain one of the two must, die." Then glorious Shamash answered the hero Enlil, "It was by your command they killed the Bull of Heaven, and killed Humbaba, and must Enkidu die although innocent?" Enlil flung round in rage at glorious Shamash, "You dare to say this, you who went about with them every day like one of themselves!"'

So Enkidu lay stretched out before Gilgamesh; his tears ran down in streams and he said to Gilgamesh, ' O my brother, so dear as you are to me, brother, yet they will take me from you.' Again he said, 'I must sit down on the threshold of the dead and never again will I see my dear brother with my eyes.'

While Enkidu lay alone in his sickness he cursed the gate as though it was living flesh, 'You there, wood of the gate, dull and insensible, witless, I searched for you over twenty leagues until I saw the towering cedar. There is no wood like you in our land. Seventy-two cubits high and twenty-four wide, the pivot and the ferrule and the jambs are perfect. A master craftsman from Nippur has made you; but O, if I had known the conclusion! If I had known that this was all the good that would come of it, I would have raised the axe and split you into little pieces and set up here a gate of wattle instead. Ah, if only some future king had brought you here, or some god- had fashioned you. Let him obliterate my name and write his own, and the curse fall on him instead of on Enkidu.'

With the first brightening of dawn Enkidu raised his head and wept before the Sun God, in the brilliance of the sunlight his tears streamed down. 'Sun God, I beseech you, about that vile Trapper, that Trapper of nothing because of whom I was to catch less than my comrade; let him catch least, make his game scarce, make him feeble, taking the smaller of every share, let his quarry escape from his nets.'

Enkindu Speaks Curses

When he had cursed the Trapper to his heart's content he turned on the harlot. He was roused to curse her also. 'As for you, woman, with a great curse I curse you! I will promise you a destiny to all eternity. My curse shall come on you soon and sudden. You shall be without a roof for your commerce, for you shall not keep house with other girls in the tavern, but do your business in places fouled by the vomit of the drunkard. Your hire will be potter's earth, your thievings will be flung into the hovel, you will sit at the crossroads in the dust of the potter's quarter, you will make your bed on the dung-hill at night, and by day take your stand in the wall's shadow. Brambles and thorns will tear your feet, the drunk and the dry will strike your cheek and your mouth will ache. Let you be stripped of your purple dyes, for I too once in the wilderness with my wife had all the treasure I wished.'

When Shamash heard the words of Enkidu he called to him from heaven: 'Enkidu, why are you cursing the woman, he mistress who taught you to eat bread fit for gods and drink wine of kings? She who put upon you a 'magnificent garment, did she not give you glorious Gilgamesh for your companion, and has not Gilgamesh, your own brother, made you rest on a 'royal bed and recline on a couch at his left hand? He has made the princes of the earth kiss your feet, and now all the people of Uruk lament and wail over you. When you are dead he will let his hair grow long for your sake, he will wear a lion's pelt and wander through the desert.'

When Enkidu heard glorious Shamash his angry heart grew quiet, he called back the curse and said, 'Woman, I promise you another destiny. The mouth which cursed you shall bless you! Kings, princes and nobles shall adore you. On your account a man though twelve miles off will clap his hand to his thigh and his hair will twitch. For you he will undo his belt and open his treasure and you shall have your desire; lapis lazuli, gold and' carnelian from the heap in the treasury. A ring for your hand and a robe shall be yours. The priest will lead you into the presence of the gods. On your account a wife, a mother of seven, was forsaken.'

Enkindu's Becomes Sick

As Enkidu slept alone in his sickness, in bitterness of spirit he poured out his heart to his friend. 'It was I who cut down the cedar, I who leveled the forest, I who slew Humbaba and now see what has become of me. Listen, my friend, this is the dream I dreamed last night. The heavens roared, and earth rumbled back an answer; between them stood I before an awful being, the sombre-faced man-bird; he had directed on me his purpose. His was a vampire face, his foot was a lion's foot, his hand was an eagle's talon. He fell on me and his claws were in my hair, he held me fast and I smothered; then he transformed me so that my arms became wings covered with feathers. He turned his stare towards me, and he led me away to the palace of Irkalla, the Queen of Darkness, to the house from which none who enters ever returns, down the road from which there is no coming back. 'There is the house whose people sit in darkness; dust is their food and clay their meat. They are clothed like birds " with wings for covering, they see no light, they sit in darkness. I entered the house of dust and I saw the kings of the earth, their crowns put away for ever; rulers and princes, all those who once wore kingly crowns and ruled the world in the days of old. They who had stood in the place of the gods like Ann and Enlil stood now like servants to fetch baked meats in the house of dust, to carry cooked meat and cold water from the water-skin. In the house of dust which I entered were high priests and acolytes, priests of the incantation and of ecstasy; there were servers of the temple, and there was Etana, that king of Dish whom the eagle carried to heaven in the days of old. I saw also Samuqan, god of cattle, and there was Ereshkigal the Queen of the Underworld; and Befit-Sheri squatted in front of her, she who is recorder of the gods and keeps the book of death. She held a tablet from which she read. She raised her head, she saw me and spoke:" Who has brought this one here?" Then I awoke like a man drained of blood who wanders alone in a waste of rashes; like one whom the bailiff has seized and his heart pounds with terror.'

Gilgamesh had peeled off his clothes, he listened to his words and wept quick tears, Gilgamesh listened and his tears flowed. He opened his mouth and spoke to Enkidu: 'Who is there in strong-walled Uruk who has wisdom like this? Strange things have been spoken, why does your heart speak strangely? The dream was marvellous but the terror was great; we must treasure the dream whatever the terror; for the dream has shown that misery comes at last to the healthy man, the end of life is sorrow.' And Gilgamesh lamented, 'Now I will pray to the great gods, for my friend had an ominous dream.'

This day on which Enkidu dreamed came to an end and be lay stricken with sickness. One whole day he lay on his bed and his suffering increased. He said to Gilgamesh, the friend on whose account he had left the wilderness, 'Once I ran for you, for the water of life, and I now have nothing:' A second day he lay on his bed and Gilgamesh watched over him but the sickness increased. A third day he lay on his bed, he called out to Gilgamesh, rousing him up. Now he was weak and his eyes were blind with weeping. Ten days he lay and his suffering increased, eleven and twelve days he lay on his bed of pain. Then he called to Gilgamesh, 'My friend, the great goddess cursed me and I must die in shame. I shall not die like a man fallen in battle; I feared to fall, but happy is the man who falls in the battle, for I must die in shame.' And Gilgamesh wept over Enkidu. With the first light of dawn he raised his voice and said to the counselors of Uruk:

'Hear me, great ones of Uruk,
I weep for Enkidu, my friend,
Bitterly moaning like a woman mourning
I weep for my brother.
O Enkidu, my brother,
You were the axe at my side,
My hand's strength, the sword in my belt,
The shield before me,
A glorious robe, my fairest ornament;
An evil Fate has robbed me.
The wild ass and the gazelle
That were father and mother,
All long-tailed creatures that nourished you
Weep for you,
All the wild things of the plain and pastures;
The paths that you loved in the forest of cedars
Night and day murmur.
Let the great ones of strong-walled Uruk
Weep for you;
Let the finger of blessing
Be stretched out in mourning;
Enkidu, young brother. Hark,

There is an echo through all the country
Like a mother mourning.
Weep all the paths where we walked together;
And the beasts we hunted, the bear and hyena,
Tiger and panther, leopard and lion,
The stag and the ibex, the bull and the doe.
The river along whose banks we used to walk,
Weeps for you,
Ula of Elam and dear Euphrates
Where once we drew water for the water-skins.
The mountain we climbed where we slew the Watchman,
Weeps for you.
The warriors of strong-walled Uruk
Where the Bull of Heaven was killed,
Weep for you.
All the people of Eridu
Weep for you Enkidu.
Those who brought grain for your eating
Mourn for you now;
Who rubbed oil on your back
Mourn for you now;
Who poured beer for your drinking
Mourn for you now.
The harlot who anointed you with fragrant ointment
Laments for you now;
The women of the palace, who brought you a wife,
A chosen ring of good advice,
Lament for you now.
And the young men your brothers
As though they were women
Go long-haired in mourning.
What is this sleep which holds you now?
You are lost in the dark and cannot hear me.'

He touched his heart but it did not beat, nor did he lift his eyes again. When Gilgamesh touched his heart it did not beat. So Gilgamesh laid a veil, as one veils the bride, over his friend. He began to rage like a lion, like a lioness robbed of her whelps. This way and that he paced round the bed, he tore out his hair and strewed it around. He dragged of his splendid robes and flung them down as though they were abominations.

In the first light of dawn Gilgamesh cried out, 'I made you rest on a royal bed, you reclined on a couch at my left hand, the princes of the earth kissed your feet. I will cause all the people of Uruk to weep over you and raise the dirge of the dead. The joyful people will stoop with sorrow; and when you have gone to the earth I will let my hair grow long for your sake, I will wander through the wilderness in the skin of a lion.' The next day also, in the first light, Gilgamesh lamented; seven days and seven nights he wept for Enkidu, until the worm fastened on him. Only then he gave him up to the earth, for the Anunnaki, the judges, had seized him.

Then Gilgamesh issued a proclamation through the land, he summoned them all, the coppersmiths, the goldsmiths, the stone-workers, and commanded them, 'Make a statue of my friend.' The statue was fashioned with a great weight of lapis lazuli for the breast and of gold for the body. A table of hard-wood was set out, and on it a bowl of carnelian filled with honey, and a bowl of lapis lazuli filled with butter. These he exposed and offered to the Sun; and weeping he went away.

Complete the SQ3R Analysis. See Appendix.

1. How does Enkindu become ill?

2. Ishtar experiences unrequited love from Gilgamesh. Using context clues, decipher the definition of unrequited love.

3. What does Ishtar do as a result of the Gilgamesh's response?

4. Is Gilgamesh responsible for Enkidu's death? If so, how?

4

The Search for Everlasting Life

Gilgamesh Mourns Enkindu

Bitterly Gilgamesh wept for his friend Enkidu; he wandered over the wilderness as a hunter, he roamed over the plains; in his bitterness he cried, 'How can I rest, how can I be at peace? Despair is in my heart. What my brother is now, that shall I be when I am dead. Because I am afraid of death I will go as best I can to find Utnapishtim whom they call the Faraway, for he has entered the assembly of the gods.' So Gilgamesh travelled over the wilderness, he wandered over the grasslands, a long journey, in search of Utnapishtim, whom the gods took after the deluge; and they set him to live in the land of Dilmun, in the garden of the sun; and to him alone of men they gave everlasting life.

At night when he came to the mountain passes Gilgamesh prayed: 'In these mountain passes long ago I saw lions, I was afraid and I lifted my eyes to the moon; I prayed and my prayers went up to the gods, so now, O moon god Sin, protect me.' When he had prayed he lay down to sleep, until he was woken from out of a dream. He saw the lions round him glorying in life; then he took his axe in his hand, he drew his sword from his belt, and he fell upon them like an arrow from the string, and struck and destroyed and scattered them.

So at length Gilgamesh came to Mashu, the great mountains about which he had heard many things, which guard the rising and the setting sun. Its twin peaks are as high as the wall of heaven and its paps reach down to the underworld. At its gate the Scorpions stand guard, half man and half dragon; their glory is terrifying, their stare strikes death into men, their shimmering halo sweeps the mountains that guard the rising sun. When Gilgamesh saw them he shielded his eyes for the length of a moment only; then he took courage and approached. When they saw him so undismayed the Man-Scorpion called to his mate, 'This one who comes to us now is flesh of the gods.' The mate of the Man-Scorpion answered, 'Two thirds is god but one third is man.'

Then he called to the man Gilgamesh, he called to the child of the gods: ' Why have you come so great a journey; for what have you travelled so far, crossing the dangerous waters; tell me the reason for your coming?' Gilgamesh answered, 'For Enkidu; I loved him dearly, together we endured all kinds of hardships; on his account I have come, for the common lot of man has taken him. I have wept for him day and night, I would not give up his body for burial, I thought my friend would come back because of my weeping. Since he went, my life is nothing; that is why I have travelled here in search of Utnapishtim my father; for men say he has entered the assembly of the gods, and has found everlasting life: I have a desire to question him, concerning the living and the dead.' The Man-Scorpion opened his mouth and said, speaking to Gilgamesh, 'No man born of woman has done what you have asked, no mortal man has gone into the mountain; the length of it is twelve leagues of darkness; in it there is no light, but the heart is oppressed with darkness.

From the rising of the sun to the setting of the sun there is no light.' Gilgamesh said, 'Although I should go in sorrow and in pain, with sighing and with weeping, still I must go. Open the gate ' of the mountain:' And the Man-Scorpion said, 'Go, Gilgamesh, I permit you to pass through the mountain of Mashu and through the high ranges; may your feet carry you safely home. The gate of the mountain is open.'

When Gilgamesh heard this he did as the Man-Scorpion had said, he followed the sun's road to his rising, through the mountain. When he had gone one league the darkness became thick around him, for there was no light, he could see nothing ahead and nothing behind him. After two leagues the darkness was thick and there was no light, he could see nothing ahead and nothing behind him. After three leagues the darkness was thick, and there was no w light, he could see nothing ahead and nothing behind him. After four leagues the darkness was thick and there was no light, he could see nothing ahead and nothing behind him. At the end of five leagues the darkness was thick and there was no light, he could see nothing ahead and nothing behind him. At the end of six leagues the darkness was thick and there was no light, he could see nothing ahead and nothing behind him. When he had gone seven leagues the darkness was thick and there was no light, he could see nothing ahead and nothing behind him. When he had gene eight leagues Gilgamesh gave a great cry, for the darkness was thick and he could see nothing ahead and nothing behind him. After nine leagues he felt the northwind on his face, but the darkness was thick and there was no light, he could see nothing ahead and nothing behind him.

Gilgamesh Searches for Everlasting Life

After ten leagues the end was near: After eleven leagues the dawn light appeared. At the end of twelve leagues the sun streamed out. There was the garden of the gods; all round him stood bushes bearing gems. Seeing it he went down at once, for there was fruit of carnelian with the vine hanging from it, beautiful to look at; lapis lazuli leaves hung thick with fruit, sweet to see. For thorns and thistles there were rare stones, a gate, and pearls from out of the sea. While Gilgamesh walked in the garden by the edge of the sea Shamash saw him, and he saw that he was dressed in the skins of animals and ate their flesh. He was distressed, and he spoke and said, 'No mortal man has gone this way before, nor will, as long as the winds drive over the sea.' And to Gilgamesh he said, 'You will never find the life for which you are searching.' Gilgamesh said to glorious Shamash, 'Now that I have toiled and strayed so far over the wilderness, am I to sleep, and let the earth cover my head for ever? Let my eyes see the sun until they are dazzled with looking. Although I am no better than a dead man, still let me see the light of the sun.'

Beside the sea she lives, the woman of the vine, the maker, of wine; Siduri sits in the garden at the edge of the sea, with the golden bowl and the golden vats that the gods gave her. She is covered with a veil; and where she sits she sees Gilgamesh coming towards her, wearing skins, the flesh of the gods in his body, but despair in his heart, and his face like the face of one who has made a long journey. She looked, and as she scanned the distance she said in her own heart, 'Surely this is some felon; where is he going now? And she barred her gate against him with the cross-bar and shot home the bolt. But Gilgamesh, hearing the sound of the bolt, threw up his head and lodged his foot in the gate; he called to her, 'Young woman, maker of wine, why do you bolt your door; what did you see that made you bar your gate? I will break in your door and burst in your gate, for I am Gilgamesh who seized and killed the Bull of Heaven, I killed the watchman of the cedar forest, I overthrew Humbaba who lived in the forest, and I killed the lions in the passes of the mountain.'

Then Siduri said to him, 'If you are that Gilgamesh who seized and killed the Bull of Heaven, who killed the watchman of the cedar forest, who overthrew Humbaba that lived in the forest, and killed the lions in the passes of the mountain, why are your cheeks so starved and why is your face so drawn? Why is despair in your heart and your face like the face of one who has made a long journey? Yes, why is your face burned from heat and cold, and why do you come here wandering over the pastures in search of the wind?

Gilgamesh answered her, 'And why should not my cheeks be starved and my face drawn? Despair is in my heart and my face is the face of one who has made a long journey, it was burned with heat and with cold. Why should I not wander over the pastures in search of the wind? My friend, my younger brother, he who hunted the wild ass of the wilderness and the panther of the plains, nay friend, my younger brother who seized and killed the Bull of Heaven and overthrew Humbaba in the cedar forest, my friend who was very dear to me and who endured dangers beside me, Enkidu my brother, whom I laved, the end of mortality has overtaken him. I wept far him seven days and nights till the worm fastened on him. Because of my brother I am afraid of death, because of my brother I stray through the wilderness and cannot rest.

But now, young woman, maker of wine, since I have seen your face do not let me see the face of death which I dread so much.' She answered, 'Gilgamesh, where are you hurrying to? You will never find that life for which you are looking. When the gods created man they allotted to him death, but life they retained in their own keeping. As for you, Gilgamesh, fill your belly with good things; day and night, night and day, dance and be merry, feast and rejoice. Let your clothes be fresh, bathe yourself in water, cherish the little child that holds your hand, and make your wife happy in your embrace; for this too is the lot of man.'

But Gilgamesh said to Siduri, the young woman, 'How can I be silent, how can I rest, when Enkidu whom I love is dust, and I too shall die and be laid in the earth. You live by the sea-shore and look into the heart of it; young woman, tell me now, which is the way to Utnapishtim, the son of Ubara-Tutu? What directions are there for the passage; give me, oh, give me directions. I will cross the Ocean if it is possible; if it is not I will wander still farther in the wilderness.' The winemaker said to him, 'Gilgamesh, there is no crossing the Ocean; whoever has come, since the days of old, has not been able to pass that sea. The Sun in his glory crosses the Ocean, but who beside Shamash has ever crossed it? The place and the passage are difficult, and the waters of death are deep which flow between. Gilgamesh, how will you cross the Ocean?

When you come to the waters of death what will you do? But Gilgamesh, down in the woods you will find Urshanabi, the ferryman of Utnapishtim; with him are the holy things, the things of stone. He is fashioning the serpent prow of the boat. Look at him well, and if it is possible, perhaps you will cross the waters with him; but if it is not possible, then you must go back.'

When Gilgamesh heard this he was seized with anger. He took his axe in his hand, and his dagger from his belt. He crept forward and he fell on them like a javelin. Then he went into the forest and sat down. Urshanabi saw the dagger flash and heard the axe, and he beat his head, for Gilgamesh had shattered the tackle of the boat in his rage. Urshanabi said to him, 'Tell me, what is your name? I am Urshanabi, the ferryman of Utnapishtim the Faraway." He replied to him, 'Gilgamesh is my name, I am from Uruk, from the house of Anu.' Then Urshanabi said to him, 'Why are your cheeks so starved and your face drawn? Why is despair in your heart and your face like the face of one who has made a long journey; yes, why is your face burned with heat and with cold, and why do you come here wandering over the pastures in search of the wind?

Gilgamesh said to him, 'Why should not my cheeks be starved and my face drawn? Despair is in my heart, and my face is the face of one who has made a long journey. I was burned with heat and with cold. Why should I not wander over the pastures? My friend, my younger brother who seized and killed the Bull of Heaven, and overthrew Humbaba in the cedar forest, my friend who was very dear to me, and who endured dangers beside me, Enkidu my brother whom I loved, the end of mortality has overtaken him. I wept for him seven days and nights till the worm fastened on him. Because of my brother I am afraid of death, because of my brother I stray through the wilderness. His fate lies heavy upon me. How can I be silent, how can I rest? He is dust and I too shall die and be laid in the earth for ever. I am afraid of death, therefore, Urshanabi, tell me which is the road to Utnapishtim? If it is possible I will cross the waters of death; if not I will wander still farther through the wilderness.'

Urshanabi said to him, 'Gilgamesh, your own hands have prevented you from crossing the Ocean; when you destroyed the tackle of the boat you destroyed its safety.' Then the two of them talked it over and Gilgamesh said, 'Why are you so angry with me, Urshanabi, for you yourself cross the sea by day and night, at all seasons you cross it' 'Gilgamesh, those things you destroyed, their property is to carry me over the water, to prevent the waters of death from touching me. It was for this reason that I preserved them, but you have destroyed them, and the urnu snakes with them. But now, go into the forest, Gilgamesh; with your axe cut poles, one hundred and twenty, cut them sixty cubits long, paint them with bitumen, set on them ferrules and bring them back.'

When Gilgamesh heard this he went into the forest, he cut poles one hundred and twenty; he cut them sixty cubits long, he painted them with bitumen, he set on them ferrules, and he brought them to Urshanabi. Then they boarded the boat, Gilgamesh and Urshanabi together, launching it out on the waves of Ocean. For three days they ran on as it were a journey of a month and fifteen days, and at last Urshanabi brought the boat to the waters of death: Then Urshanabi said to
Gilgamesh, 'Press on, take a pole and thrust it in, but do not let your hands touch the waters. Gilgamesh, take a second pole, take a third, take a fourth pole. Now, Gilgamesh, take a fifth, take a sixth and seventh pole. Gilgamesh, take an eighth, and ninth, a tenth pole. Gilgamesh, take an eleventh, take a twelfth pole.' After one hundred and twenty thrusts Gilgamesh had used the last pole. Then he stripped himself, he held up his arms for a mast and his covering for a sail. So Urshanabi the

ferryman brought Gilgamesh to Utnapishtim, whom they call the Faraway, who lives in Dihnun at the place of the sun's transit, eastward of the mountain. To him alone of men the gods had given everlasting life.

Gilgamesh and Utnapishtim

Now Utnapishtim, where he lay at ease, looked into the distance and he said in his heart, musing to himself, 'Whydoes the boat sail here without tackle and mast; why are the sacred stones destroyed, and why does the master not sail the boat? That man who comes is none of mine; where I look I see a man whose body is covered with skins of beasts. Who is this who walks up the shore behind Urshanabi, for surely he is no man of mine? So Utnapishtim looked at him and said, 'What is your name, you who come here wearing the skins of beasts, with your cheeks starved and your face drawn?

Where are you hurrying to now? For what reason have you made this great journey, crossing "the seas whose passage is difficult? Tell me the reason for your coming.' He replied, 'Gilgamesh is my name. I am from Uruk, from the house of Anu.' Then Utnapishtim said to him, 'If you are Gilgamesh, why are your cheeks so starved and your face drawn? Why is despair in your heart and your face like the face of one who has made a long journey? Yes, why is your face burned with heat and cold; and why do you come here, wandering over the wilderness in search of the wind?

Gilgamesh said to him, 'Why should not my cheeks be starved and my face drawn?

Despair is in my heart and my face is the face of one who has made a long journey. It was burned with heat and with cold. Why should I not wander over the pastures? My friend, my younger brother who seized and killed the Bull of Heaven and overthrew Humbaba in the cedar forest, my friend who was very dear to me and endured dangers beside me, Enkidu, my brother whom I loved, the end of mortality has overtaken him. I wept for him seven days and nights till the worm fastened on him. Because of my brother I am afraid of death; because of my brother I stray through the wilderness. His fate lies heavy upon me. How can I be silent, how can I rest? He is dust and I shall die also and be laid in the . earth for ever.' Again Gilgamesh said, speaking to Utnapishtim, 'It is to see Utnapishtim whom we call the Faraway that I have come this journey. For. this I have wandered over the world, I have crossed many difficult ranges, I have crossed the seas, I have wearied myself with travelling; my joints are aching, and I have lost acquaintance with sleep which is sweet. My clothes were worn out before

I came to the house of Siduri. I have killed the bear and hyena, the lion and panther, the tiger, the stag and the ibex, all sorts of wild game and the small creatures of the pastures. I ate their flesh and I wore their skins; and that was how I came to the gate of the young woman, the maker of wine, who barred her gate of pitch and bitumen against me. But from her I had news of the journey; so then I came to Urshanabi the ferryman, and with him I crossed over the waters of death. Oh, father Utnapishtim, you who have entered the assembly of the gods, I wish to question you concerning the living and the dead, how shall I find the life for which I am searching?

Utuapishtim said, 'There is no permanence. Do we build a house to stand for ever, do we seal a contract to hold for all time? Do brothers divide an inheritance to keep for ever, does the flood-time of rivers endure? It is only the nymph of the dragon-fly who sheds her larva and sees the sun in his glory. From the days of old there is no permanence. The sleeping and the dead, how alike they are, they are like a painted death. What is there between the master and the servant when both have fulfilled their doom? When the Anunnaki, the judges, come together, and Mammetun the mother of destinies, together they decree the fates of men. Life and death they allot but the day of death they do not disclose.'

Then Gilgamesh said to Utnapishtim the Faraway, 'I look at you now, Utnapishtim, and your appearance is no different from mine; there is nothing strange in your features. I thought I should find, you like a hero prepared for battle, but you he here taking your ease on your back. Tell me truly, how was it that you came to enter the company of the gods and to possess everlasting life?' Utnapishtim said to Gilgamesh, 'I will reveal to you a mystery, I will tell you a secret of the gods.'

Complete the SQ3R Analysis. See Appendix.

Short Answer Questions – Gilgamesh – Chapter 4

1. Who is Siduri and why is she significant?

2. What does Gilgamesh learn about everlasting life for mortal men?

3. How much of Gilgamesh mortal, and how much of Gilgamesh god?

4. Who is Utnapishtim, and what do you predict he will tell Gilgamesh about "the secret of the gods?"

5

The Story of the Flood

'You know the city Shurrupak, it stands on the banks of Euphrates? That city grew old and the gods that were in it were old. There was Anu,-lord of the firmament, their father, and warrior Enlil their counselor, Ninurta the helper, and Ennugi watcher over canals; and with them also was Ea. In those days the world teemed, the people multiplied, the world bellowed like a wild bull, and the great god was aroused by the clamor. Enlil heard the clamour and he said to the gods in council, "The uproar of mankind is intolerable and sleep is no longer possible by reason of the babel." So the gods agreed to exterminate mankind. Enlil did this, but Ea because of his oath warned me in a dream. He whispered their words to my house of reeds, "Reed-house, reed-house! Wall, O wall, hearken reed-house, wall reflect; O man of Shurrupak, son of Ubara-Tutu; tear down your house and build a boat, abandon possessions and look for life, despise worldly goods and save your soul alive. Tear down your house, I say, and build a boat. These are the measurements of the barque as you shall build her: let hex beam equal her length, let her deck be roofed like the vault that covers the abyss; then take up into the boat the seed of all living creatures."

'When I had understood I said to my lord, "Behold, what you have commanded I will honor and perform, but how shall I answer the people, the city, the elders?" Then Ea opened his mouth and said to me, his servant, "Tell them this: I have learned that Enlil is wrathful against me, I dare no longer walk in his land nor live in his city; I will go down to the Gulf to dwell with Ea my lord. But on you he will rain down abundance, rare fish and shy wild-fowl, a rich harvest-tide. In the evening the rider of the storm will bring you wheat in torrents."

Building the Ark

'In the first light of dawn all my household gathered round me, the children brought pitch and the men whatever was necessary. On the fifth day I laid the keel and the ribs, then I made fast the planking. The ground-space was one acre, each side of the deck measured one hundred and twenty cubits, making a square. I built six decks below, seven in all, I divided them into nine sections with bulkheads between. I drove in wedges where needed, I saw to the punt poles, and laid in supplies. The carriers brought oil in baskets, I poured pitch into the furnace and asphalt and oil; more oil was consumed in caulking, and more again the master of the boat took into his stores. I slaughtered bullocks for the people and every day I killed sheep. I gave the shipwrights wine to drink as though it were river water, raw wine and red wine and oil and white wine. There was feasting then as -there is at the time of the New Year's festival; I myself anointed my head. On the seventh day the boat was complete.

'Then was the launching full of difficulty; there was shifting of ballast above and below till two thirds was submerged. I loaded into her all that 1 had of gold and of living things, my family, my kin, the beast of the field both wild and tame, and all the craftsmen. I sent them on board, for the time that Shamash had ordained was already fulfilled when he said, "in the evening, when the rider of the storm sends down the destroying rain, enter the boat and batten her down." The time was fulfilled, the evening came, the rider of the storm sent down the rain. I looked out at the weather and it was terrible, so I too boarded the boat and battened her down. All was now complete, the battening and the caulking; so I handed the tiller to Puzur-Amurri the steersman, with the navigation and the care of the whole boat.

'With the first light of dawn a black cloud came from the horizon; it thundered within where Adad, lord of the storm was riding. In front over hill and plain Shullat and Hanish, heralds of the storm, led on. Then the gods of the abyss rose up; Nergal pulled out the dams of the nether waters, Ninurta the war-lord threw down the dykes, and the seven judges of hell, the Annunaki, raised their torches, lighting the land with their livid flame. A stupor of despair went up to heaven when the god of the storm turned daylight to darkness, when he smashed the land like a cup. One whole day the tempest raged, gathering fury as .it went, it poured over the people like the tides of battle; an imam could not see his brother nor the people be seen from heaven. Even the gods were terrified at the flood, they fled to the highest heaven, the firmament of Ann; they crouched against the walls, cowering like curs. Then Ishtar the sweet-voiced Queen of Heaven cried out like a woman in travail:

"Alas the days -of old are turned to dust because I commanded evil; why did I command thus evil in the council of all the gods? I commanded wars to destroy the people, but are they not my people, for I brought them forth? Now like the spawn of fish they float in the ocean." The great gods of heaven and of hell wept, they covered their mouths.

A Week Long Flood

'For six days and six nights the winds blew, torrent and tempest and flood overwhelmed the world, tempest and flood raged together like warring hosts. When the seventh day dawned the storm from the south subsided, the sea grew calm, the, flood was stilled; I looked at the face of the world and there was silence, all mankind was turned to clay. The surface of the sea stretched as flat as a roof-top; I opened a hatch and the light fell on my face. Then I bowed low, I sat down and I wept, the tears streamed down my face, for on every side was the waste of water. I looked for land in vain, but fourteen leagues distant there appeared a mountain, and there the boat grounded; on the mountain of Nisir the boat held fast, she held fast and did not budge. One day she held, and -a second day on the mountain of Nisir she held fast and did not budge. A third day, and a fourth day she held fast on the mountain and did not budge; a fifth day and a sixth day she held fast on the mountain. When the seventh day dawned I loosed a dove and let her go. She flew away, but finding no resting-place she returned. Then I loosed a swallow, and she flew away but finding no resting-place she returned. I loosed a raven, she saw that the waters had retreated, she ate, she flew around, she cawed, and she did not come back. Then I threw everything open to the four winds, I made a sacrifice and poured out a libation on the mountaintop. Seven and again seven cauldrons I set up on their stands, I heaped up wood and cane and cedar and myrtle. When the gods smelled the sweet savor, they gathered like flies over the sacrifice. Then, at last, Ishtar also came, she lifted her necklace with the jewels of heaven that once Anu had made to please her. "O you gods here present, by the lapis lazuli round my neck I shall remember these days as I remember the jewels of my throat; these last days I shall not forget. Let all the gods gather round the sacrifice, except Enlil. He shall not approach this offering, for without reflection he brought the flood; he consigned my people to destruction."

'When Enlil had come, when he saw the boat, he was wrath and swelled with anger at the gods, the host of heaven, "Has any of these mortals escaped? Not one was to have survived the destruction." Then the god of the wells and canals Ninurta opened his mouth and said to the warrior Enlil, "Who is there of the gods that can devise without Ea? It is Ea alone who knows all things." Then Ea opened his mouth and spoke to warrior Enlil, "Wisest of gods, hero Enlil, how could you so senselessly bring down the flood?

Lay upon the sinner his sin,
Lay upon the transgressor his transgression,
Punish him a little when he breaks loose,
Do not drive him too hard or he perishes,
Would that a lion had ravaged mankind
Rather than the f loud,
Would that a wolf had ravaged mankind
Rather than the flood,
Would that famine had wasted the world
Rather than the flood,
Would that pestilence had wasted mankind
Rather than the flood.

It was not I that revealed the secret of the gods; the wise man learned it in a dream. Now take your counsel what shall be done with him."

'Then Enlil went up into the boat, he took me by the hand and my wife and made us enter the boat and kneel down on either side, he standing between us. He touched our foreheads to bless us saying, "In time past Utnapishtim was a mortal man; henceforth he and his wife shall live in the distance at the mouth of the rivers." Thus it was that the gods took me and placed me here to live in the distance, at the mouth of the rivers.'

Complete the SQ3R Analysis. See Appendix.

Essay Topic – Gilgamesh – Chapter 5

Compare and Contrast and the Gilgamesh flood narrative to the Greek Mythology account of the Flood. What are the similarities and what are the differences.

6

The Return

UTNAPISHTIM said, 'As for you, Gilgamesh, who will assemble the gods for your sake, so that you may find that life for which you are searching? But if you wish, come and put into the test: only prevail against sleep for six days and seven nights.' But while Gilgamesh sat there resting on his haunches, a mist of sleep like soft wool teased from the fleece drifted over him, and Utnapishtim said to his wife, 'Look at him now, the strong man who would have everlasting life, even now the mists of sleep are drifting over him.' His wife replied, 'Touch the man to wake him, so that he may return to his own land in peace, going back through the gate by which he came.' Utnapishtim said to his wife, 'All men are deceivers, even you he will attempt to deceive; therefore bake loaves of bread, each day one loaf, and put it beside his head; and make a mark on the wall to number the days he has slept.'

The Loaves of Bread

So she baked loaves of bread, each day one loaf, and put it beside his head, and she marked on the wall the days that he slept; and there came a day when the first loaf was hard, the second loaf was like leather, the third was soggy, the crust of the fourth had mold, the fifth was mildewed, the sixth was fresh, and the seventh was still on the embers. Then Utnapishtim touched him and he woke. Gilgamesh said to Utnapishtim the Faraway, 'I hardly slept when you touched and roused me.' But Utnapishtim said, 'Count these loaves and learn how many days you slept, for your first is hard, your second like leather, your third is soggy, the crust of your fourth has mold, your fifth is mildewed, your sixth is fresh and your seventh was still over the glowing embers when I touched and woke you.' Gilgamesh said, 'What shall I do, O Utnapishtim, where shall I go? Already the thief in the night has hold of my limbs, death inhabits my room; wherever my foot rests, there I find death.'

Then Utnapishtim spoke to Urshanabi the ferryman: 'Woe to you Urshanabi, now and for ever more you have become hateful to this harborage; it is not for you, nor for you are the crossings of this sea. Go now, banished from the shore. But this man before whom you walked, bringing him here, whose body is covered with foulness and the grace of whose limbs has been spoiled by wild skins, take him to the washing-place. There he shall wash his long hair clean as snow in the water, he shall throve off his skins and let the sea carry them away, and the beauty of his body shall be shown, the fillet on his forehead shall be renewed, and he shall be given clothes to cover his nakedness. Till he reaches his own city and his journey is accomplished, these clothes will show no sign of age, they will wear like a new garment.' So Urshanabi took Gilgamesh and led him to the washing-place, he washed his long hair as clean as snow in the water, he threw off his skins, which the sea carried away, and showed the beauty of his body. He renewed the fillet on his forehead, and to cover his nakedness gave him clothes which would show no sign of age, but would war like a new garment till he reached his own city, and his journey was accomplished.

Then Gilgamesh and Urshanabi launched the boat on to the water and boarded it, and they made ready to sail away; but the wife of Utnapishtim the Faraway said to him, `Gilgamesh came here wearied out, he is worn out; what will you give him to carry him back to his own country? So Utnapishtim spoke, and Gilgamesh took a pole and brought the boat into the bank. `Gilgamesh, you came here a man wearied out, you have worn yourself out; what shall I give you to carry you back to your own country? Gilgamesh, I shall reveal a secret thing, it is a mystery of the gods that I am telling you.

There is a plant that grows under the water, it has a prickle like a thorn, like a rose; it will wound your hands, but if yousucceed in taking it, then your hands will hold that which restores his lost youth to a man: 'When Gilgamesh heard this he opened the sluices so that a sweet water current might carry him out to the deepest channel; he tied heavy stones to his feet and they dragged him down to the water-bed. There he saw the plant growing; although it pricked him he took it in his hands; then he cut the heavy stones from his feet, and the sea carried him and threw him on to the shore. Gilgamesh said to Urshanabi the ferryman, `Come here, and see this marvelous plant. By its virtue a man may win back all his former strength. I will take it to Uruk of the strong walls; there I will give it to the old men to eat. Its name shall be "The Old Men Are Young Again"; and at last I shall eat it myself and have back all my lost youth.' So Gilgamesh returned by the gate through which he had come, Gilgamesh and Urshanabi went together. They travelled their twenty leagues and then they broke their fast; after thirty leagues they stopped for the night.

Gigamesh and the Serpent

Gilgamesh saw a well of cool water and he went down and bathed; but deep in the pool there was lying a serpent, and the serpent sensed the sweetness of the flower. It rose out of the water and snatched it away, and immediately it sloughed its skin and returned to the well. Then Gilgamesh sat down and wept, the tears ran down his face, and he took the hand of Urshanabi; 'O Urshanabi, was it for this that I toiled with my hands, is it for this I have wrung out my heart's blood? For myself I have gained nothing; not I, but the beast of the earth has joy of it now. Already the stream has carried it twenty leagues back to the channels where I found it. I found a sign and now I have lost it. Let us leave the boat on the bank and go.'

After twenty leagues they broke their fast, after thirty leagues they stopped for the night; in three days they had walked as much as a journey of a month and fifteen days. When the journey was accomplished they arrived at Uruk, the strong-walled city. Gilgamesh spoke to him, to Urshanabi the ferryman, 'Urshanabi, climb up on to the wall of Uruk, inspect its foundation terrace, and examine well the brickwork; see if it is not of burnt bricks; and did not the seven wise men lay these foundations?

Ishtar's Garden

One third of the whole is city, one third is garden, and one third is field, with the precinct of the goddess Ishtar. These parts and the precinct are all Uruk.' This too was the work of Gilgamesh, the king, who knew the countries of the world. He was wise„ he saw mysteries and knew secret things, he brought us a tale of the days before the flood. He went a long journey, was weary, worn out with labor, and returning engraved on a stone the whole story.

Complete the SQ3R Analysis. See Appendix.

Short Answer Questions – Gilgamesh – Chapter 6

1. What does Ishtar's garden represent in this text?

2. Why does Gilgamesh cry after the snake sheds its skin?

3. What does is the symbolism behind the loaves of bread in this section?

7

The Death of Gilgamesh

The destiny was fulfilled which the father of the gods, Enlil of the mountain, had decreed for Gilgamesh: 'In nether-earth the darkness will show him a light: of mankind, all that are known, none will leave a monument for generations to come to compare with his. The heroes, the wise men, like the new moon have their waxing and waning. Men will say, "Who has ever ruled with might and with power like him?" As in the dark month, the month of shadows, so without him there is no light.

O Gilgamesh, this was the meaning of your dream. You were given the kingship, such was your destiny, everlasting life was not your destiny. Because of this do not be sad at heart, do not be grieved or oppressed; he has given you power to bind and to loose, to be the darkness and the light of mankind. He has given unexampled supremacy over the people, victory in battle from which no fugitive returns, in forays and assaults from which there is no going back. But do not abuse this power, deal justly with your servants in the palace, deal justly before the face of the Sun.'

The king has laid himself down and will not rise again,
The Lord of Kullab will not rise again;
He overcame evil, he will not come again;
Though he was strong of arm he will not rise again;
He had wisdom and a comely face, he will not come again;
He is gone into the mountain, he will not come again;
On the bed of fate he lies, he will not rise again,
Front the couch of many colors he will not come again.

The people of the city, great and small, are not silent; they lift up, the lament, all men of flesh and blood lift up the lament. Fate has spoken; like a hooked fish he lies stretched on the bed, like a gazelle that is caught in a noose. Inhuman Namtar is heavy upon him, Namtar that has neither hand nor foot, that drinks no water and eats no meat.

For Gilgamesh, son of Ninsun, they weighed out their offerings; his dear wife, his son, his concubine, his musicians, his jester, and all his household; his servants, his stewards, all who lived in the palace weighed out their offerings for Gilgamesh the son of Ninsun, the heart of Uruk. They weighed out their offerings to Ereshkigal, the Queen of Death, and to all the gods of the dead. To Namtar, who is fate, they weighed out the offering. Bread for Ned the Keeper of the Gate, bread for Ningizzida the god of the serpent, the lord of the Tree of Life; for Dumuzi also, the young shepherd, for Enki and Ninki, for Endukugga and Nindukugga, for Enmul and Nimnul, all the ancestral gods, forbears of Enlil. A feast for Shulpae the god of feasting. For Samuqan, god of the herds, for die mother Ninhursag, and the gods of creation in the place of creation, for the host of heaven, priest and priestess weighed out the offering of the dead.

Gilgamesh, the son of Ninsun, lies in the tomb. At the place of offerings he weighed the bread-offering, at the place of libation he poured out the wine. In those days the lord Gilgamesh departed, the son of Ninsun, the king, peerless, without an equal among men, who did not neglect Enlil his master. O Gilgamesh, lord of Kullab, great is thy praise.

Complete the SQ3R Analysis. See Appendix.

GILGAMESH, King Of Babylon., and Stephen Herbert. LANGDON. The Epic of Gilgamish . By Stephen Langdon. University Museum: Philadelphia, 1917. Print.

Essay Assignment – Gilgamesh – Chapter 7

Writers like Rick Riordan, author of Percy Jackson and the Lightening Thief, rework Greek Mythology narratives using contemporary faces, spaces, ideas and scenarios.

Re-write The Epic of Gilgamesh using contemporary words in a contemporary setting. Be sure to include elements of narrative style by providing and introduction which includes the setting and characters. Body paragraphs should follow the rising action, climax and falling action format. The conclusion should provide a resolution for your protagonist and readers.

C H A R T

KNOW • WANT • LEARN

KW

ALREADY KNOW	WANT TO KNOW	WHAT I LEARNED

The Biblical Account
Noah and the Flood

Genesis 6

The Wickedness and Judgment of Man

6 Now it came to pass, when men began to multiply on the face of the earth, and daughters were born to them, 2 that the sons of God saw the daughters of men, that they were beautiful; and they took wives for themselves of all whom they chose.

3 And the Lord said, "My Spirit shall not strive with man forever, for he is indeed flesh; yet his days shall be one hundred and twenty years." 4 There were giants on the earth in those days, and also afterward, when the sons of God came in to the daughters of men and they bore children to them. Those were the mighty men who were of old, men of renown.

5 Then the Lord saw that the wickedness of man was great in the earth, and that every intent of the thoughts of his heart was only evil continually. 6 And the Lord was sorry that He had made man on the earth, and He was grieved in His heart. 7 So the Lord said, "I will destroy man whom I have created from the face of the earth, both man and beast, creeping thing and birds of the air, for I am sorry that I have made them." 8 But Noah found grace in the eyes of the Lord.

Noah Pleases God

9 This is the genealogy of Noah. Noah was a just man, perfect in his generations. Noah walked with God. 10 And Noah begot three sons: Shem, Ham, and Japheth.

11 The earth also was corrupt before God, and the earth was filled with violence. 12 So God looked upon the earth, and indeed it was corrupt; for all flesh had corrupted their way on the earth.

The Ark Prepared

13 And God said to Noah, "The end of all flesh has come before Me, for the earth is filled with violence through them; and behold, I will destroy them with the earth. 14 Make yourself an ark of gopherwood; make rooms in the ark, and cover it inside and outside with pitch. 15 And this is how you shall make it: The length of the ark shall be three hundred cubits, its width fifty cubits, and its height thirty cubits. 16 You shall make a window for the ark, and you shall finish it to a cubit from above; and set the door of the ark in its side. You shall make it with lower, second, and third decks. 17 And behold, I Myself am bringing floodwaters on the earth, to destroy from under heaven all flesh in which is the breath of life; everything that is on the earth shall die. 18 But I will establish My covenant with you; and you shall go into the ark—you, your sons, your wife, and your sons' wives with you. 19 And of every living thing of all flesh you shall bring two of every sort into the ark, to keep them alive with you; they shall

be male and female. 20 Of the birds after their kind, of animals after their kind, and of every creeping thing of the earth after its kind, two of every kind will come to you to keep them alive. 21 And you shall take for yourself of all food that is eaten, and you shall gather it to yourself; and it shall be food for you and for them."

22 Thus Noah did; according to all that God commanded him, so he did.

The Great Flood

Chapter 7

1 Then the Lord said to Noah, "Come into the ark, you and all your household, because I have seen that you are righteous before Me in this generation. 2 You shall take with you seven each of every clean animal, a male and his female; two each of animals that are unclean, a male and his female; 3 also seven each of birds of the air, male and female, to keep the species alive on the face of all the earth. 4 For after seven more days I will cause it to rain on the earth forty days and forty nights, and I will destroy from the face of the earth all living things that I have made." 5 And Noah did according to all that the Lord commanded him. 6 Noah was six hundred years old when the floodwaters were on the earth.

7 So Noah, with his sons, his wife, and his sons' wives, went into the ark because of the waters of the flood. 8 Of clean animals, of animals that are unclean, of birds, and of everything that creeps on the earth, 9 two by two they went into the ark to Noah, male and female, as God had commanded Noah. 10 And it came to pass after seven days that the waters of the flood were on the earth. 11 In the six hundredth year of Noah's life, in the second month, the seventeenth day of the month, on that day all the fountains of the great deep were broken up, and the windows of heaven were opened. 12 And the rain was on the earth forty days and forty nights.

13 On the very same day Noah and Noah's sons, Shem, Ham, and Japheth, and Noah's wife and the three wives of his sons with them, entered the ark— 14 they and every beast after its kind, all cattle after their kind, every creeping thing that creeps on the earth after its kind, and every bird after its kind, every bird of every sort. 15 And they went into the ark to Noah, two by two, of all flesh in which is the breath of life. 16 So those that entered, male and female of all flesh, went in as God had commanded him; and the Lord shut him in.

17 Now the flood was on the earth forty days. The waters increased and lifted up the ark, and it rose high above the earth. 18 The waters prevailed and greatly increased on the earth, and the ark moved about on the surface of the waters. 19 And the waters prevailed exceedingly on the earth, and all the high hills under the whole heaven were covered. 20 The waters prevailed fifteen cubits upward, and the mountains were covered. 21 And all flesh died that moved on the earth: birds and cattle and beasts and every creeping thing that creeps on the earth, and every man. 22 All in whose nostrils was the breath of the spirit of life, all that was on the dry land, died. 23 So He destroyed all living things which were on the face of the ground: both man and cattle, creeping thing and bird of the air. They were destroyed from the earth. Only Noah and

those who were with him in the ark remained alive. 24 And the waters prevailed on the earth one hundred and fifty days.

Noah's Deliverance

Chapter 8

1 Then God remembered Noah, and every living thing, and all the animals that were with him in the ark. And God made a wind to pass over the earth, and the waters subsided. 2 The fountains of the deep and the windows of heaven were also stopped, and the rain from heaven was restrained. 3 And the waters receded continually from the earth. At the end of the hundred and fifty days the waters decreased. 4 Then the ark rested in the seventh month, the seventeenth day of the month, on the mountains of Ararat. 5 And the waters decreased continually until the tenth month. In the tenth month, on the first day of the month, the tops of the mountains were seen.

6 So it came to pass, at the end of forty days, that Noah opened the window of the ark which he had made. 7 Then he sent out a raven, which kept going to and fro until the waters had dried up from the earth. 8 He also sent out from himself a dove, to see if the waters had receded from the face of the ground. 9 But the dove found no resting place for the sole of her foot, and she returned into the ark to him, for the waters were on the face of the whole earth. So he put out his hand and took her, and drew her into the ark to himself. 10 And he waited yet another seven days, and again he sent the dove out from the ark. 11 Then the dove came to him in the evening, and behold, a freshly plucked olive leaf was in her mouth; and Noah knew that the waters had receded from the earth. 12 So he waited yet another seven days and sent out the dove, which did not return again to him anymore.
13 And it came to pass in the six hundred and first year, in the first month, the first day of the month, that the waters were dried up from the earth; and Noah removed the covering of the ark and looked, and indeed the surface of the ground was dry. 14 And in the second month, on the twenty-seventh day of the month, the earth was dried.

15 Then God spoke to Noah, saying, 16 "Go out of the ark, you and your wife, and your sons and your sons' wives with you. 17 Bring out with you every living thing of all flesh that is with you: birds and cattle and every creeping thing that creeps on the earth, so that they may abound on the earth, and be fruitful and multiply on the earth." 18 So Noah went out, and his sons and his wife and his sons' wives with him. 19 Every animal, every creeping thing, every bird, and whatever creeps on the earth, according to their families, went out of the ark.

God's Covenant with Creation

20 Then Noah built an altar to the Lord, and took of every clean animal and of every clean bird, and offered burnt offerings on the altar. 21 And the Lord smelled a soothing aroma. Then the Lord said in His heart, "I will never again curse the ground for man's sake, although the imagination of man's heart is evil from his youth; nor will I again destroy every living thing as I have done.
22 "While the earth remains,
Seedtime and harvest,
Cold and heat,

Winter and summer,
And day and night
Shall not cease."

God's Promise to Noah

Chapter 9

1 So God blessed Noah and his sons, and said to them: "Be fruitful and multiply, and fill the earth. 2 And the fear of you and the dread of you shall be on every beast of the earth, on every bird of the air, on all that move on the earth, and on all the fish of the sea. They are given into your hand. 3 Every moving thing that lives shall be food for you. I have given you all things, even as the green herbs. 4 But you shall not eat flesh with its life, that is, its blood. 5 Surely for your lifeblood I will demand a reckoning; from the hand of every beast I will require it, and from the hand of man. From the hand of every man's brother I will require the life of man.

6 "Whoever sheds man's blood,
By man his blood shall be shed;
For in the image of God
He made man.
7 And as for you, be fruitful and multiply;
Bring forth abundantly in the earth
And multiply in it."

8 Then God spoke to Noah and to his sons with him, saying: 9 "And as for Me, behold, I establish My covenant with you and with your descendants after you, 10 and with every living creature that is with you: the birds, the cattle, and every beast of the earth with you, of all that go out of the ark, every beast of the earth. 11 Thus I establish My covenant with you: Never again shall all flesh be cut off by the waters of the flood; never again shall there be a flood to destroy the earth."

12 And God said: "This is the sign of the covenant which I make between Me and you, and every living creature that is with you, for perpetual generations: 13 I set My rainbow in the cloud, and it shall be for the sign of the covenant between Me and the earth. 14 It shall be, when I bring a cloud over the earth, that the rainbow shall be seen in the cloud; 15 and I will remember My covenant which is between Me and you and every living creature of all flesh; the waters shall never again become a flood to destroy all flesh. 16 The rainbow shall be in the cloud, and I will look on it to remember the everlasting covenant between God and every living creature of all flesh that is on the earth." 17 And God said to Noah, "This is the sign of the covenant which I have established between Me and all flesh that is on the earth."

Noah and His Sons

18 Now the sons of Noah who went out of the ark were Shem, Ham, and Japheth. And Ham was the father of Canaan. 19 These three were the sons of Noah, and from these the whole earth was populated.

20 And Noah began to be a farmer, and he planted a vineyard. 21 Then he drank of the wine and was drunk, and became uncovered in his tent. 22 And Ham, the father of Canaan, saw the nakedness of his father, and told his two brothers outside. 23 But Shem and Japheth took a garment, laid it on both their shoulders, and went backward and covered the nakedness of their father. Their faces were turned away, and they did not see their father's nakedness.

24 So Noah awoke from his wine, and knew what his younger son had done to him. 25 Then he said:

"Cursed be Canaan;
A servant of servants
He shall be to his brethren."
26 And he said:

"Blessed be the Lord,
The God of Shem,
And may Canaan be his servant.
27 May God enlarge Japheth,
And may he dwell in the tents of Shem;
And may Canaan be his servant."
28 And Noah lived after the flood three hundred and fifty years. 29 So all the days of Noah were nine hundred and fifty years; and he died.

Complete the SQ3R Analysis. See Appendix.

New King James Version (NKJV)
Scripture taken from the New King James Version®. Copyright © 1982 by Thomas Nelson. Used by permission. All rights reserved.

Short Answer Questions – Biblical Account of Noah and the Flood

1. Why does Noah curse Ham?

2. What do you believe was Noah's greatest difficulty in building the ark?

3. What covenant did God establish with Noah?

4. What is the symbol used for God's promise to never flood the world again? How is that symbol used now?

Essay Topic

1. Compare and contrast the Biblical Account of the Flood narrative to the flood myth in Gilgamesh. What are the similarities and differences in the account?

2. Why did Noah curse his son, and what was his punishment? Reflect on the Cain and Abel narrative to discover any parallels in the treatment of siblings by their parents. Write an essay where you compare the treatment of children due to their behavior.

3. Discuss a time when your parents punished you because you disrespected them or rewarded you because you were obedient.

C H A R T

KNOW • WANT • LEARN

KWL

WHAT I LEARNED	WANT TO KNOW	ALREADY KNOW

The Story of Prometheus

How Fire Was Given to Man

In those old, old times, there lived two brothers who were not like other men, nor yet like those Mighty Ones who lived upon the mountain top. They were the sons of one of those Titans who had fought against Jupiter and been sent in chains to the strong prison-house of the Lower World.

The name of the elder of these brothers was Prometheus, or Forethought; for he was always thinking of the future and making things ready for what might happen to-morrow, or next week, or next year, or it may be in a hundred years to come. The younger was called Epimetheus, or Afterthought; for he was always so busy thinking of yesterday, or last year, or a hundred years ago, that he had no care at all for what might come to pass after a while.

For some cause Jupiter had not sent these brothers to prison with the rest of the Titans.

Prometheus did not care to live amid the clouds on the mountain top. He was too busy for that. While the Mighty Folk were spending their time in idleness, drinking nectar and eating ambrosia, he was intent upon plans for making the world wiser and better than it had ever been before.

He went out amongst men to live with them and help them; for his heart was filled with sadness when he found that they were no longer happy as they had been during the golden days when Saturn was king. Ah, how very poor and wretched they were! He found them living in caves and in holes of the earth, shivering with the cold because there was no fire, dying of starvation, hunted by wild beasts and by one another-the most miserable of all living creatures.

"If they only had fire," said Prometheus to himself, "they could at least warm themselves and cook their food; and after a while they could learn to make tools and build themselves houses. Without fire, they are worse off than the beasts."

Then he went boldly to Jupiter and begged him to give fire to men, that so they might have a little comfort through the long, dreary months of winter.

"Not a spark will I give," said Jupiter. "No, indeed! Why, if men had fire they might become strong and wise like ourselves, and after a while they would drive us out of our kingdom. Let them shiver with cold, and let them live like the beasts. It is best for them to be poor and ignorant, that so we Mighty Ones may thrive and be happy."

Prometheus made no answer; but he had set his heart on helping mankind, and he did not give up. He turned away, and left Jupiter and his mighty company forever.

As he was walking by the shore of the sea he found a reed, or, as some say, a tall stalk of fennel, growing; and when he had broken it off he saw that its hollow center was filled with a dry, soft pith which would burn slowly and keep on fire a long time. He took the long stalk in his hands, and started with it towards the dwelling of the sun in the far east.

"Mankind shall have fire in spite of the tyrant who sits on the mountain top," he said.

He reached the place of the sun in the early morning just as the glowing, golden orb was rising from the earth and beginning his daily journey through the sky. He touched the end of the long reed to the flames, and the dry pith caught on fire and burned slowly. Then he turned and hastened back to his own land, carrying with him the precious spark hidden in the hollow center of the plant.

He called some of the shivering men from their caves and built a fire for them, and showed them how to warm themselves by it and how to build other fires from the coals. Soon there was a cheerful blaze in every rude home in the land, and men and women gathered round it and were warm and happy, and thankful to Prometheus for the wonderful gift which he had brought to them from the sun.

It was not long until they learned to cook their food and so to eat like men instead of like beasts. They began at once to leave off their wild and savage habits; and instead of lurking in the dark places of the world, they came out into the open air and the bright sunlight, and were glad because life had been given to them.

After that, Prometheus taught them, little by little, a thousand things. He showed them how to build houses of wood and stone, and how to tame sheep and cattle and make them useful, and how to plow and sow and reap, and how to protect themselves from the storms of winter and the beasts of the woods. Then he showed them how to dig in the earth for copper and iron, and how to melt the ore, and how to hammer it into shape and fashion from it the tools and weapons which they needed in peace and war; and when he saw how happy the world was becoming he cried out:

"A new Golden Age shall come, brighter and better by far than the old!"

How Diseases and Cares Came to Man

Things might have gone on very happily indeed, and the Golden Age might really have come again, had it not been for Jupiter. But one day, when he chanced to look down upon the earth, he saw the fires burning, and the people living in houses, and the flocks feeding on the hills, and the grain ripening in the fields, and this made him very angry.

"Who has done all this?" he asked.

And some one answered, "Prometheus!"

"What! that young Titan!" he cried. "Well, I will punish him in a way that will make him wish I had shut him up in the prison-house with his kinsfolk. But as for those puny men, let them keep their fire. I will make them ten times more miserable than they were before they had it."

Of course it would be easy enough to deal with Prometheus at any time, and so Jupiter was in no great haste about it. He made up his mind to distress mankind first; and he thought of a plan for doing it in a very strange, roundabout way.

In the first place, he ordered his blacksmith Vulcan, whose forge was in the crater of a burning mountain, to take a lump of clay which he gave him, and mold it into the form of a woman. Vulcan did as he was bidden; and when he had finished the image, he carried it up to Jupiter, who was sitting among the clouds with all the Mighty Folk around him. It was nothing but a mere lifeless body, but the great blacksmith had given it a form more perfect than that of any statue that has ever been made.

"Come now!" said Jupiter, "let us all give some goodly gift to this woman;" and he began by giving her life.

Then the others came in their turn, each with a gift for the marvelous creature. One gave her beauty; and another a pleasant voice; and another good manners; and another a kind heart; and another skill in many arts; and, lastly, some one gave her curiosity. Then they called her Pandora, which means the all-gifted, because she had received gifts from them all.

Pandora was so beautiful and so wondrously gifted that no one could help loving her. When the Mighty Folk had admired her for a time, they gave her to Mercury, the light-footed; and he led her down the mountain side to the place where Prometheus and his brother were living and toiling for the good of mankind. He met Epimetheus first, and said to him:

"Epimetheus, here is a beautiful woman, whom Jupiter sent to you to be your wife."

Prometheus had often warned his brother to beware of any gift that Jupiter might send, for he knew that the mighty tyrant could not be trusted; but when Epimetheus saw Pandora, how lovely and wise she was, he forgot all warnings, and took her home to live with him and be his wife.

Pandora was very happy in her new home; and even Prometheus, when he saw her, was pleased with her loveliness. She had brought with her a golden casket, which Jupiter had given her at parting, and which he had told her held many precious things; but wise Athena, the queen of the air, had warned her never, never to open it, nor look at the things inside.

"They must be jewels," she said to herself; and then she thought of how they would add to her beauty if only she could wear them. "Why did Jupiter give them to me if I should never use them, nor so much as look at them?" she asked.

The more she thought about the golden casket, the more curious she was to see what was in it; and every day she took it down from its shelf and felt of the lid, and tried to peer inside of it without opening it.

"Why should I care for what Athena told me?" she said at last. "She is not beautiful, and jewels would be of no use to her. I think that I will look at them, at any rate. Athena will never know. Nobody else will ever know."

She opened the lid a very little, just to peep inside. All at once there was a whirring, rustling sound, and before she could shut it down again, out flew ten thousand strange creatures with death-like faces and gaunt and dreadful forms, such as nobody in all the world had ever seen. They fluttered for a little while about the room, and then flew away to find dwelling-places wherever there were homes of men. They were diseases and cares; for up to that time mankind had not had any kind of sickness, nor felt any troubles of mind, nor worried about what the morrow might bring forth.

These creatures flew into every house, and, without any one seeing them, nestled down in the bosoms of men and women and children, and put an end to all their joy; and ever since that day they have been flitting and creeping, unseen and unheard, over all the land, bringing pain and sorrow and death into every household.

If Pandora had not shut down the lid so quickly, things would have gone much worse. But she closed it just in time to keep the last of the evil creatures from getting out. The name of this creature was Foreboding, and although he was almost half out of the casket, Pandora pushed him back and shut the lid so tight that he could never escape. If he had gone out into the world, men would have known from childhood just what troubles were going to come to them every day of their lives, and they would never have had any joy or hope so long as they lived.

And this was the way in which Jupiter sought to make mankind more miserable than they had been before Prometheus had befriended them.

How the Friend of Man was Punished

The next thing that Jupiter did was to punish Prometheus for stealing fire from the sun. He bade two of his servants, whose names were Strength and Force, to seize the bold Titan and carry him to the topmost peak of the Caucasus Mountains. Then he sent the blacksmith Vulcan to bind him with iron chains and fetter him to the rocks so that he could not move hand or foot.

Vulcan did not like to do this, for he was a friend of Prometheus, and yet he did not dare to disobey. And so the great friend of men, who had given them fire and lifted them out of their wretchedness and shown them how to live, was chained to the mountain peak; and there he hung, with the storm-winds whistling always around

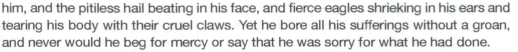

him, and the pitiless hail beating in his face, and fierce eagles shrieking in his ears and tearing his body with their cruel claws. Yet he bore all his sufferings without a groan, and never would he beg for mercy or say that he was sorry for what he had done.

Year after year, and age after age, Prometheus hung there. Now and then old Helios, the driver of the sun car, would look down upon him and smile; now and then flocks of birds would bring him messages from far-off lands; once the ocean nymphs came and sang wonderful songs in his hearing; and oftentimes men looked up to him with pitying eyes, and cried out against the tyrant who had placed him there.

Then, once upon a time, a white cow passed that way,-a strangely beautiful cow, with large sad eyes and a face that seemed almost human. She stopped and looked up at the cold gray peak and the giant body which was chained there. Prometheus saw her and spoke to her kindly:

"I know who you are," he said. "You are Io who was once a fair and happy **maiden** in distant Argos; and now, because of the **tyrant** Jupiter and his jealous queen, you are doomed to wander from land to land in that unhuman form. But do not lose hope. Go on to the southward and then to the west; and after many days you shall come to the great river Nile. There you shall again become a maiden, but fairer and more beautiful than before; and you shall become the wife of the king of that land, and shall give birth to a son, from whom shall spring the hero who will break my chains and set me free. As for me, I bide in patience the day which not even Jupiter can hasten or delay. Farewell!"

Poor Io would have spoken, but she could not. Her sorrowful eyes looked once more at the suffering hero on the peak, and then she turned and began her long and **tiresome** journey to the land of the Nile.

Ages passed, and at last a great hero whose name was Hercules came to the land of the Caucasus. In spite of Jupiter's dread thunderbolts and fearful storms of snow and sleet, he climbed the rugged mountain peak; he slew the fierce eagles that had so long tormented the helpless prisoner on those craggy heights; and with a mighty blow, he broke the fetters of Prometheus and set the grand old hero free.

"I knew that you would come," said Prometheus. "Ten generations ago I spoke of you to Io, who was afterwards the queen of the land of the Nile."

"And Io," said Hercules, "was the mother of the race from which I am sprung."

Complete the SQ3R Analysis. See Appendix.

Baldwin, James. The Golden Fleece: More Old Greek Stories. New York: American Book, 1905. Print.

Short Answers - Prometheus

1. Name some of the differences between humans and gods in this story.

2. What role does Pandora play in this myth?

3. What was Prometheus' flaw?

4. What was Prometheus' punishment?

5. What can we learn from Prometheus that may be relevant to contemporary society?

Essay Topic

In an essay, compare and contrast the Prometheus myth to the Biblical narrative of Adam and Eve. What are the similarities, and what are the differences?

The Flood
According to Greek Mythology

In those very early times there was a man named Deucalion, and he was the son of Prometheus. He was only a common man and not a Titan like his great father, and yet he was known far and wide for his good deeds and the uprightness of his life. His wife's name was Pyrrha, and she was one of the fairest of the daughters of men.

After Jupiter had bound Prometheus on Mount Caucasus and had sent diseases and cares into the world, men became very, very wicked. They no longer built houses and tended their flocks and lived together in peace; but every man was at war with his neighbor, and there was no law nor safety in all the land. Things were in much worse case now than they had been before Prometheus had come among men, and that was just what Jupiter wanted. But as the world became wickeder and wickeder every day, he began to grow weary of seeing so much bloodshed and of hearing the cries of the oppressed and the poor.

"These men," he said to his mighty company, "are nothing but a source of trouble. When they were good and happy, we felt afraid lest they should become greater than ourselves; and now they are so terribly wicked that we are in worse danger than before. There is only one thing to be done with them, and that is to destroy them every one."

The Flood Begins

So he sent a great rain-storm upon the earth, and it rained day and night for a long time; and the sea was filled to the brim, and the water ran over the land and covered first the plains and then the forests and then the hills. But men kept on fighting and robbing, even while the rain was pouring down and the sea was coming up over the land.

No one but Deucalion, the son of Prometheus, was ready for such a storm. He had never joined in any of the wrong doings of those around him, and had often told them that unless they left off their evil ways there would be a day of reckoning in the end. Once every year he had gone to the land of the Caucasus to talk with his father, who was hanging chained to the mountain peak.

"The day is coming," said Prometheus, "when Jupiter will send a flood to destroy mankind from the earth. Be sure that you are ready for it, my son."

And so when the rain began to fall, Deucalion drew from its shelter a boat which he had built for just such a time. He called fair Pyrrha, his wife, and the two sat in the boat and were floated safely on the rising waters. Day and night, day and night, I cannot tell how long, the boat drifted hither and thither. The tops of the trees were hidden by the flood, and then the hills and then the mountains; and Deucalion and Pyrrha could see nothing anywhere but water, water, water-and they knew that all the people in the land had been drowned.

The Rain Stopped

After a while the rain stopped falling, and the clouds cleared away, and the blue sky and the golden sun came out overhead. Then the water began to sink very fast and to run off the land towards the sea; and early the very next day the boat was drifted high upon a mountain called Parnassus, and Deucalion and Pyrrha stepped out upon the dry land. After that, it was only a short time until the whole country was laid bare, and the trees shook their leafy branches in the wind, and the fields were carpeted with grass and flowers more beautiful than in the days before the flood.

But Deucalion and Pyrrha were very sad, for they knew that they were the only persons who were left alive in all the land. At last they started to walk down the mountain side towards the plain, wondering what would become of them now, all alone as they were in the wide world. While they were talking and trying to think what they should do, they heard a voice behind them. They turned and saw a noble young prince standing on one of the rocks above them. He was very tall, with blue eyes and yellow hair. There were wings on his shoes and on his cap, and in his hands he bore a staff with golden serpents twined around it. They knew at once that he was Mercury, the swift messenger of the Mighty Ones, and they waited to hear what he would say.

"Is there anything that you wish?" he asked. "Tell me, and you shall have whatever you desire."

"We should like, above all things," said Deucalion, "to see this land full of people once more; for without neighbors and friends, the world is a very lonely place indeed."

The Casting of Mother Earth's Bones

"Go on down the mountain," said Mercury, "and as you go, cast the bones of your mother over your shoulders behind you;" and, with these words, he leaped into the air and was seen no more.

"What did he mean?" asked Pyrrha.

"Surely I do not know," said Deucalion. "But let us think a moment. Who is our mother, if it is not the Earth, from whom all living things have sprung? And yet what could he mean by the bones of our mother?"

"Perhaps he meant the stones of the earth," said Pyrrha. "Let us go on down the mountain, and as we go, let us pick up the stones in our path and throw them over our shoulders behind us."

"It is rather a silly thing to do," said Deucalion; "and yet there can be no harm in it, and we shall see what will happen."

And so they walked on, down the steep slope of Mount Parnassus, and as they walked they picked up the loose stones in their way and cast them over their shoulders; and strange to say, the stones which Deucalion threw sprang up as full-grown men, strong, and handsome, and brave; and the stones which Pyrrha threw sprang up as full-grown women, lovely and fair. When at last they reached the plain they found themselves at the head of a noble company of human beings, all eager to serve them.

So Deucalion became their king, and he set them in homes, and taught them how to till the ground, and how to do many useful things; and the land was filled with people who were happier and far better than those who had dwelt there before the flood. And they named the country Hellas, after Hellen, the son of Deucalion and Pyrrha; and the people are to this day called **Hellenes**.

But we call the country GREECE.

Complete the SQ3R Analysis. See Appendix.

Baldwin, James. *The Golden Fleece: More Old Greek Stories.* New York: American Book, 1905. Print.

Short Answer Questions – The Flood According to Greek Mythology

1. What is a synonym for Hellenes?

2. What role does Mercury play in the Flood myth?

3. How is Deucalion related to Prometheus? What kind of relationship do they have?

4. How are the bones renewed and revived in the Greek Flood myth?

Essay Topic

1. How do the Greeks account for the flood in contrast to the Gilgamesh and Biblical Flood narratives? What is the same in all narratives, and what is different.

2. Think about the stories that represent the "Fall of Man," the punishment of man, and the renewal of man through immersion in water. Consider narratives you are familiar with, and write a comparative account of these narratives as a critical assessment of your own.

THE SELFISH NATURE

Notes

Chapter 2

❧

The Selfish Nature

Comparing and Contrasting Cultures

Webster's dictionary defines the term selfish as "excessively or exclusively with oneself : seeking or concentrating on one's own advantage, pleasure, or well-being without regard for others." Its second definition says that it arises from "concern with one's own welfare or advantage in disregard of others <a selfish act>." In scientific terms it is "actively replicating repetitive sequence of nucleic acid that serves no known function <selfish DNA>; also: being genetic material solely concerned with its own replication <selfish genes>". Each of these ideas can be used to explain human nature's need to preserve one's own best interest.

Each of the selected stories selected in the chapter manifest the selfish nature of ancient man, specifically as it relates to jealousy, self-interest, and judgment. The "Cain and Abel" accounts are Hebrew, Christian, Islamic and Armenian, and show similarities in theme and structure. Likewise, the accounts of "Solomon and the Two Women" and "Future Buddha as a Wise Judge" show similarities in theme. Determining contrasts in storytelling based upon religious point of view is the subject of this chapter.

As you explore this chapter, look for the following:

- What are the contrasts in the method of storytelling?

- What are the differences in the deity and how they deal with the acts of selfishness and punishment?

- Who are the characters, and what is their historical significance?

- Decipher the judgments according to the religious norms of the time. How to they compare on contrast with one another?

INSTRUCTIONS

1. Complete the KWL chart to see what information you know about the stories you will read.

2. After completing the KWL chart, and doing a research on the story you about to read, write an introduction to introduce this text.

3. At the end of each section, you will complete an outlining notetaking exercise to help you study texts in this chapter. Afterwards, you will write a chapter summary.

C H A R T

KNOW • WANT • LEARN

KWL

ALREADY KNOW	WANT TO KNOW	WHAT I LEARNED

The Biblical Record of Cain and Abel

Genesis 4 (NKJV)

Cain Murders Abel

1 Now Adam knew Eve his wife, and she conceived and bore Cain, and said, "I have acquired a man from the Lord." 2 Then she bore again, this time his brother Abel. Now Abel was a keeper of sheep, but Cain was a tiller of the ground. 3 And in the process of time it came to pass that Cain brought an offering of the fruit of the ground to the Lord. 4 Abel also brought of the firstborn of his flock and of their fat. And the Lord respected Abel and his offering, 5 but He did not respect Cain and his offering. And Cain was very angry, and his countenance fell.

6 So the Lord said to Cain, "Why are you angry? And why has your countenance fallen? 7 If you do well, will you not be accepted? And if you do not do well, sin lies at the door. And its desire is for you, but you should rule over it."

8 Now Cain talked with Abel his brother; and it came to pass, when they were in the field, that Cain rose up against Abel his brother and killed him.

9 Then the Lord said to Cain, "Where is Abel your brother?"

He said, "I do not know. Am I my brother's keeper?"

10 And He said, "What have you done? The voice of your brother's blood cries out to Me from the ground. 11 So now you are cursed from the earth, which has opened its mouth to receive your brother's blood from your hand. 12 When you till the ground, it shall no longer yield its strength to you. A fugitive and a vagabond you shall be on the earth."

13 And Cain said to the Lord, "My punishment is greater than I can bear! 14 Surely You have driven me out this day from the face of the ground; I shall be hidden from Your face; I shall be a fugitive and a vagabond on the earth, and it will happen that anyone who finds me will kill me."

15 And the Lord said to him, "Therefore, whoever kills Cain, vengeance shall be taken on him sevenfold." And the Lord set a mark on Cain, lest anyone finding him should kill him.

The Family of Cain

16 Then Cain went out from the presence of the Lord and dwelt in the land of Nod on the east of Eden. 17 And Cain knew his wife, and she conceived and bore Enoch. And he built a city, and called the name of the city after the name of his son—Enoch. 18 To Enoch was born Irad; and Irad begot Mehujael, and Mehujael begot Methushael, and Methushael begot Lamech.

Notes

19 Then Lamech took for himself two wives: the name of one was Adah, and the name of the second was Zillah. 20 And Adah bore Jabal. He was the father of those who dwell in tents and have livestock. 21 His brother's name was Jubal. He was the father of all those who play the harp and flute. 22 And as for Zillah, she also bore Tubal-Cain, an instructor of every craftsman in bronze and iron. And the sister of Tubal-Cain was Naamah.

23 Then Lamech said to his wives:

> "Adah and Zillah, hear my voice;
> Wives of Lamech, listen to my speech!
> For I have killed a man for wounding me,
> Even a young man for hurting me.
> 24 If Cain shall be avenged sevenfold,
> Then Lamech seventy-sevenfold."

A New Son

25 And Adam knew his wife again, and she bore a son and named him Seth, "For God has appointed another seed for me instead of Abel, whom Cain killed." 26 And as for Seth, to him also a son was born; and he named him Enosh. Then men began to call on the name of the Lord.

New King James Version (NKJV)
Scripture taken from the New King James Version®. Copyright © 1982 by Thomas Nelson. Used by permission. All rights reserved.

Practice the outline notetaking skill here. Then write a summary of "The Biblical Record of Cain and Abel"

OUTLINE AND NOTES

_____
_____
_____
_____
_____
_____
_____
_____
_____
_____
_____
_____
_____
_____
_____
_____
_____
_____
_____
_____
_____
_____
_____
_____
_____

Write a summary of "The Biblical Record of Cain and Abel

The Story of the Two Sons of Adam

The Quran

The Quran, 5:27-31

Recite to them the story of the two sons of Adam; truly when they offered an offering, and it was accepted from one of them, and was not accepted from the other, that one said, "I will surely kill thee;" he said, "God only accepts from those who fear. If thou dost stretch forth to me thine hand to kill me, I will not stretch forth mine hand to kill thee; verily, I fear God, the Lord of the worlds; verily, I wish that thou mayest draw upon thee my sin and thy sin, and be of the fellows of the Fire, for that is the reward of the unjust."

But his soul allowed him to slay his brother, and he slew him, and in the morning he was of those who lose. And God sent a crow to scratch in the earth and show him how he might hide his brother's shame, he said, "Alas, for me! Am I too helpless to become like this crow and hide my brother's shame?" and in the morning he was of those who did repent.

Copied from the English Translated Holy Quran.
http://www.usc.edu/org/cmje/religious-texts/quran/verses/005-qmt.php#005.027

Practice the outline notetaking skill here. Then write a summary of "The Two Sons of Adam According to the Quran"

OUTLINE AND NOTES

_____
_____
_____
_____
_____
_____
_____
_____
_____
_____

Write a summary of "The Two Sons of Adam According to the Quran"

_____
_____
_____
_____
_____
_____
_____
_____
_____
_____
_____
_____
_____

Cain and Abel

Turkey (Armenian)

One day Eve called to her Cain and Abel, who, still little children, were playing on the grass.

She held out to her firstborn her right arm, and to her second son her left, and said, "Bite them, I command you."

The elder boy bit till he drew blood, but Abel merely imprinted a long lingering kiss on his mother's arm.

Then said Eve to her husband, "Our Cain will be a wicked man."

Adam and Eve loved Abel dearly. Cain was jealous of their partiality. He wished to kill his brother, but knew not how. Satan took the form of a raven, picked a quarrel with another raven, and in Cain's presence cut his opponent's throat with a pointed black pebble. Cain picked up the stone, hid it in his girdle, proposed to his brother a walk on the mountain, and there cut his throat with the pebble. The peasants of Armenia to this day call flints "Satan's nails," and conscientiously break every pointed black one they may find.

Cain, after his crime, dared not return to his parents; the blood of his brother still adhered to his hands. In vain did he hold them all day long immersed in a neighboring spring; the stain was still there. Night came on, and, not being able to sleep, he wandered long and far, seeking a waterfall. Guided at last to one by the noise of its waters in the still night, he lay down on the bank and held his reddened hands under the cascade. There he held them, day and night, summer and winter, during a whole year, without sleep and without food, but at the end of that time they were still as crimson as on the day of the crime.

And so long as Cain lived, he was never able to get rid of the proof of his fratricide.

·······• ⟲⟳ •·······

Source: Lucy M. J. Garnett, The Women of Turkey and Their Folk-Lore (London: David Nutt, 1890), pp. 273-74.

Practice the outline notetaking skill here. Then write a summary of "Cain and Abel (Armenian)"

OUTLINE AND NOTES

_____

_____

_____

_____

_____

_____

_____

_____

_____

_____

_____

_____

Write a summary of "Cain and Abel (Armenian)"

_____

_____

_____

_____

_____

_____

_____

_____

_____

_____

Short Answer Questions "Cain and Abel"

1. What is consistent in each of the Cain and Abel narratives?

2. When contrasting the "Cain and Abel" stories, what are the differences between the narratives? Create a chart or an outline to show the differences in the narratives.

3. Based upon what you know about the oral tradition, why do you think there are differences in the accounts of "Cain and Abel?"

Essay Topics

1. Which of the "Cain and Abel" accounts do you believe is the most consistent with the way the original story was told? Was the "Biblical Cain and Abel", the "Quran Cain and Abel" or the "Armenian Cain and Abel" the most reliable? Compare and contrast these texts to support your claim.

2. In the "Biblical account of Cain and Abel", Cain asks God, "Am I my brother's keeper"? This quote has been used over time to question one's individual responsibility to make the world a better place. Write an essay on the topic of social responsibility or social justice based upon the question, "Am I my brother's keeper?" Consider the "Biblical Account of Cain and Abel" in your response.

3. What does the "Cain and Abel" story tell us today? How can we apply it in our families, relationships, community, nation and world?

C H A R T

KNOW • WANT • LEARN

KWL

ALREADY KNOW	WANT TO KNOW	WHAT I LEARNED

The Biblical Account of Solomon and the Two Women

I Kings 3:16-28 (NKJV)

Then came there two women, that were harlots, unto King Solomon, and stood before him. And the one woman said, "Oh my lord, I and this woman dwell in one house; and I was delivered of a child with her in the house. And it came to pass the third day after that I was delivered, that this woman was delivered also: and we were together; there was no stranger with us in the house, save we two in the house. And this woman's child died in the night; because she overlaid it. And she arose at midnight, and took my son from beside me, while thine handmaid slept, and laid it in her bosom, and laid her dead child in my bosom. And when I rose in the morning to give my child suck, behold, it was dead: but when I had considered it in the morning, behold, it was not my son, which I did bear."

And the other woman said, "Nay; but the living is my son, and the dead is thy son."

And this said, "No; but the dead is thy son, and the living is my son." Thus they spake before the king.

Then said the king, "The one saith, 'This is my son that liveth, and thy son is the dead'; and the other saith, 'Nay; but thy son is the dead, and my son is the living.'" And the king said, "Bring me a sword." And they brought a sword before the king. And the king said, "Divide the living child in two, and give half to the one, and half to the other."

Then spake the woman whose the living child was unto the king, for her bowels yearned upon her son, and she said, "Oh my lord, give her the living child, and in no wise slay it."

But the other said, "Let it be neither mine nor thine, but divide it."

Then the king answered and said, "Give her the living child, and in no wise slay it: she is the mother thereof."

And all Israel heard of the judgment which the king had judged; and they feared the king: for they saw that the wisdom of God was in him, to do judgment.

New King James Version (NKJV)
Scripture taken from the New King James Version®. Copyright © 1982 by Thomas Nelson. Used by permission. All rights reserved.

Practice the outline notetaking skill here. Then write a summary of "The Biblical Account of Solomon and the Two Women"

OUTLINE AND NOTES

Write a summary of "The Biblical Account of Solomon and the Two Women"

The Future Buddha as a Wise Judge

Jakata Tales

A woman, carrying her child, went to the future Buddha's tank to wash. And having first bathed the child, she put on her upper garment and descended into the water to bathe herself. Then a Yakshini, seeing the child, had a craving to eat it. And taking the form of a woman, she drew near, and asked the mother, "Friend, this is a very pretty child. Is it one of yours?" And when she was told it was, she asked if she might nurse it. And this being allowed, she nursed it a little, and then carried it off. But when the mother saw this, she ran after her, and cried out, "Where are you taking my child to?" and caught hold of her.

The Yakshini boldly said, "Where did you get the child from? It is mine!" And so quarreling, they passed the door of the future Buddha's Judgment Hall.

He heard the noise, sent for them, inquired into the matter, and asked them whether they would abide by his decision. And they agreed. Then he had a line drawn on the ground; and told the Yakshini to take hold of the child's arms, and the mother to take hold of its legs; and said, "The child shall be hers who drags him over the line."

But as soon as they pulled at him, the mother, seeing how he suffered, grieved as if her heart would break. And letting him go, she stood there weeping.

Then the future Buddha asked the bystanders, "Whose hearts are tender to babes? Those who have borne children, or those who have not?"

And they answered, "Oh sire! The hearts of mothers are tender."

Then he said, "Who, think you, is the mother? She who has the child in her arms, or she who has let go?"

And they answered, "She who has let go is the mother."

And he said, "Then do you all think that the other was the thief?"

And they answered, "Sire! We cannot tell."

And he said, "Verily, this is a Yakshini, who took the child to eat it."

And he replied, "Because her eyes winked not, and were red, and she knew no fear, and had no pity, I knew it."

And so saying, he demanded of the thief, "Who are you?"

And she said, "Lord! I am a Yakshini."

And he asked, "Why did you take away this child?"

And she said, "I thought to eat him, Oh my Lord!"

And he rebuked her, saying, "Oh foolish woman! For your former sins you have been born a Yakshini, and now do you still sin!" And he laid a vow upon her to keep the Five Commandments, and let her go.

But the mother of the child exalted the future Buddha, and said, "Oh my Lord! Oh great physician! May your life be long!" And she went away, with her babe clasped to her bosom.

Buddhist Birth-Stories; or, Jataka Tales, edited by V. Fausbøll and translated by T. W. Rhys Davids, vol. 1 (London: Trübner and Company, 1880), pp. xiv-xvi. This tale is one of several stories included in the multi-part Jataka no. 546.

Practice the outline notetaking skill here. Then write a summary of "Future Buddha as Wise Judge"

OUTLINE AND NOTES

Write a summary of "The Biblical Account of "Future Buddha as Wise Judge"

Short Answer Questions

1. What are the similarities and differences in the stories of the wise king and two women?

2. What are the differences in the descriptions of the two women in both of the narratives? Define the terms used to describe the women in your response.

3. How does the position of the women in the community impact the reader's perspective of the women?

4. In the biblical account of "Solomon and the Two Women" there is evidence of a violation of the Mosaic Ten Commandments. Which commandments are broken and how are they violated.

5. How is the common theme of both of these narratives relevant today, especially as it relates to family relationships and world issues?

Essay Topics

1. In the Biblical account of "Solomon and the Two Women," do you believe that Solomon would have killed the child if the mother did not respond as she did? What information leads you to this conclusion? To answer this question, do a "background check" on King Solomon. Research information about King Solomon's reign and family. Introduce new information not found in the story to support your position. Combine both new researched information and evidence from I Kings 3:16-28 to support your claim.

2. "The Future Buddha as a Wise Judge" is based upon moral precepts in Pali Buddhism. Read "The Five Moral Precepts of Pali Buddhism" and explain how the five precepts are at work in "The Future Buddha as a Wise Judge" text.

BELIEF SYSTEMS FOR SOCIAL MORALITY

The Five Moral Precepts of Pali Buddhism

The Biblical Account of The Mosaic Ten Commandments

Notes

Chapter 3

❧

Belief Systems for Social Morality

Considering Cause and Effect

Have you ever heard the statement, "When in Rome, do as the Romans"? Imagine if you were actually in Rome and you didn't know the laws or culture of the city. It would be virtually impossible to "DO as the Romans."

The Romans were one of the most legally minded people in history. The development of their law was Rome's GREATEST and most enduring achievement. We base much of our current legal system on ideas found in the Romans Twelve Tablets of Law.

Around 450 B.C., the Romans placed the Twelve Tables of Law on view in the Forum, a public meeting area for the civic, religious and commercial activities of Rome to provide its citizens instructions with the civil code for their empire. When the Empire declined, it was carried forward into the legal system of the Middle Ages, where it became the model for European and South American law codes until the 20th century.

Roman law was based on the concept of justice and the rights for the individual. It is from the Romans that we inherited the following beliefs:

- A man should not be accused anonymously
- He should not be penalized for what he thinks
- He should be considered innocent until he is proven guilty.
- A man should be given everything which is his own.

Remarkably, Rome's legal system developed in a pagan society, in which slave labor was common, turned out to be adaptable to the Christian society of the Middle Ages, the capitalists of the 17century, and to us today. Research the Twelve Tables of Law to learn more about the effects of Roman law on the Roman Empire and the American justice system.

In this chapter we will look at the origins of the law in the Mosaic Ten Commandments and the moral code of Pali Buddhism. This chapter emphasizes the cause and effect relationships between the laws and of the ancient world and their effects on our modern methods of law.

As you read the sections in the chapter, consider the following ideas:

- How does Pali Buddhism compare to the Mosaic Ten Commandments in terms of producing a moral code?
- How has the Mosaic Ten Commandments impacted the basic laws in the American legal system?
- Why are the Mosaic Ten Commandments a part of the American legal system?
- Is there really a separation of church and state?

These are the questions to explore as you read the next chapter.

INSTRUCTIONS

1. Complete the KWL chart to see what information you know about the stories you will read.
2. After completing the KWL chart, and doing a research on the story you about to read, write an introduction to introduce this text.
3. At the end of each section, you will complete an outlining notetaking exercise to help you study texts in this chapter. Afterwards, you will write a chapter summary

C H A R T

KNOW • WANT • LEARN

KWL

ALREADY KNOW	WANT TO KNOW	WHAT I LEARNED

Notes

The Five Moral Precepts of Pali Buddhism

I undertake the training rule to abstain from killing.
I undertake the training rule to abstain from taking what is not given.
I undertake the training rule to avoid sexual misconduct.
I undertake the training rule to abstain from false speech.
I undertake the training rule to abstain from fermented drink that causes heedlessness.

Practice the outline notetaking skill here. Then write a summary of "Five Precepts of Pali Buddhism"

OUTLINE AND NOTES

_____
_____
_____
_____
_____
_____
_____
_____
_____
_____
_____

Write a summary of "The Five Precepts of Pali Buddhism"

_____
_____
_____
_____
_____
_____
_____
_____
_____
_____
_____
_____
_____

CHART

KNOW • WANT • LEARN

KWL

ALREADY KNOW	WANT TO KNOW	WHAT I LEARNED

The Biblical Account of the The Mosaic Ten Commandments

Exodus 20 (NKJV)

1 And God spoke all these words, saying:

2 "I am the Lord your God, who brought you out of the land of Egypt, out of the house of bondage.

3 "You shall have no other gods before Me.

4 "You shall not make for yourself a carved image—any likeness of anything that is in heaven above, or that is in the earth beneath, or that is in the water under the earth; 5 you shall not bow down to them nor serve them. For I, the Lord your God, am a jealous God, visiting the iniquity of the fathers upon the children to the third and fourth generations of those who hate Me, 6 but showing mercy to thousands, to those who love Me and keep My commandments.

7 "You shall not take the name of the Lord your God in vain, for the Lord will not hold him guiltless who takes His name in vain.

8 "Remember the Sabbath day, to keep it holy. 9 Six days you shall labor and do all your work, 10 but the seventh day is the Sabbath of the Lord your God. In it you shall do no work: you, nor your son, nor your daughter, nor your male servant, nor your female servant, nor your cattle, nor your stranger who is within your gates. 11 For in six days the Lord made the heavens and the earth, the sea, and all that is in them, and rested the seventh day. Therefore the Lord blessed the Sabbath day and hallowed it.

12 "Honor your father and your mother, that your days may be long upon the land which the Lord your God is giving you.

13 "You shall not murder.

14 "You shall not commit adultery.

15 "You shall not steal.

16 "You shall not bear false witness against your neighbor.

17 "You shall not covet your neighbor's house; you shall not covet your neighbor's wife, nor his male servant, nor his female servant, nor his ox, nor his donkey, nor anything that is your neighbor."

New King James Version (NKJV)
Scripture taken from the New King James Version®. Copyright © 1982 by Thomas Nelson. Used by permission. All rights reserved.

Practice the outline notetaking skill here. Then write a summary of "The Ten Commandments"

OUTLINE AND NOTES

Write a summary of "The Ten Commandments"

Short Answer Responses

1. Discuss three common ideas in "The Five Moral Precepts of Pali Buddhism" and "The Mosaic Ten Commandments".

2. How do these principles work today in American government? Explain five laws and how they function in today's society.

3. Why do you think "The Five Moral Precepts of Pali Buddhism" and the "Mosaic Ten Commandments" are similar although they represent different religions?

4. If you could change any of "The Five Moral Precepts of Pail Buddhism" which would you change to fit your personal moral code?

_____

_____

_____

_____

_____

_____

_____

_____

_____

_____

_____

_____

_____

_____

_____

_____

_____

_____

_____

_____

Essay Topics

1. Which of the laws in the "Mosaic Ten Commandments" are the least respected today? What does it say about our current culture? Research customs and penalties for breaking the law in ancient Hebrew culture. How does our culture treat its citizens who break the law in contrast to ancient Hebrew citizens? Discuss penalties for breaking these laws as evidence to support your claims.

2. Envision a world where the penalty for killing, adultery and theft were punishable by death. Do you think the world would be safer, and if so, how? Who do you think the death penalty effect most in this world? What potential solutions or problems could this society face in terms of ensuring social justice?

3. If you had the ability to create your own legal code, which of the "Mosaic Ten Commandments" or "The Five Moral Precepts of Pali Buddhism" would you keep, and which would you discard? Write a cause and effect essay where you predict the outcome of the society you create based upon including or omitting certain laws.

Chapter 4

❧

Ancient Ideas of Social Responsibility

Deciphering Meaning in Ancient Texts

The idea that those in an advantageous position, either in terms of money or power, should conduct in a socially responsible way can be traced back to classical Athens of 500 B.C. This ancient concept of the wealthy should share a portion of their accumulated wealth with their fellow citizens is rooted in the idea that the Greek citizens helped the wealthy become wealthy through purchasing their goods. Therefore, as a result of their accumulation of money from the Greek citizens, the wealthy ought to be benevolent and share their wealth with fellow citizens.

The donations made to the general public were called liturgies. Although they worked similar to the taxation we know today, they were not mandatory.

- They were only imposed on the very wealthy
- They very wealthy had to own substantial land.
- They were signs of honor.
- Most who donated gave more than what was required.
- There were two forms of liturgies. The most common were religious and the least common were military.

Another form of ancient social responsibility is the idea that one should help others because they received help from others. Aristotle, in his Nicomachean Ethics and Politics, presents the two basic types of benefactors in the Hellenistic world.

- The great souled man is a member of the upper class who engages in the providing gifts to other wealthy people.

- The magnificent man is noble in character and provides gifts to his community out of his own wealth.
- They often have inherited wealth and residual income because they
- provide a necessary service for the city.
- In exchange for their access to the city and citizens to provide these necessary services, the city would expect the *"noble man"* to provide various services to the city in exchange for public honor from the citizens.
- In the Art of Rhetoric, Aristotle states that true wealth consists in doing good; that is, in monetary handouts, giving of scarce and costly gifts, and helping others to maintain an existence.

Greek mythology provides us with worthwhile examples of benefactors. As we learned in the first chapter of Mythology and Belief, the first benefactor was Prometheus. He is the first benefactor to give man the gift of fire. Athena, the goddess of wisdom and war, gave the olive branch as a symbol of peace and prosperity, and thus had Athens named in her honor.

A famous ancient Grecian affiliated with social responsibility and benevolence is Hippocrates, from whom doctors today thank for the Hippocratic Oath. Upon this oath, doctors agree to treat the total human and not just the ailments. Hippocrates advised doctors to, "Sometimes give your services for nothing, calling to mind a previous benefaction or present satisfaction. And if there be an opportunity of serving one who is a stranger in financial straits, give full assistance to all such."

In this chapter, we will explore the stories of social responsibility in the ancient world. In an excerpt of Roman writer Ovid's text, Metamorphoses, we will explore the myths of "Philemon and Baucis." Then we will explore the Biblical Old Testament story of the prophet "Elijah and the Widow of Zarephath" as well as the "Biblical New Testament story of Paul and Barnabus in Lystra."

We will analyze these texts for the characters display of social responsibility as it relates to their fellow man or lack there of. As you read this section, you should ask the following questions:

- What is the significant theme of each story?
- Why are the deities represented a crucial part of the story?
- What lessons do these stories teach us about responsibility for our fellow man?

These are the questions to explore as you read the next chapter.

INSTRUCTIONS

1. Complete the KWL chart to see what information you know about the stories you will read.
2. After completing the KWL chart, and doing a research on the story you about to read, write an introduction to introduce this text.
3. At the end of each section, you will complete an SQ3R exercise to study the texts in this chapter.

CHART

KNOW • WANT • LEARN

KWL

ALREADY KNOW	WANT TO KNOW	WHAT I LEARNED

Notes

Metamorphoses Book VIII

Philemon and Baucis
Ovid

Fable VI

Jupiter and Mercury, disguised in human shape, are received by Philemon and Baucis, after having been refused admittance by their neighbors. The Gods, in acknowledgment of their hospitality, transform their cottage into a temple, of which, at their own request, they are made the priest and priestess; and, after a long life, the worthy couple are changed into trees. The village where they live is laid under water, on account of the impiety of the inhabitants, and is turned into a lake. Acheloüs here relates the surprising changes of Proteus.

After these things the river was silent. The wondrous deed .had astonished them all. The son of Ixion laughed at them, believing the story; and as he was a despiser of the Gods, and of a haughty disposition, he said, "Acheloüs, thou dost relate a fiction, and dost deem the Gods more powerful than they are, if they both give and take away the form of things." At this all were amazed, and did not approve of such language; and before all, Lelex, ripe in understanding and age, spoke thus: "The power of heaven is immense, and has no limits; and whatever the Gods above will, 'tis done.

"And that thou mayst the less doubt of this, there is upon the Phrygian hills, an oak near to the lime tree, enclosed by a low wall. I, myself, have seen the spot; for Pittheus sent me into the land of Pelops, once governed by his father, Pelops. Not far thence is a standing water, formerly habitable ground, but now frequented by cormorants and coots, that delight in fens. Jupiter came hither in the shape of a man, and together with his parent, the grandson of Atlas, Mercury, the bearer of the Caduceus, having laid aside his wings. To a thousand houses did they go, asking for lodging and for rest. A thousand houses did the bolts fasten against them. Yet one received them, a small one indeed, thatched with straw, and the reeds of the marsh. But a pious old woman named Baucis, and Philemon of a like age, were united in their youthful years in that cottage, and in it, they grew old together; and by owning their poverty, they rendered it light, and not to be endured with discontented mind. It matters not, whether you ask for the masters there, or for the servants; the whole family are but two; the same persons both obey and command. When, therefore, the inhabitants of heaven reached this little abode, and, bending their necks, entered the humble door, the old man bade them rest their limbs on a bench set there; upon which the attentive Baucis threw a coarse cloth. Then she moves the warm embers on the hearth, and stirs up the fire they had had the day before, and supplies it with leaves and dry bark, and with her aged breath kindles it into a flame; and brings out of the house dry bits of branches, and breaks them, and puts them beneath a small boiler. Some pot-herbs, too, which her husband has gathered in the well-watered garden, she strips of their leaves.

"With a two-pronged fork Philemon lifts down a rusty side of bacon, that hangs from a black beam; and cuts off a small portion from the chine that has been kept so long; and when cut, softens it in boiling water. In the meantime, with discourse they beguile the intervening hours; and suffer not the length of time to be perceived.

There is a beechen trough there that hangs on a peg by its crooked handle; this is filled with warm water, and receives their limbs to refresh them. On the middle of the couch, its feet and frame being made of willow, is placed a cushion of soft sedge. This they cover with cloths, which they have not been accustomed to place there but on festive occasions; but even these cloths are coarse and old, though not unfitting for a couch of willow. The Gods seat themselves. The old woman, wearing an apron, and shaking with palsy, sets the table before them. But the third leg of the table is too short; a potsherd, placed beneath, makes it equal. After this, being placed beneath, has taken away the inequality, green mint rubs down the table thus made level. Here are set the double-tinted berries of the chaste Minerva, and cornel-berries, gathered in autumn, and preserved in a thin pickle; endive, too, and radishes, and a large piece of curdled milk, and eggs, that have been gently turned in the slow embers; all served in earthenware. After this, an embossed goblet of similar clay is placed there; cups, too, made of beech wood, varnished, where they are hollowed out, with yellow wax.

"There is now a short pause; the fire then sends up the warm repast; and wine kept no long time, is again put on; and then, set aside for a little time, it gives place to the second course. Here are nuts, and here are dried figs mixed with wrinkled dates, plums too, and fragrant apples in wide baskets, and grapes gathered from the purple vines. In the middle there is white honey-comb. Above all, there are welcome looks, and no indifferent and niggardly feelings. In the meanwhile, as oft as Baucis and the alarmed Philemon behold the goblet, when drunk off, replenish itself of its own accord, and the wine increase of itself, astonished at this singular event, they are frightened, and, with hands held up, they offer their prayers, and entreat pardon for their entertainment, and their want of preparation. There was a single goose, the guardian of their little cottage, which its owners were preparing to kill for the Deities, their guests. Swift with its wings, it wearied them, rendered slow by age, and it escaped them a long time, and at length seemed to fly for safety to the Gods themselves. The immortals forbade it to be killed, and said, 'We are Divinities, and this impious neighborhood shall suffer deserved punishment. To you it will be allowed to be free from this calamity; only leave your habitation, and attend our steps, and go together to the summit of the mountain.'

"They both obeyed; and, supported by staffs, they endeavored to place their feet on the top of the high hill. They were now as far from the top, as an arrow discharged can go at once, when they turned their eyes, and beheld the other parts sinking in a morass, and their own abode alone remaining. While they were wondering at these things, and while they were bewailing the fate of their fellow countrymen, that old cottage of theirs too little for even two owners, was changed into a temple. Columns took the place of forked stakes, the thatch grew yellow, and the earth was covered with marble; the doors appeared carved, and the roof to be of gold. Then, the son of Saturn uttered such words as these with benign lips: 'Tell us, good old man, and thou, wife, worthy of a husband so good, what it is you desire?' Having spoken a few words to Baucis, Philemon discovered their joint request to the Gods: 'We desire to be your priests, and to have the care of your temple; and, since we have passed our years in harmony, let the same hour take us off both together; and let me not ever see the tomb of my wife, nor let me be destined to be buried by her.' Their wishes were fulfilled. So long as life was granted, they were the keepers of the temple; and when, enervated by years and old age, they were standing, by chance, before the sacred steps, and were relating the fortunes of the spot, Baucis beheld Philemon, and the aged Philemon saw Baucis, too, shooting into leaf. And now the tops of the trees growing above their two faces, so long as they could they exchanged words with each other, and said together, 'Farewell! my spouse;' and at the same moment the branches covered their concealed faces. The inhabitants of Tyana still shew these adjoining trees, made of their two bodies. Old men, no romancers, (and there was no reason why they should wish to deceive me) told me this. I, indeed, saw garlands hanging on the branches, and placing there some fresh ones myself, I said, 'The good are the peculiar care of the Gods, and those who worshipped the Gods, are now worshipped themselves.'"

He had now ceased; and the thing itself and the relator of it had astonished them all; and especially Theseus, whom, desiring to hear of the wonderful actions of the Gods, the Calydonian river leaning on his elbow, addressed in words such as these: "There are, O most valiant hero, some things, whose form has been once changed, and then has continued under that change. There are some whose privilege it is to pass into many shapes, as thou, Proteus, inhabitant of the sea that embraces the earth. For people have seen thee one while a young man, and again a lion; at one time thou wast a furious boar, at another a serpent, which they dreaded to touch; and sometimes, horns rendered thee a bull. Oft times thou mightst be seen as a stone; often, too, as a tree. Sometimes imitating the appearance of flowing water, thou wast a river; sometimes fire, the very contrary of water."

Complete the SQ3R Analysis. See Appendix.

Ovid, and Henry T. Riley. The Metamorphoses of Ovid. Philadelphia: D. McKay, 1899. Print.

C H A R T

KNOW • WANT • LEARN

KWL

ALREADY KNOW	WANT TO KNOW	WHAT I LEARNED

The Biblical Account of The Prophet Elijah and the Widow of Zarephath

1 Kings 17 (NKJV)

Elijah Proclaims a Drought

17 And Elijah the Tishbite, of the inhabitants of Gilead, said to Ahab, "As the Lord God of Israel lives, before whom I stand, there shall not be dew nor rain these years, except at my word."

2 Then the word of the Lord came to him, saying, 3 "Get away from here and turn eastward, and hide by the Brook Cherith, which flows into the Jordan. 4 And it will be that you shall drink from the brook, and I have commanded the ravens to feed you there."

5 So he went and did according to the word of the Lord, for he went and stayed by the Brook Cherith, which flows into the Jordan. 6 The ravens brought him bread and meat in the morning, and bread and meat in the evening; and he drank from the brook. 7 And it happened after a while that the brook dried up, because there had been no rain in the land.

Elijah and the Widow

8 Then the word of the Lord came to him, saying, 9 "Arise, go to Zarephath, which belongs to Sidon, and dwell there. See, I have commanded a widow there to provide for you." 10 So he arose and went to Zarephath. And when he came to the gate of the city, indeed a widow was there gathering sticks. And he called to her and said, "Please bring me a little water in a cup, that I may drink." 11 And as she was going to get it, he called to her and said, "Please bring me a **morsel** of bread in your hand."

12 So she said, "As the Lord your God lives, I do not have bread, only a handful of flour in a bin, and a little oil in a jar; and see, I am gathering a couple of sticks that I may go in and prepare it for myself and my son, that we may eat it, and die."

13 And Elijah said to her, "Do not fear; go and do as you have said, but make me a small cake from it first, and bring it to me; and afterward make some for yourself and your son. 14 For thus says the Lord God of Israel: 'The bin of flour shall not be used up, nor shall the jar of oil run dry, until the day the Lord sends rain on the earth.'"

15 So she went away and did according to the word of Elijah; and she and he and her household ate for many days. 16 The bin of flour was not used up, nor did the jar of oil run dry, according to the word of the Lord which He spoke by Elijah.

Notes

Elijah Revives the Widow's Son

17 Now it happened after these things that the son of the woman who owned the house became sick. And his sickness was so serious that there was no breath left in him. 18 So she said to Elijah, "What have I to do with you, O man of God? Have you come to me to bring my sin to **remembrance**, and to kill my son?"

19 And he said to her, "Give me your son." So he took him out of her arms and carried him to the upper room where he was staying, and laid him on his own bed. 20 Then he cried out to the Lord and said, "O Lord my God, have You also brought tragedy on the widow with whom I lodge, by killing her son?" 21 And he stretched himself out on the child three times, and cried out to the Lord and said, "O Lord my God, I pray, let this child's soul come back to him." 22 Then the Lord heard the voice of Elijah; and the soul of the child came back to him, and he revived.

23 And Elijah took the child and brought him down from the upper room into the house, and gave him to his mother. And Elijah said, "See, your son lives!"

24 Then the woman said to Elijah, "Now by this I know that you are a man of God, and that the word of the Lord in your mouth is the truth."

Complete the SQ3R Analysis. See Appendix.

New King James Version (NKJV)
Scripture taken from the New King James Version®. Copyright © 1982 by Thomas Nelson. Used by permission. All rights reserved.

C H A R T
KNOW • WANT • LEARN

KWL

ALREADY KNOW	WANT TO KNOW	WHAT I LEARNED

The Biblical Account of Paul and Barnabus at Lystra

Acts 14 New King James Version (NKJV)

At Iconium

14 Now it happened in Iconium that they went together to the synagogue of the Jews, and so spoke that a great multitude both of the Jews and of the Greeks believed. 2 But the unbelieving Jews stirred up the **Gentiles** and poisoned their minds against the brethren. 3 Therefore they stayed there a long time, speaking boldly in the Lord, who was bearing witness to the word of His grace, granting signs and wonders to be done by their hands.

4 But the multitude of the city was divided: part sided with the Jews, and part with the apostles. 5 And when a violent attempt was made by both the Gentiles and Jews, with their rulers, to abuse and stone them, 6 they became aware of it and fled to Lystra and Derbe, cities of Lycaonia, and to the surrounding region. 7 And they were preaching the gospel there.

Idolatry at Lystra

8 And in Lystra a certain man without strength in his feet was sitting, a cripple from his mother's womb, who had never walked. 9 This man heard Paul speaking. Paul, observing him intently and seeing that he had faith to be healed, 10 said with a loud voice, "Stand up straight on your feet!" And he leaped and walked. 11 Now when the people saw what Paul had done, they raised their voices, saying in the Lycaonian language, "The gods have come down to us in the likeness of men!" 12 And Barnabas they called Zeus, and Paul, Hermes, because he was the chief speaker. 13 Then the priest of Zeus, whose temple was in front of their city, brought oxen and **garlands** to the gates, intending to sacrifice with the multitudes.

14 But when the **apostles** Barnabas and Paul heard this, they tore their clothes and ran in among the multitude, crying out 15 and saying, "Men, why are you doing these things? We also are men with the same nature as you, and preach to you that you should turn from these useless things to the living God, who made the heaven, the earth, the sea, and all things that are in them, 16 who in bygone generations allowed all nations to walk in their own ways. 17 Nevertheless He did not leave Himself without witness, in that He did good, gave us rain from heaven and fruitful seasons, filling our hearts with food and gladness." 18 And with these sayings they could scarcely restrain the **multitudes** from sacrificing to them.

Stoning, Escape to Derbe

19 Then Jews from Antioch and Iconium came there; and having persuaded the multitudes, they stoned Paul and dragged him out of the city, supposing him to be dead. 20 However, when the disciples gathered around him, he rose up and went into the city. And the next day he departed with Barnabas to Derbe.

Complete the SQ3R Analysis. See Appendix.

New King James Version (NKJV)
Scripture taken from the New King James Version®. Copyright © 1982 by Thomas Nelson. Used by permission. All rights reserved.

Short Answer Questions – "Metamorphoses", "Paul and Barnabus", and "Elijah and the Widow of Zarapheth"

1. How does Ovid's depiction of true love manifest symbolically in the "Metamorphoses Philemon and Baucis"?

2. What is the primary similarity in the two main characters in "Metamorphoses Book VIII Philemon and Baucis" and "Paul and Barnabus at Lystra"? What is the differences in the characters' responses?

3. What is ironic about the ravens bringing Elijah food in "The Prophet Elijah and the Widow of Zarapheth"?

_____

_____

_____

_____

_____

_____

_____

_____

_____

_____

_____

_____

_____

_____

_____

_____

_____

_____

Essay Topics

1. Although both "The Prophet Elijah and the Widow of Zarapheth" and "Paul and Barnabus at Lystra" are both in the bible, the main characters Elijah and Paul handle themselves differently when giving and receiving help from the communities they serve. How do you account for the differences in the men who are both doing the work of God? Write a comparison/contrast essay comparing the biblical accounts.

2. Write and essay illustrating the idea of social responsibility in "Metamorphoses Philemon and Baucis", "Paul and Barnabus at Lystra", and "The Prophet Elijah and the Widow of Zarapheth.

CIVIL DISOBEDIENCE
and Social Justice

Notes

Chapter 5

Civil Disobedience and Social Justice

Exploring the Rhetoric of Nonviolent Resistance

Henry David Thoreau defines civil disobedience as "the refusal to obey certain laws or governmental demands for the purpose of influencing legislation or government policy, characterized by the employment of such nonviolent techniques as boycotting, picketing, and nonpayment of taxes." This definition was penned in 1848 in his essay "Resistance to Civil Government," where he declared: "That government is best which governs least." He further expresses that people who find it necessary to break the law in protest so that they can follow their own conscience, must be prepared to suffer the consequences affiliated with the action. In other words, they should be prepared to pay penalties, including imprisonment. Thoreau exemplifies this in his personal story by refusing to pay taxes to support the Mexican War. He was imprisoned as a result.

Thoreau's example has had a profound impact on civil activists worldwide. Of the list of human rights activists and social justice engineers are Mahatma Gandhi and Martin Luther King Jr.

In Martin Luther King's "Letter From a Birmingham Jail" his famous quote "Injustice anywhere is a threat to justice everywhere," has received worldwide acclaim and has been used as a justification for the fight civil rights and civil disobedience. In Mahatma

Gandhi's Non-violence in Peace and War 1942-49, he states "An unjust law is itself a species of violence. Arrest for its breach is more so. Now the law of nonviolence says that violence should be resisted not by counter-violence but by nonviolence. This I do by breaking the law and by peacefully submitting to arrest and imprisonment." Both of these important figures in social history fought vigorously, yet nonviolently for what the believed, even to the point of imprisonment.

To sway people to move toward nonviolent protest, Thoreau, Gandhi, and King used Aristotle's three appeals, pathos, ethos and logos to move people to action through calm and peaceful protest.

- Pathos – an appeal to one's emotions
- Ethos – an appeal to character
- Logos – an appeal to logic or reason

This chapter will explore the idea of civil disobedience from the pens of some of the greatest social thinkers of the 19th and 20th centuries. As you read, consider the following questions:

- What exactly is civil disobedience?
- Why has civil disobedience gained worldwide traction?
- What is the rhetoric of civil disobedience?
- How does Aristotle's three appeals work in the essays and letters in this chapter?
- How does civil disobedience speak to social responsibility?

These are the questions to explore as you read the next chapter.

INSTRUCTIONS

1. Complete the KWL chart to see what information you know about the stories you will read.
2. After completing the KWL chart, and doing a research on the story you about to read, write an introduction to introduce this text.
3. At the end of each section, you will complete an outlining notetaking exercise to help you study texts in this chapter. Afterwards, you will write a chapter summary.

C H A R T

KNOW • WANT • LEARN

WHAT I LEARNED	WANT TO KNOW	ALREADY KNOW

On the Duty of Civil Disobedience

Henry David Thoreau

I heartily accept the motto,—"That government is best which governs least"; and I should like to see it acted up to more rapidly and systematically. Carried out, it finally amounts to this, which also I believe,—"That government is best which governs not at all"; and when men are prepared for it, that will be the kind of government which they will have. Government is at best but an expedient; but most governments are usually, and all governments are sometimes, **inexpedient**. The objections which have been brought against a standing army, and they are many and weighty, and deserve to prevail, may also at last be brought against a standing government. The standing army is only an arm of the standing government. The government itself, which is only the mode which the people have chosen to execute their will, is equally liable to be abused and **perverted** before the people can act through it. Witness the present **Mexican War**, the work of comparatively a few individuals using the standing government as their tool; for, in the outset, the people would not have consented to this measure.

This American government—what is it but a tradition, though a recent one, endeavoring to transmit itself unimpaired to posterity, but each instant losing some of its **integrity**? It has not the **vitality** and force of a single living man; for a single man can bend it to his will. It is a sort of wooden gun to the people themselves. But it is not the less necessary for this; for the people must have some complicated machinery or other, and hear its din, to satisfy that idea of government which they have. Governments show thus how successfully men can be imposed on, even impose on themselves, for their own advantage. It is excellent, we must all allow. Yet this government never of itself furthered any enterprise, but by the alacrity with which it got out of its way. It does not keep the country free. It does not settle the West. It does not educate. The character inherent in the American people has done all that has been accomplished; and it would have done somewhat more, if the government had not sometimes got in its way. For government is an expedient by which men would fain succeed in letting one another alone; and, as has been said, when it is most expedient, the governed are most let alone by it. Trade and commerce, if they were not made of India rubber, would never manage to bounce over the obstacles which legislators are continually putting in their way; and, if one were to judge these men wholly by the effects of their actions, and not partly by their intentions, they would deserve to be classed and punished with those mischievous persons who put obstructions on the railroads.

But, to speak practically and as a citizen, unlike those who call themselves no-government men, I ask for, not at once no government, but at once a better government. Let every man make known what kind of government would command his respect, and that will be one step toward obtaining it.

After all, the practical reason why, when the power is once in the hands of the people, a majority are permitted, and for a long period continue, to rule, is not because they are most likely to be in the right, nor because this seems fairest to the minority, but because they are physically the strongest. But a government in which the majority rule in all cases cannot be based on justice, even as far as men understand it. Can there not be a government in which majorities do not virtually decide right and wrong, but conscience?—in which majorities decide only those questions to which the rule of expediency is applicable? Must the citizen ever for a moment, or in the least degree, resign his conscience to the legislator? Why has every man a **conscience**, then? I think that we should be men first, and subjects afterward. It is not desirable to cultivate a respect for the law, so much as for the right. The only obligation which I have a right to assume is to do at any time what I think right. It is truly enough said that a corporation has no conscience; but a corporation of conscientious men is a corporation with a conscience. Law never made men a whit more just; and, by means of their respect for it, even the well-disposed are daily made the agents of injustice. A common and natural result of an undue respect for law is, that you may see a file of soldiers, colonel, captain, corporal, privates, powder-monkeys, and all, marching in admirable order over hill and dale to the wars, against their wills, ay, against their common sense and consciences, which makes it very steep marching indeed, and produces a palpitation of the heart. They have no doubt that it is a damnable business in which they are concerned; they are all peaceably inclined. Now, what are they? Men at all? or small movable forts and magazines, at the service of some unscrupulous man in power? Visit the Navy Yard, and behold a marine, such a man as an American government can make, or such as it can make a man with its black arts—a mere shadow and reminiscence of humanity, a man laid out alive and standing, and already, as one may say, buried under arms with funeral accompaniments, though it may be,—

> "Not a drum was heard, not a funeral note,
> As his corpse to the rampart we hurried;
> Not a soldier discharged his farewell shot
> O'er the grave where our hero we buried."

The mass of men serve the state thus, not as men mainly, but as machines, with their bodies. They are the standing army, and the militia, jailers, constables, posse **comitatus**, etc. In most cases there is no free exercise whatever of the judgment or of the moral sense; but they put themselves on a level with wood and earth and stones; and wooden men can perhaps be manufactured that will serve the purpose as well. Such command no more respect than men of straw or a lump of dirt. They have the same sort of worth only as horses and dogs. Yet such as these even are commonly esteemed good citizens. Others, as most legislators, politicians, lawyers, ministers, and office-holders, serve the state chiefly with their heads; and, as they rarely make any moral distinctions, they are as likely to serve the devil, without intending it, as God. A very few, as heroes, patriots, **martyrs**, reformers in the great sense, and men, serve the state with their consciences also, and so necessarily resist it for the most part; and they are commonly treated as enemies by it. A wise man will only be useful as a man, and will not submit to be "clay," and "stop a hole to keep the wind away," but leave that office to his dust at least:—

> "I am too high-born to be propertied,
> To be a secondary at control,
> Or useful serving-man and instrument
> To any sovereign state throughout the world."

He who gives himself entirely to his fellow-men appears to them useless and selfish; but he who gives himself partially to them is pronounced a benefactor and philanthropist.

How does it become a man to behave toward this American government today? I answer, that he cannot without disgrace be associated with it. I cannot for an instant recognize that political organization as my government which is the slave's government also.

All men recognize the right of revolution; that is, the right to refuse allegiance to, and to resist, the government, when its tyranny or its inefficiency are great and unendurable. But almost all say that such is not the case now. But such was the case, they think, in the **Revolution of '75**. If one were to tell me that this was a bad government because it taxed certain foreign commodities brought to its ports, it is most probable that I should not make an ado about it, for I can do without them. All machines have their friction; and possibly this does enough good to counterbalance the evil. At any rate, it is a great evil to make a stir about it. But when the friction comes to have its machine, and oppression and robbery are organized, I say, let us not have such a machine any longer. In other words, when a sixth of the population of a nation which has undertaken to be the refuge of liberty are slaves, and a whole country is unjustly overrun and conquered by a foreign army, and subjected to military law, I think that it is not too soon for honest men to rebel and revolutionize. What makes this duty the more urgent is the fact that the country so overrun is not our own, but ours is the invading army.

Paley, a common authority with many on moral questions, in his chapter on the "Duty of Submission to Civil Government," resolves all civil obligation into expediency; and he proceeds to say that "so long as the interest of the whole society requires it, that is, so long as the established government cannot be resisted or changed without public inconveniency, it is the will of God... that the established government be obeyed, and no longer.... This principle being admitted, the justice of every particular case of resistance is reduced to a computation of the quantity of the danger and grievance on the one side, and of the probability and expense of redressing it on the other." Of this, he says, every man shall judge for himself. But Paley appears never to have contemplated those cases to which the **rule of expediency** does not apply, in which a people, as well as an individual, must do justice, cost what it may. If I have unjustly wrested a plank from a drowning man, I must restore it to him though I drown myself. This, according to Paley, would be inconvenient. But he that would save his life, in such a case, shall lose it. This people must cease to hold slaves, and to make war on Mexico, though it cost them their existence as a people.

In their practice, nations agree with Paley; but does any one think that Massachusetts does exactly what is right at the present crisis?

> "A drab of state, a cloth-o'-silver slut,
> To have her train borne up, and her soul trail in the dirt."

Practically speaking, the opponents to a reform in Massachusetts are not a hundred thousand politicians at the South, but a hundred thousand merchants and farmers

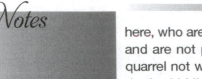

here, who are more interested in commerce and agriculture than they are in humanity, and are not prepared to do justice to the slave and to Mexico, cost what it may. I quarrel not with far-off foes, but with those who, near at home, cooperate with, and do the bidding of those far away, and without whom the latter would be harmless. We are accustomed to say, that the mass of men are unprepared; but improvement is slow, because the few are not materially wiser or better than the many. It is not so important that many should be as good as you, as that there be some absolute goodness somewhere; for that will leaven the whole lump. There are thousands who are in opinion opposed to slavery and to the war, who yet in effect do nothing to put an end to them; who, esteeming themselves children of Washington and Franklin, sit down with their hands in their pockets, and say that they know not what to do, and do nothing; who even postpone the question of freedom to the question of free-trade, and quietly read the prices-current along with the latest advices from Mexico, after dinner, and, it may be, fall asleep over them both. What is the price-current of an honest man and patriot today? They hesitate, and they regret, and sometimes they petition; but they do nothing in earnest and with effect. They will wait, well disposed, for others to remedy the evil, that they may no longer have it to regret. At most, they give only a cheap vote, and a feeble countenance and Godspeed, to the right, as it goes by them. There are nine hundred and ninety-nine patrons of virtue to one virtuous man; but it is easier to deal with the real possessor of a thing than with the temporary guardian of it.

All voting is a sort of gaming, like checkers or backgammon, with a slight moral tinge to it, a playing with right and wrong, with moral questions; and betting naturally accompanies it. The character of the voters is not staked. I cast my vote, perchance, as I think right; but I am not vitally concerned that that right should prevail. I am willing to leave it to the majority. Its obligation, therefore, never exceeds that of expediency. Even voting for the right is doing nothing for it. It is only expressing to men feebly your desire that it should prevail. A wise man will not leave the right to the mercy of chance, nor wish it to prevail through the power of the majority. There is but little virtue in the action of masses of men. When the majority shall at length vote for the abolition of slavery, it will be because they are indifferent to slavery, or because there is but little slavery left to be abolished by their vote. They will then be the only slaves. Only his vote can hasten the abolition of slavery who asserts his own freedom by his vote.

I hear of a convention to be held at Baltimore, or elsewhere, for the selection of a candidate for the Presidency, made up chiefly of editors, and men who are politicians by profession; but I think, what is it to any independent, intelligent, and respectable man what decision they may come to? Shall we not have the advantage of his wisdom and honesty, nevertheless? Can we not count upon some independent votes? Are there not many individuals in the country who do not attend conventions? But no: I find that the respectable man, so called, has immediately drifted from his position, and despairs of his country, when his country has more reason to despair of him. He forthwith adopts one of the candidates thus selected as the only available one, thus proving that he is himself available for any purposes of the **demagogue**. His vote is of no more worth than that of any unprincipled foreigner or hireling native, who may have been bought. Oh for a man who is a man, and, as my neighbor says, has a bone in his back which you cannot pass your hand through! Our statistics are at fault: the population has been returned too large. How many men are there to a square thousand miles in this country? Hardly one. Does not America offer any inducement for men to settle here? The American has dwindled into an Odd Fellow—one who may be known by the development of his organ of gregariousness, and a manifest lack of intellect and cheerful self-reliance; whose first and chief concern, on coming into the world, is to see that the almshouses are in good repair; and, before yet he has lawfully donned the virile garb, to collect a fund for the support of the widows and orphans that may be; who, in short ventures to live only by the aid of the Mutual Insurance company, which has promised to bury him decently.

It is not a man's duty, as a matter of course, to devote himself to the eradication of any, even the most enormous wrong; he may still properly have other concerns to engage him; but it is his duty, at least, to wash his hands of it, and, if he gives it no thought longer, not to give it practically his support. If I devote myself to other pursuits and contemplations, I must first see, at least, that I do not pursue them sitting upon another man's shoulders. I must get off him first, that he may pursue his contemplations too. See what gross inconsistency is tolerated. I have heard some of my townsmen say, "I should like to have them order me out to help put down an insurrection of the slaves, or to march to Mexico;—see if I would go"; and yet these very men have each, directly by their allegiance, and so indirectly, at least, by their money, furnished a substitute. The soldier is applauded who refuses to serve in an unjust war by those who do not refuse to sustain the unjust government which makes the war; is applauded by those whose own act and authority he disregards and sets at naught; as if the state were **penitent** to that degree that it hired one to scourge it while it sinned, but not to that degree that it left off sinning for a moment. Thus, under the name of Order and Civil Government, we are all made at last to pay homage to and support our own meanness. After the first blush of sin comes its indifference; and from immoral it becomes, as it were, unmoral, and not quite unnecessary to that life which we have made.

The broadest and most prevalent error requires the most disinterested virtue to sustain it. The slight reproach to which the virtue of patriotism is commonly liable, the noble are most likely to incur. Those who, while they disapprove of the character and measures of a government, yield to it their allegiance and support are undoubtedly its most **conscientious** supporters, and so frequently the most serious obstacles to reform. Some are petitioning the State to dissolve the Union, to disregard the requisitions of the President. Why do they not dissolve it themselves—the union between themselves and the State—and refuse to pay their quota into its treasury? Do not they stand in the same relation to the State, that the State does to the Union? And have not the same reasons prevented the State from resisting the Union, which have prevented them from resisting the State?

How can a man be satisfied to entertain an opinion merely, and enjoy it? Is there any enjoyment in it, if his opinion is that he is aggrieved? If you are cheated out of a single dollar by your neighbor, you do not rest satisfied with knowing that you are cheated, or with saying that you are cheated, or even with petitioning him to pay you your due; but you take effectual steps at once to obtain the full amount, and see that you are never cheated again. Action from principle—the perception and the performance of right—changes things and relations; it is essentially revolutionary, and does not consist wholly with anything which was. It not only divides states and churches, it divides families; ay, it divides the individual, separating the **diabolical** in him from the divine.

Unjust laws exist; shall we be content to obey them, or shall we endeavor to amend them, and obey them until we have succeeded, or shall we transgress them at once? Men generally, under such a government as this, think that they ought to wait until they have persuaded the majority to alter them. They think that, if they should resist, the remedy would be worse than the evil. But it is the fault of the government itself that the remedy is worse than the evil. It makes it worse. Why is it not more apt to anticipate and provide for reform? Why does it not cherish its wise minority? Why does it cry and resist before it is hurt? Why does it not encourage its citizens to be on the alert to point out its faults, and do better than it would have them? Why does it always crucify Christ, and excommunicate Copernicus and Luther, and pronounce Washington and Franklin rebels?

One would think, that a deliberate and practical denial of its authority was the only offence never contemplated by government; else, why has it not assigned its definite, its suitable and proportionate, penalty? If a man who has no property refuses but once to earn nine shillings for the State, he is put in prison for a period unlimited by any law that I know, and determined only by the **discretion** of those who placed him there; but if he should steal ninety times nine shillings from the State, he is soon permitted to go at large again.

If the injustice is part of the necessary friction of the machine of government, let it go, let it go; perchance it will wear smooth—certainly the machine will wear out. If the injustice has a spring, or a pulley, or a rope, or a crank, exclusively for itself, then perhaps you may consider whether the remedy will not be worse than the evil; but if it is of such a nature that it requires you to be the agent of injustice to another, then, I say, break the law. Let your life be a counter friction to stop the machine. What I have to do is to see, at any rate, that I do not lend myself to the wrong which I condemn.

As for adopting the ways which the State has provided for remedying the evil, I know not of such ways. They take too much time, and a man's life will be gone. I have other affairs to attend to. I came into this world, not chiefly to make this a good place to live in, but to live in it, be it good or bad. A man has not everything to do, but something; and because he cannot do everything, it is not necessary that he should do something wrong. It is not my business to be petitioning the Governor or the Legislature any more than it is theirs to petition me; and if they should not hear my petition, what should I do then? But in this case the State has provided no way; its very Constitution is the evil. This may seem to be harsh and stubborn and **unconciliatory**; but it is to treat with the utmost kindness and consideration the only spirit that can appreciate or deserves it. So is an change for the better, like birth and death which **convulse** the body.

I do not hesitate to say, that those who call themselves **Abolitionists** should at once effectually withdraw their support, both in person and property, from the government of Massachusetts, and not wait till they constitute a majority of one, before they suffer the right to prevail through them. I think that it is enough if they have God on their side, without waiting for that other one. Moreover, any man more right than his neighbors constitutes a majority of one already.

I meet this American government, or its representative, the State government, directly, and face to face, once a year—no more—in the person of its tax-gatherer;

this is the only mode in which a man situated as I am necessarily meets it; and it then says distinctly, Recognize me; and the simplest, the most effectual, and, in the present posture of affairs, the **indispensablest** mode of treating with it on this head, of expressing your little satisfaction with and love for it, is to deny it then. My civil neighbor, the tax-gatherer, is the very man I have to deal with—for it is, after all, with men and not with parchment that I quarrel—and he has voluntarily chosen to be an agent of the government. How shall he ever know well what he is and does as an officer of the government, or as a man, until he is obliged to consider whether he shall treat me, his neighbor, for whom he has respect, as a neighbor and well-disposed man, or as a maniac and disturber of the peace, and see if he can get over this obstruction to his neighborliness without a ruder and more **impetuous** thought or speech corresponding with his action? I know this well, that if one thousand, if one hundred, if ten men whom I could name—if ten honest men only—ay, if one HONEST man, in this State of Massachusetts, ceasing to hold slaves, were actually to withdraw from this co-partnership, and be locked up in the county jail therefor, it would be the abolition of slavery in America. For it matters not how small the beginning may seem to be: what is once well done is done forever. But we love better to talk about it: that we say is our mission. Reform keeps many scores of newspapers in its service, but not one man. If my **esteemed** neighbor, the State's **ambassador**, who will devote his days to the settlement of the question of human rights in the Council Chamber, instead of being threatened with the prisons of Carolina, were to sit down the prisoner of Massachusetts, that State which is so anxious to foist the sin of slavery upon her sister—though at present she can discover only an act of inhospitality to be the ground of a quarrel with her—the Legislature would not wholly waive the subject the following winter.

Under a government which imprisons any unjustly, the true place for a just man is also a prison. The proper place today, the only place which Massachusetts has provided for her freer and less desponding spirits, is in her prisons, to be put out and locked out of the State by her own act, as they have already put themselves out by their principles. It is there that the fugitive slave, and the Mexican prisoner on parole, and the Indian come to plead the wrongs of his race, should find them; on that separate, but more free and honorable ground, where the State places those who are not with her, but against her—the only house in a slave State in which a free man can abide with honor. If any think that their influence would be lost there, and their voices no longer afflict the ear of the State, that they would not be as an enemy within its walls, they do not know by how much truth is stronger than error, nor how much more eloquently and effectively he can combat injustice who has experienced a little in his own person. Cast your whole vote, not a strip of paper merely, but your whole influence. A minority is powerless while it conforms to the majority; it is not even a minority then; but it is **irresistible** when it clogs by its whole weight. If the alternative is to keep all just men in prison, or give up war and slavery, the State will not hesitate which to choose. If a thousand men were not to pay their tax-bills this year, that would not be a violent and bloody measure, as it would be to pay them, and enable the State to commit violence and shed innocent blood. This is, in fact, the definition of a peaceable revolution, if any such is possible. If the tax-gatherer, or any other public officer, asks me, as one has done, "But what shall I do?" my answer is, "If you really wish to do anything, resign your office." When the subject has refused allegiance, and the officer has resigned his office, then the revolution is accomplished. But even

Notes

suppose blood should flow. Is there not a sort of blood shed when the **conscience** is wounded? Through this wound a man's real manhood and immortality flow out, and he bleeds to an everlasting death. I see this blood flowing now.

I have contemplated the imprisonment of the offender, rather than the seizure of his goods—though both will serve the same purpose—because they who assert the purest right, and consequently are most dangerous to a corrupt State, commonly have not spent much time in accumulating property. To such the State renders comparatively small service, and a slight tax is wont to appear exorbitant, particularly if they are obliged to earn it by special labor with their hands. If there were one who lived wholly without the use of money, the State itself would hesitate to demand it of him. But the rich man—not to make any **invidious** comparison—is always sold to the institution which makes him rich. Absolutely speaking, the more money, the less virtue; for money comes between a man and his objects, and obtains them for him; and it was certainly no great virtue to obtain it. It puts to rest many questions which he would otherwise be taxed to answer; while the only new question which it puts is the hard but superfluous one, how to spend it. Thus his moral ground is taken from under his feet. The opportunities of living are diminished in proportion as what are called the "means" are increased. The best thing a man can do for his culture when he is rich is to endeavor to carry out those schemes which he entertained when he was poor. Christ answered the **Herodians** according to their condition. "Show me the tribute-money," said he;—and one took a penny out of his pocket;—if you use money which has the image of **Ceasar** on it, and which he has made current and valuable, that is, if you are men of the State, and gladly enjoy the advantages of Ceasar's government, then pay him back some of his own when he demands it; "Render therefore to Ceasar that which is Ceasar's, and to God those things which are God's"—leaving them no wiser than before as to which was which; for they did not wish to know.

When I **converse** with the freest of my neighbors, I perceive that, whatever they may say about the magnitude and seriousness of the question, and their regard for the public tranquility, the long and the short of the matter is, that they cannot spare the protection of the existing government, and they dread the consequences to their property and families of disobedience to it. For my own part, I should not like to think that I ever rely on the protection of the State. But, if I deny the authority of the State when it presents its tax-bill, it will soon take and waste all my property, and so harass me and my children without end. This is hard. This makes it impossible for a man to live honestly, and at the same time comfortably in outward respects. It will not be worth the while to accumulate property; that would be sure to go again. You must hire or squat somewhere, and raise but a small crop, and eat that soon. You must live within yourself, and depend upon yourself always tucked up and ready for a start, and not have many affairs. A man may grow rich in Turkey even, if he will be in all respects a good subject of the Turkish government. **Confucius** said, "If a state is governed by the principles of reason, poverty and misery are subjects of shame; if a state is not governed by the principles of reason, riches and honors are the subjects of shame." No: until I want the protection of Massachusetts to be extended to me in some distant Southern port, where my liberty is endangered, or until I am bent solely on building up an estate at home by peaceful enterprise, I can afford to refuse allegiance to Massachusetts, and her right to my property and life. It costs me less in every sense to incur the penalty of disobedience to the State than it would to obey. I should feel as if I were worth less in that case.

Some years ago, the State met me in behalf of the Church, and commanded me to pay a certain sum toward the support of a clergyman whose preaching my father attended, but never I myself. "Pay," it said, "or be locked up in the jail." I declined to pay. But, unfortunately, another man saw fit to pay it. I did not see why the schoolmaster should be taxed to support the priest, and not the priest the schoolmaster: for I was not the State's schoolmaster, but I supported myself by voluntary subscription. I did not see why the lyceum should not present its tax-bill, and have the State to back its demand, as well as the Church. However, at the request of the selectmen, I **condescended** to make some such statement as this in writing:—"Know all men by these presents, that I, Henry Thoreau, do not wish to be regarded as a member of any incorporated society which I have not joined." This I gave to the town clerk; and he has it. The State, having thus learned that I did not wish to be regarded as a member of that church, has never made a like demand on me since; though it said that it must adhere to its original presumption that time. If I had known how to name them, I should then have signed off in detail from all the societies which I never signed on to; but I did not know where to find a complete list.

I have paid no poll-tax for six years. I was put into a jail once on this account, for one night; and, as I stood considering the walls of solid stone, two or three feet thick, the door of wood and iron, a foot thick, and the iron grating which strained the light, I could not help being struck with the foolishness of that institution which treated me as if I were mere flesh and blood and bones, to be locked up. I wondered that it should have concluded at length that this was the best use it could put me to, and had never thought to avail itself of my services in some way. I saw that, if there was a wall of stone between me and my townsmen, there was a still more difficult one to climb or break through, before they could get to be as free as I was. I did not for a moment feel confined, and the walls seemed a great waste of stone and mortar. I felt as if I alone of all my townsmen had paid my tax. They plainly did not know how to treat me, but behaved like persons who are **underbred**. In every threat and in every compliment there was a **blunder**; for they thought that my chief desire was to stand the other side of that stone wall. I could not but smile to see how **industriously** they locked the door on my meditations, which followed them out again without let or hindrance, and they were really all that was dangerous. As they could not reach me, they had resolved to punish my body; just as boys, if they cannot come at some person against whom they have a spite, will abuse his dog. I saw that the State was half-witted, that it was timid as a lone woman with her silver spoons, and that it did not know its friends from its foes, and I lost all my remaining respect for it, and pitied it.

Thus the State never intentionally confronts a man's sense, intellectual or moral, but only his body, his senses. It is not armed with superior wit or honesty, but with superior physical strength. I was not born to be forced. I will breathe after my own fashion. Let us see who is the strongest. What force has a multitude? They only can force me who obey a higher law than I. They force me to become like themselves. I do not hear of men being forced to have this way or that by masses of men. What sort of life were that to live? When I meet a government which says to me, "Your money or your life," why should I be in haste to give it my money? It may be in a great strait, and not know what to do: I cannot help that. It must help itself; do as I do. It is not worth the while to snivel about it. I am not responsible for the successful working of the machinery of society. I am not the son of the engineer. I perceive that, when an

Notes

acorn and a chestnut fall side by side, the one does not remain inert to make way for the other, but both obey their own laws, and spring and grow and flourish as best they can, till one, perchance, overshadows and destroys the other. If a plant cannot live according to its nature, it dies; and so a man.

The night in prison was novel and interesting enough. The prisoners in their shirt-sleeves were enjoying a chat and the evening air in the doorway, when I entered. But the jailer said, "Come, boys, it is time to lock up"; and so they dispersed, and I heard the sound of their steps returning into the hollow apartments. My roommate was introduced to me by the jailer as "a first-rate fellow and a clever man." When the door was locked, he showed me where to hang my hat, and how he managed matters there. The rooms were whitewashed once a month; and this one, at least, was the whitest, most simply furnished, and probably the neatest apartment in the town. He naturally wanted to know where I came from, and what brought me there; and, when I had told him, I asked him in my turn how he came there, presuming him to be an honest man, of course; and, as the world goes, I believe he was. "Why," said he, "they accuse me of burning a barn; but I never did it." As near as I could discover, he had probably gone to bed in a barn when drunk, and smoked his pipe there; and so a barn was burnt. He had the reputation of being a clever man, had been there some three months waiting for his trial to come on, and would have to wait as much longer; but he was quite domesticated and contented, since he got his board for nothing, and thought that he was well treated.

He occupied one window, and I the other; and I saw that if one stayed there long, his principal business would be to look out the window. I had soon read all the tracts that were left there, and examined where former prisoners had broken out, and where a grate had been sawed off, and heard the history of the various occupants of that room; for I found that even here there was a history and a gossip which never circulated beyond the walls of the jail. Probably this is the only house in the town where verses are composed, which are afterward printed in a circular form, but not published. I was shown quite a long list of verses which were composed by some young men who had been detected in an attempt to escape, who avenged themselves by singing them.

I pumped my fellow-prisoner as dry as I could, for fear I should never see him again; but at length he showed me which was my bed, and left me to blow out the lamp.

It was like travelling into a far country, such as I had never expected to behold, to lie there for one night. It seemed to me that I never had heard the town-clock strike before, nor the evening sounds of the village; for we slept with the windows open, which were inside the grating. It was to see my native village in the light of the Middle Ages, and our Concord was turned into a Rhine stream, and visions of knights and castles passed before me. They were the voices of old burghers that I heard in the streets. I was an involuntary spectator and auditor of whatever was done and said in the kitchen of the **adjacent** village-inn—a wholly new and rare experience to me. It was a closer view of my native town. I was fairly inside of it. I never had seen its institutions before. This is one of its peculiar institutions; for it is a shire town. I began to comprehend what its **inhabitants** were about.

In the morning, our breakfasts were put through the hole in the door, in small oblong-square tin pans, made to fit, and holding a pint of chocolate, with brown bread, and an iron spoon. When they called for the vessels again, I was green enough to return what bread I had left; but my **comrade** seized it, and said that I should lay that up for lunch or dinner. Soon after he was let out to work at haying in a neighboring field, whither he went every day, and would not be back till noon; so he bade me good-day, saying that he doubted if he should see me again.

When I came out of prison—for some one interfered, and paid that tax—I did not perceive that great changes had taken place on the common, such as he observed who went in a youth and emerged a tottering and gray-headed man; and yet a change had to my eyes come over the scene—the town, and State, and country—greater than any that mere time could effect. I saw yet more distinctly the State in which I lived. I saw to what extent the people among whom I lived could be trusted as good neighbors and friends; that their friendship was for summer weather only; that they did not greatly propose to do right; that they were a distinct race from me by their prejudices and **superstitions**, as the Chinamen and Malays are; that in their sacrifices to humanity, they ran no risks, not even to their property; that after all they were not so noble but they treated the thief as he had treated them, and hoped, by a certain outward observance and a few prayers, and by walking in a particular straight though useless path from time to time, to save their souls. This may be to judge my neighbors harshly; for I believe that many of them are not aware that they have such an institution as the jail in their village.

It was formerly the custom in our village, when a poor debtor came out of jail, for his acquaintances to salute him, looking through their fingers, which were crossed to represent the grating of a jail window, "How do ye do?" My neighbors did not thus salute me, but first looked at me, and then at one another, as if I had returned from a long journey. I was put into jail as I was going to the shoemaker's to get a shoe which was mended. When I was let out the next morning, I proceeded to finish my errand, and, having put on my mended shoe, joined a **huckleberry party**, who were impatient to put themselves under my conduct; and in half an hour—for the horse was soon tackled—was in the midst of a huckleberry field, on one of our highest hills, two miles off, and then the State was nowhere to be seen. This is the whole history of "My Prisons."

I have never declined paying the highway tax, because I am as desirous of being a good neighbor as I am of being a bad subject; and as for supporting schools, I am doing my part to educate my fellow-countrymen now. It is for no particular item in the tax-bill that I refuse to pay it. I simply wish to refuse allegiance to the State, to withdraw and stand **aloof** from it effectually. I do not care to trace the course of my dollar, if I could, till it buys a man or a musket to shoot one with—the dollar is innocent—but I am concerned to trace the effects of my allegiance. In fact, I quietly declare war with the State, after my fashion, though I will still make what use and get what advantage of her I can, as is usual in such cases.

If others pay the tax which is demanded of me, from a sympathy with the State, they do but what they have already done in their own case, or rather they abet injustice to a greater extent than the State requires. If they pay the tax from a mistaken interest in the individual taxed, to save his property, or prevent his going to jail, it is because

Notes

they have not considered wisely how far they let their private feelings interfere with the public good.

This, then, is my position at present. But one cannot be too much on his guard in such a case, lest his action be biased by obstinacy or an undue regard for the opinions of men. Let him see that he does only what belongs to himself and to the hour.

I think sometimes, Why, this people mean well; they are only ignorant; they would do better if they knew how: why give your neighbors this pain to treat you as they are not inclined to? But I think, again, This is no reason why I should do as they do, or permit others to suffer much greater pain of a different kind. Again, I sometimes say to myself, When many millions of men, without heat, without ill-will, without personal feeling of any kind, demand of you a few shillings only, without the possibility, such is their constitution, of retracting or altering their present demand, and without the possibility, on your side, of appeal to any other millions, why expose yourself to this overwhelming brute force? You do not resist cold and hunger, the winds and the waves, thus **obstinately**; you quietly submit to a thousand similar necessities. You do not put your head into the fire. But just in proportion as I regard this as not wholly a brute force, but partly a human force, and consider that I have relations to those millions as to so many millions of men, and not of mere brute or **inanimate** things, I see that appeal is possible, first and instantaneously, from them to the Maker of them, and, secondly, from them to themselves. But, if I put my head deliberately into the fire, there is no appeal to fire or to the Maker of fire, and I have only myself to blame. If I could convince myself that I have any right to be satisfied with men as they are, and to treat them accordingly, and not according, in some respects, to my requisitions and expectations of what they and I ought to be, then, like a good Muslim and **fatalist**, I should endeavor to be satisfied with things as they are, and say it is the will of God. And, above all, there is this difference between resisting this and a purely brute or natural force, that I can resist this with some effect; but I cannot expect, like **Orpheus**, to change the nature of the rocks and trees and beasts.

I do not wish to quarrel with any man or nation. I do not wish to split hairs, to make fine distinctions, or set myself up as better than my neighbors. I seek rather, I may say, even an excuse for conforming to the laws of the land. I am but too ready to conform to them. Indeed, I have reason to suspect myself on this head; and each year, as the tax-gatherer comes round, I find myself disposed to review the acts and position of the general and State governments, and the spirit of the people, to discover a pretext for **conformity**.

> "We must affect our country as our parents,
> And if at any time we alienate
> Our love or industry from doing it honor,
> We must respect effects and teach the soul
> Matter of **conscience** and religion,
> And not desire of rule or benefit."

I believe that the State will soon be able to take all my work of this sort out of my hands, and then I shall be no better a **patriot** than my fellow-countrymen. Seen from a lower point of view, the Constitution, with all its faults, is very good; the law and the courts are very respectable; even this State and this American government are, in many respects, very admirable and rare things, to be thankful for, such as a great many have described them; but seen from a point of view a little higher, they are what I have described them; seen from a higher still, and the highest, who shall say what they are, or that they are worth looking at or thinking of at all?

However, the government does not concern me much, and I shall bestow the fewest possible thoughts on it. It is not many moments that I live under a government, even in this world. If a man is thought-free, fancy-free, imagination-free, that which is not never for a long time appearing to be to him, unwise rulers or reformers cannot fatally interrupt him.

I know that most men think differently from myself; but those whose lives are by profession devoted to the study of these or **kindred** subjects, content me as little as any. Statesmen and legislators, standing so completely within the institution, never distinctly and nakedly behold it. They speak of moving society, but have no resting-place without it. They may be men of a certain experience and discrimination, and have no doubt invented ingenious and even useful systems, for which we sincerely thank them; but all their wit and usefulness lie within certain not very wide limits. They are wont to forget that the world is not governed by policy and **expediency**. Webster never goes behind government, and so cannot speak with authority about it. His words are wisdom to those legislators who contemplate no essential reform in the existing government; but for thinkers, and those who legislate for all time, he never once glances at the subject. I know of those whose serene and wise speculations on this theme would soon reveal the limits of his mind's range and hospitality. Yet, compared with the cheap professions of most reformers, and the still cheaper wisdom and **eloquence** of politicians in general, his are almost the only sensible and valuable words, and we thank Heaven for him. Comparatively, he is always strong, original, and, above all, practical. Still, his quality is not wisdom, but prudence. The lawyer's truth is not truth, but consistency or a consistent expediency. Truth is always in harmony with herself, and is not concerned chiefly to reveal the justice that may consist with wrong-doing. He well deserves to be called, as he has been called, the Defender of the Constitution. There are really no blows to be given by him but defensive ones. He is not a leader, but a follower. His leaders are the men of '87. "I have never made an effort," he says, "and never propose to make an effort; I have never countenanced an effort, and never mean to countenance an effort, to disturb the arrangement as originally made, by which the various States came into the Union." Still thinking of the **sanction** which the Constitution gives to slavery, he says, "Because it was a part of the original compact—let it stand."

Notwithstanding his special **acuteness** and ability, he is unable to take a fact out of its merely political relations, and behold it as it lies absolutely to be **disposed** of by the intellect—what, for instance, it behooves a man to do here in America today with regard to slavery, but ventures, or is driven, to make some such desperate answer as the following, while professing to speak absolutely, and as a private man—from which what new and singular code of social duties might be inferred? "The manner," says he, "in which the governments of those States where slavery exists are to regulate it is for their own consideration, under their responsibility to their constituents, to the general laws of **propriety**, humanity, and justice, and to God. Associations formed elsewhere, springing from a feeling of humanity, or any other cause, have nothing whatever to do with it. They have never received any encouragement from me, and they never will."

They who know of no purer sources of truth, who have traced up its stream no higher, stand, and wisely stand, by the Bible and the Constitution, and drink at it there with reverence and humility; but they who behold where it comes trickling into this lake or that pool, gird up their loins once more, and continue their **pilgrimage** toward its fountain-head.

No man with a **genius** for legislation has appeared in America. They are rare in the history of the world. There are orators, politicians, and **eloquent** men, by the thousand; but the speaker has not yet opened his mouth to speak who is capable of settling the much-vexed questions of the day. We love eloquence for its own sake, and not for any truth which it may utter, or any **heroism** it may inspire. Our legislators have not yet learned the comparative value of free-trade and of freedom, of union, and of rectitude, to a nation. They have no genius or talent for comparatively humble questions of taxation and finance, **commerce** and manufacturers and agriculture. If we were left solely to the wordy wit of legislators in Congress for our guidance, uncorrected by the seasonable experience and the effectual complaints of the people, America would not long retain her rank among the nations. For eighteen hundred years, though perchance I have no right to say it, the New Testament has been written; yet where is the legislator who has wisdom and practical talent enough to avail himself of the light which it sheds on the science of legislation?

The authority of government, even such as I am willing to submit to—for I will cheerfully obey those who know and can do better than I, and in many things even those who neither know nor can do so well—is still an impure one: to be strictly just, it must have the sanction and consent of the governed. It can have no pure right over my person and property but what I concede to it. The progress from an absolute to a limited **monarchy**, from a limited monarchy to a **democracy**, is a progress toward a true respect for the individual. Even the Chinese philosopher was wise enough to regard the individual as the basis of the empire. Is a democracy, such as we know it, the last improvement possible in government? Is it not possible to take a step further towards recognizing and organizing the rights of man? There will never be a really free and **enlightened** State until the State comes to recognize the individual as a higher and independent power, from which all its own power and authority are derived, and treats him accordingly. I please myself with imagining a State at least which can afford to be just to all men, and to treat the individual with respect as a neighbor; which even would not think it inconsistent with its own repose if a few were to live aloof from it, not meddling with it, nor embraced by it, who fulfilled all the duties of neighbors and fellow-men. A State which bore this kind of fruit, and suffered it to drop off as fast as it ripened, would prepare the way for a still more perfect and glorious State, which also I have imagined, but not yet anywhere seen.

Walden and On the Duty of Civil Disobedience was written in 1849 by Henry David Thoreau and are available in the public domain.

Notes and Outline of "On the Duty of Civil Disobedience".

Summary of "On the Duty of Civil Disobedience".

Short Answer Questions – Henry David Thoreau

1. **What is Thoreau's definition of civil disobedience?**

2. **What prompts Thoreau to write this speech?**

3. **Briefly describe the content of each of the three major sections.**

4. **Why was Thoreau's night in jail "like traveling into a far country"?**

5. **What is the significance of the shoes and huckleberry party?**

6. **Interpret the metaphor of the "wooden gun" in paragraph two.**

Essay Topics

1. In a well-developed essay, discuss the theoretical foundations of civil disobedience, drawing from specific details in Thoreau's texts.

2. In a carefully constructed argument, support, refute, or qualify Thoreau's claim from

- Civil Disobedience that "we should be men first and subjects afterward."

3. In an essay discuss which of Thoreau's arguments do you find convincing and which do you disagree?

4. Interpret, "That government is best which governs least…that government is best which governs not at all." In an essay, discuss Thoreau's view of the role of government? How would this idea work in American government? What areas of government would change in contemporary society if it completely adopted Thoreau's point of view regarding its function in society.

C H A R T
KNOW • WANT • LEARN

KWL

WHAT I LEARNED	WANT TO KNOW	ALREADY KNOW

Notes

On Civil Disobedience

Mahatma Ghandi

"There are two ways of countering injustice. One way is to smash the head of the man who perpetrates injustice and to get your own head smashed in the process. All strong people in the world adopt this course. Everywhere wars are fought and millions of people are killed. The consequence is not the progress of a nation but its decline. Soldiers returning from the front have become so bereft of reason that they indulge in various antisocial activities. One does not have to go far for examples. In the Boer War, when the British won a victory at Mafeking, the whole of England, and London in particular, went so mad with joy that for days on end everyone did nothing but dance night and day! They freely indulged in wickedness and rowdyism and did not leave a single bar with a drop of liquor in it. The Times, commenting, said that no words could describe the way those few days were spent, that all that could be said was that "the English nation went amafficking (a- Mafeking)". Pride makes a victorious nation bad-tempered. It falls into luxurious ways of living. Then for a time, it may be conceded, peace prevails. But after a short while, it comes more and more to be realized that the seeds of war have not been destroyed but have become a thousand times more nourished and mighty. No country has ever become, or will ever become, happy through victory in war. A nation does not rise that way, it only falls further. In fact, what comes to it is defeat, not victory. And if, perchance, either our act or our purpose was ill-conceived, it brings disaster to both belligerents.

But through the other method of combating injustice, we alone suffer the consequences of our mistakes, and the other side is wholly spared. This other method is **satyagraha**. One who resorts to it does not have to break another's head; he may merely have his own head broken. He has to be prepared to die himself suffering all the pain. In opposing the atrocious laws of the Government of South Africa, it was this method that we adopted. We made it clear to the said Government that we would never bow to its outrageous laws. No clapping is possible without two hands to do it, and no quarrel without two persons to make it. Similarly, no State is possible without two entities (the rulers and the ruled). You are our sovereign, our Government, only so long as we consider ourselves your subjects. When we are not subjects, you are not the sovereign either. So long as it is your endeavor to control us with justice and love, we will let you do so. But if you wish to strike at us from behind, we cannot permit it. Whatever you do in other matters, you will have to ask our opinion about the laws that concern us. If you make laws to keep us suppressed in a wrongful manner and without taking us into confidence, these laws will merely adorn the statute-books. We will never obey them. Award us for it what punishment you like, we will put up with it. Send us to prison and we will live there as in a paradise. Ask us to mount the scaffold and we will do so laughing. Shower what sufferings you like upon us, we will calmly endure all and not hurt a hair of your body. We will gladly die and will not so much as touch you. But so long as there is yet life in these our bones, we will never comply with your arbitrary laws."

Gandhi. Freedom's Battle, Being a Comprehensive Collection of Writings and Speeches on the Present Situation. Madras: Ganesh, 1922. Print.

Notes and Outline of "On Civil Disobedience"

Write a summary of "On Civil Disobedience"

Short Answer Questions

1. What is Gandhi's definition of civil disobedience?

2. How is Gandhi's satyagraha different from Thoreau's civil disobedience?

3. Discuss Ghandi's perspectives on war and prosperous nations.

Essay Topics

1. How can Gandhi's ideas work for today? Think of specific examples.

2. Gandhi translated a version of Thoreau's essay for Indian Opinion, while crediting. Thoreau's piece as "the chief cause of the abolition of slavery in America." Additionally, Gandhi stated: "Thoreau was a great writer, philosopher, poet, and withal a most practical man, that is, he taught nothing he was not prepared to practice in himself. He was one of the greatest and most moral men America has produced. At the time of the abolition of slavery movement, he wrote his famous essay "On the Duty of Civil Disobedience". He went to "gaol", or jail, for the sake of his principles and suffering humanity. His essay has, therefore, been sanctified by suffering. Moreover, it is written for all time. Its incisive logic is unanswerable." In an essay explain how Ghandi may have been able to understand Thoreau and his motives to abolish slavery in the United States. Where do these men connect in their motives and methods?

CHART

KNOW • WANT • LEARN

KWL

ALREADY KNOW	WANT TO KNOW	WHAT I LEARNED

A Letter from a Birmingham Jail

Public Statement by Eight Alabama Clergymen
April 12, 1963

We the undersigned clergymen are among those who, in January, issued "An Appeal for Law and Order and Common Sense," in dealing with racial problems in Alabama. We expressed understanding that honest convictions in racial matters could properly be pursued in the courts, but urged that decisions of those courts should in the meantime be peacefully obeyed.

Since that time there had been some evidence of increased forbearance and a willingness to face facts. Responsible citizens have undertaken to work on various problems which cause racial friction and unrest. In Birmingham, recent public events have given indication that we all have opportunity for a new constructive and realistic approach to racial problems.

However, we are now confronted by a series of demonstrations by some of our Negro citizens, directed and led in part by outsiders. We recognize the natural impatience of people who feel that their hopes are slow in being realized. But we are convinced that these demonstrations are unwise and untimely.

We agree rather with certain local Negro leadership which has called for honest and open negotiation of racial issues in our area. And we believe this kind of facing of issues can best be accomplished by citizens of our own metropolitan area, white and Negro, meeting with their knowledge and experience of the local situation. All of us need to face that responsibility and find proper channels for its accomplishment.Just as we formerly pointed out that "hatred and violence have no sanction in our religious and political traditions," we also point out that such actions as incite to hatred and violence, however technically peaceful those actions may be, have not contributed to the resolution of our local problems. We do not believe that these days of new hope are days when extreme measures are justified in Birmingham.

We commend the community as a whole, and the local news media and law enforcement in particular, on the calm manner in which these demonstrations have been handled. We urge the public to continue to show restraint should the demonstrations continue, and the law enforcement official to remain calm and continue to protect our city from violence.

We further strongly urge our own Negro community to withdraw support from these demonstrations, and to unite locally in working peacefully for a better Birmingham. When rights are consistently denied, a cause should be pressed in the courts and in negotiations among local leaders, and not in the streets. We appeal to both our white and Negro citizenry to observe the principles of law and order and common sense.

C. C. J. Carpenter, D.D., LL.D.
Bishop of Alabama

Joseph A. Durick, D.D.
Auxiliary Bishop, Diocese of Mobile, Birmingham

Rabbi Hilton L. Grafman
Temple Emanu-El, Birmingham, Alabama

Bishop Paul Hardin
Bishop of the Alabama-West Florida Conference

Bishop Nolan B. Harmon
Bishop of the North Alabama Conference of the Methodist Church

George M. Murray, D.D., LL.D.
Bishop Coadjutor, Episcopal Diocese of Alabama

Edward V. Ramage
Moderator, Synod of the Alabama Presbyterian Church in the United States

Earl Stallings
Pastor, First Baptist Church, Birmingham, Alabama

Letter From a Birmingham Jail

Rev. Dr. Martin Luther King, Jr.
Birmingham City Jail April 16, 1963

My dear Fellow Clergymen,

While confined here in the Birmingham City Jail, I came across your recent statement calling our present activities "unwise and untimely." Seldom, if ever, do I pause to answer criticism of my work and ideas. If I sought to answer all the criticisms that cross my desk, my secretaries would be engaged in little else in the course of the day and I would have no time for constructive work. But since I feel that you are men of genuine goodwill and your criticisms are sincerely set forth, I would like to answer your statement in what I hope will be patient and reasonable terms.

I think I should give the reason for my being in Birmingham, since you have been influenced by the argument of "outsiders coming in." I have the honor of serving as president of the Southern Christian Leadership Conference, an organization operating in every Southern state with headquarters in Atlanta, Georgia. We have some eighty-five affiliate organizations all across the South -- one being the Alabama Christian Movement for Human Rights. Whenever necessary and possible we share staff, educational, and financial resources with our affiliates. Several months ago our local affiliate here in Birmingham invited us to be on call to engage in a nonviolent direct action program if such were deemed necessary. We readily consented and when the hour came we lived up to our promises. So I am here, along with several members of my staff, because we were invited here. I am here because I have basic organizational ties here. Beyond this, I am in Birmingham because injustice is here. Just as the eighth century prophets left their little villages and carried their "thus saith the Lord" far beyond the boundaries of their home town, and just as the Apostle Paul left his little village of Tarsus and carried the gospel of Jesus Christ to practically every hamlet and city of the Greco-Roman world, I too am compelled to carry the gospel of freedom beyond my particular home town. Like Paul, I must constantly respond to the Macedonian call for aid.

Moreover, I am cognizant of the interrelatedness of all communities and states. I cannot sit idly by in Atlanta and not be concerned about what happens in Birmingham. *Injustice anywhere is a threat to justice everywhere.* We are caught in an inescapable network of mutuality tied in a single garment of destiny. Whatever affects one directly affects all indirectly. Never again can we afford to live with the narrow, provincial "outside agitator" idea. Anyone who lives inside the United States can never be considered an outsider anywhere in this country.

You deplore the demonstrations that are presently taking place in Birmingham. But I am sorry that your statement did not express a similar concern for the conditions that brought the demonstrations into being. I am sure that each of you would want to go beyond the superficial social analyst who looks merely at effects, and does not

Notes

grapple with underlying causes. I would not hesitate to say that it is unfortunate that so-called demonstrations are taking place in Birmingham at this time, but I would say in more emphatic terms that it is even more unfortunate that the white power structure of this city left the Negro community with no other alternative.

In any nonviolent campaign there are four basic steps: (1) Collection of the facts to determine whether injustices are alive; (2) Negotiation; (3) Self-purification; and (4)

Direct action. We have gone through all of these steps in Birmingham. There can be no gainsaying of the fact that racial injustice engulfs this community. Birmingham is probably the most thoroughly segregated city in the United States. Its ugly record of police brutality is known in every section of this country. Its unjust treatment of Negroes in the courts is a notorious reality. There have been more unsolved bombings of Negro homes and churches in Birmingham than any city in this nation. These are the hard, brutal, and unbelievable facts. On the basis of these conditions Negro leaders sought to negotiate with the city fathers. But the political leaders consistently refused to engage in good faith negotiation.

Then came the opportunity last September to talk with some of the leaders of the economic community. In these negotiating sessions certain promises were made by the merchants -- such as the promise to remove the humiliating racial signs from the stores.

On the basis of these promises Rev. Shuttlesworth and the leaders of the Alabama Christian Movement for Human Rights agreed to call a moratorium on any type of demonstrations. As the weeks and months unfolded we realized that we were the victims of a broken promise. The signs remained. As in so many experiences of the past we were confronted with blasted hopes, and the dark shadow of a deep disappointment settled upon us. So we had no alternative except that of preparing for direct action, whereby we would present our very bodies as a means of laying our case before the conscience of the local and national community. We were not unmindful of the difficulties involved. So we decided to go through a process of self-purification. We started having workshops on nonviolence and repeatedly asked ourselves the questions, "Are you able to accept blows without retaliating?" "Are you able to endure the ordeals of jail?"

We decided to set our direct-action program around the Easter season, realizing that with the exception of Christmas, this was the largest shopping period of the year. Knowing that a strong economic withdrawal program would be the by-product of direct action, we felt that this was the best time to bring pressure on the merchants for the needed changes.

Then it occurred to us that the March election was ahead, and so we speedily decided to postpone action until after election day. When we discovered that Mr. Connor was in the run-off, we decided again to postpone action so that the demonstrations could not be used to cloud the issues. At this time we agreed to begin our nonviolent witness the day after the run-off. This reveals that we did not move irresponsibly into direct action. We too wanted to see Mr. Connor defeated; so we went through postponement after postponement to aid in this community need. After this we felt that direct action could be delayed no longer.

You may well ask, Why direct action? Why sit-ins, marches, etc.? Isn't negotiation a better path?" You are exactly right in your call for negotiation. Indeed, this is the purpose of direct action. Nonviolent direct action seeks to create such a crisis and establish such creative tension that a community that has constantly refused to negotiate is forced to confront the issue. It seeks so to dramatize the issue that it can no longer be ignored. I just referred to the creation of tension as a part of the work of the nonviolent resister. This may sound rather shocking. But I must confess that I am not afraid of the word tension. I have earnestly worked and preached against violent tension, but there is a type of constructive nonviolent tension that is necessary for growth. Just as Socrates felt that it was necessary to create a tension in the mind so that individuals could rise from the bondage of myths and half-truths to the unfettered realm of creative analysis and objective appraisal, we must see the need of having nonviolent gadflies to create the kind of tension in society that will help men rise from the dark depths of prejudice and racism to the majestic heights of understanding and brotherhood. So the purpose of the direct action is to create a situation so crisis-packed that it will inevitably open the door to negotiation. We, therefore, concur with you in your call for negotiation. Too long has our beloved Southland been bogged down in the tragic attempt to live in monologue rather than dialogue.

One of the basic points in your statement is that our acts are untimely. Some have asked, "Why didn't you give the new administration time to act?" The only answer that I can give to this inquiry is that the new administration must be prodded about as much as the outgoing one before it acts. We will be sadly mistaken if we feel that the election of Mr. Boutwell will bring the millennium to Birmingham. While Mr. Boutwell is much more articulate and gentle than Mr. Connor, they are both segregationists dedicated to the task of maintaining the status quo. The hope I see in Mr. Boutwell is that he will be reasonable enough to see the futility of massive resistance to desegregation. But he will not see this without pressure from the devotees of civil rights.

My friends, I must say to you that we have not made a single gain in civil rights without determined legal and nonviolent pressure. History is the long and tragic story of the fact that privileged groups seldom give up their privileges voluntarily. Individuals may see the moral light and voluntarily give up their unjust posture; but as Reinhold Niebuhr has reminded us, groups are more immoral than individuals.

We know through painful experience that freedom is never voluntarily given by the oppressor; it must be demanded by the oppressed. Frankly I have never yet engaged in a direct action movement that was "well timed," according to the timetable of those who have not suffered unduly from the disease of segregation. For years now I have heard the word "Wait!" It rings in the ear of every Negro with a piercing familiarity. This "wait" has almost always meant "never." It has been a tranquilizing thalidomide, relieving the emotional stress for a moment, only to give birth to an ill-formed infant of frustration.

We must come to see with the distinguished jurist of yesterday that "justice too long delayed is justice denied." We have waited for more than three hundred and forty years for our constitutional and God-given rights. The nations of Asia and Africa are moving with jet-like speed toward the goal of political independence, and we still creep at horse and buggy pace toward the gaining of a cup of coffee at a lunch counter.

I guess it is easy for those who have never felt the stinging darts of segregation to say wait. But when you have seen vicious mobs lynch your mothers and fathers at will and drown your sisters and brothers at whim; when you have seen hate filled policemen curse, kick, brutalize, and even kill your black brothers and sisters with impunity; when you see the vast majority of your twenty million Negro brothers smothering in an air-tight cage of poverty in the midst of an affluent society; when you suddenly find your tongue twisted and your speech stammering as you seek to explain to your six-year-old daughter why she can't go to the public amusement park that has just been advertised on television, and see tears welling up in her little eyes when she is told that Funtown is closed to colored children, and see the depressing clouds of inferiority begin to form in her little mental sky, and see her begin to distort her little personality by unconsciously developing a bitterness toward white people; when you have to concoct an answer for a five-year-old son asking in agonizing pathos: "Daddy, why do white people treat colored people so mean?"; when you take a cross-country drive and find it necessary to sleep night after night in the uncomfortable corners of your automobile because no motel will accept you; when you are humiliated day in and day out by nagging signs reading "white" men and "colored"; when your first name becomes "nigger" and your middle name becomes "boy" (however old you are) and your last name becomes "John," and when your wife and mother are never given the respected title "Mrs."; when you are harried by day and haunted by night by the fact that you are a Negro, living constantly at tip-toe stance never quite knowing what to expect next, and plagued with inner fears and outer resentments; when you are forever fighting a degenerating sense of "nobodiness" -- then you will understand why we find it difficult to wait. There comes a time when the cup of endurance runs over, and men are no longer willing to be plunged into an abyss of injustice where they experience the bleakness of corroding despair. I hope, sirs, you can understand our legitimate and unavoidable impatience.

You express a great deal of anxiety over our willingness to break laws. This is certainly a legitimate concern. Since we so diligently urge people to obey the Supreme Court's decision of 1954 outlawing segregation in the public schools, it is rather strange and paradoxical to find us consciously breaking laws. One may well ask: "How can you advocate breaking some laws and obeying others?" The answer is found in the fact that there are two types of laws: There are just laws and there are unjust laws. I would be the first to advocate obeying just laws. One has not only a legal but moral responsibility to obey just laws. Conversely, one has a moral responsibility to disobey unjust laws. I would agree with Saint Augustine that *"An unjust law is no law at all."*

Now what is the difference between the two? How does one determine when a law is just or unjust? A *just law* is a man-made code that squares with the *moral law* or the law of God. An *unjust law* is a code that is out of harmony with the moral law. To put it in the terms of Saint Thomas Aquinas, an unjust law is a human law that is not rooted in eternal and *natural law*. Any law that uplifts human personality is just. Any law that degrades human personality is unjust. All segregation statutes are unjust because segregation distorts the soul and damages the personality. It gives the segregator a false sense of superiority and the segregated a false sense of inferiority. To use the words of Martin Buber, the great Jewish philosopher, segregation substitutes an "I-it" relationship for an "I-thou" relationship, and ends up relegating persons to the status of things. So segregation is not only politically, economically, and sociologically unsound, but it is morally wrong and sinful. Paul Tillich has said that sin is separation.

Isn't segregation an existential expression of man's tragic separation, an expression of his awful estrangement, 9 his terrible sinfulness? So I can urge men to obey the1954 decision of the Supreme Court because it is morally right, and I can urge them to disobey segregation ordinances because they are morally wrong.

Let us turn to a more concrete example of just and unjust laws. An unjust law is a code that a majority inflicts on a minority that is not binding on itself. This is difference made legal. On the other hand a just law is a code that a majority compels a minority to follow that it is willing to follow itself. This is sameness made legal.

Let me give another explanation. An unjust law is a code inflicted upon a minority which that minority had no part in enacting or creating because they did not have the unhampered right to vote. Who can say that the legislature of Alabama which set up the segregation laws was democratically elected? Throughout the state of Alabama all types of conniving methods are used to prevent Negroes from becoming registered voters and there are some counties without a single Negro registered to vote despite the fact that the Negro constitutes a majority of the population. Can any law set up in such a state be considered democratically structured?

These are just a few examples of unjust and just laws. There are some instances when a law is just on its face but unjust in its application. For instance, I was arrested Friday on a charge of parading without a permit. Now there is nothing wrong with an ordinance which requires a permit for a parade, but when the ordinance is used to preserve segregation and to deny citizens the First Amendment privilege of peaceful assembly and peaceful protest, then it becomes unjust.

I hope you can see the distinction I am trying to point out. In no sense do I advocate evading or defying the law as the rabid segregationist would do. This would lead to anarchy. One who breaks an unjust law must do it openly, lovingly (not hatefully as the white mothers did in New Orleans when they were seen on television screaming "nigger, nigger, nigger") and with a willingness to accept the penalty. I submit that an individual who breaks a law that conscience tells him is unjust, and willingly accepts the penalty by staying in jail to arouse the conscience of the community over its injustice, is in reality expressing the very highest respect for law.

Of course there is nothing new about this kind of civil disobedience. It was seen sublimely in the refusal of Shadrach, Meshach, and Abednego to obey the laws of Nebuchadnezzar because a higher moral law was involved. It was practiced superbly by the early Christians who were willing to face hungry lions and the excruciating pain of chopping blocks, before submitting to certain unjust laws of the Roman Empire. To a degree academic freedom is a reality today because Socrates practiced civil disobedience.

We can never forget that everything Hitler did in Germany was "legal" and everything the Hungarian freedom fighters did in Hungary was "illegal." It was "illegal" to aid and comfort a Jew in Hitler's Germany. But I am sure that, if I had lived in Germany during that time, I would have aided and comforted my Jewish brothers even though it was illegal. If I lived in a communist country today where certain principles dear to the Christian faith are suppressed, I believe I would openly advocate disobeying these anti-10 religious laws.

I must make two honest confessions to you, my Christian and Jewish brothers. First, I must confess that over the last few years I have been gravely disappointed with the white moderate. I have almost reached the regrettable conclusion that the Negroes' great stumbling block in the stride toward freedom is not the White Citizen's "Counciler" or the Ku Klux Klanner, but the white moderate who is more devoted to "order" than to justice; who prefers a negative peace which is the absence of tension to a positive peace which is the presence of justice; who constantly says "I agree with you in the goal you seek, but I can't agree with your methods of direct action"; who paternalistically feels that he can set the timetable for another man's freedom; who lives by the myth of time and who constantly advises the Negro to wait until a "more convenient season." Shallow understanding from people of good will is more frustrating than absolute misunderstanding from people of ill will. Lukewarm acceptance is much more bewildering than outright rejection.

I had hoped that the white moderate would understand that law and order exist for the purpose of establishing justice, and that when they fail to do this they become dangerously structured dams that block the flow of social progress. I had hoped that the white moderate would understand that the present tension in the South is merely a necessary phase of the transition from an obnoxious negative peace, where the Negro passively accepted his unjust plight, to a substance-filled positive peace, where all men will respect the dignity and worth of human personality. Actually, we who engage in nonviolent direct action are not the creators of tension. We merely bring to the surface the hidden tension that is already alive. We bring it out in the open where it can be seen and dealt with. Like a boil that can never be cured as long as it is covered up but must be opened with all its pus-flowing ugliness to the natural medicines of air and light, injustice must likewise be exposed, with all of the tension its exposing creates, to the light of human conscience and the air of national opinion before it can be cured.

In your statement you asserted that our actions, even though peaceful, must be condemned because they precipitate violence. But can this assertion be logically made? Isn't this like condemning the robbed man because his possession of money precipitated the evil act of robbery? Isn't this like condemning Socrates because his unswerving commitment to truth and his philosophical delvings precipitated the misguided popular mind to make him drink the hemlock? Isn't this like condemning Jesus because His unique God consciousness and never-ceasing devotion to His will precipitated the evil act of crucifixion? We must come to see, as federal courts have consistently affirmed, that it is immoral to urge an individual to withdraw his efforts to gain his basic constitutional rights because the quest precipitates violence. Society must protect the robbed and punish the robber.

I had also hoped that the white moderate would reject the myth of time. I received a letter this morning from a white brother in Texas which said: "All Christians know that the colored people will receive equal rights eventually, but is it possible that you are in too great of a religious hurry? It has taken Christianity almost 2,000 years to accomplish what it has. The teachings of Christ take time to come to earth." All that is said here grows out of a tragic misconception of time. It is the strangely irrational notion that there is something in the very flow of time that will inevitably cure all ills.

Actually time is neutral. It can be used either destructively or constructively. I am coming to feel that the people of ill will have used time much more effectively than the people of good will. We will have to repent in this generation not merely for the *vitriolic* words and actions of the bad people, but for the appalling silence of the good people. We must come to see that human progress never rolls in on wheels of inevitability. It comes through the tireless efforts and persistent work of men willing to be co-workers with God, and without this hard work time itself becomes an ally of the forces of *social stagnation*. We must use time creatively, and forever realize that the time is always ripe to do right. Now is the time to make real the promise of democracy, and transform our pending national elegy into a creative psalm of brotherhood. Now is the time to lift our national policy from the quicksand of racial injustice to the solid rock of human dignity.

You spoke of our activity in Birmingham as extreme. At first I was rather disappointed that fellow clergymen would see my nonviolent efforts as those of the extremist. I started thinking about the fact that I stand in the middle of two opposing forces in the Negro community. One is a force of complacency made up of Negroes who, as a result of long years of oppression, have been so completely drained of self-respect and a sense of "somebodiness" that they have adjusted to segregation, and of a few Negroes in the middle class who, because of a degree of academic and economic security, and because at points they profit by segregation, have unconsciously become insensitive to the problems of the masses. The other force is one of bitterness and hatred and comes *perilously* close to advocating violence. It is expressed in the various black nationalist groups that are springing up over the nation, the largest and best known being Elijah Muhammad's Muslim movement. This movement is nourished by the contemporary frustration over the continued existence of racial discrimination. It is made up of people who have lost faith in America, who have absolutely repudiated Christianity, and who have concluded that the white man is an incurable "devil." I have tried to stand between these two forces saying that we need not follow the "do-nothingism" of the complacent or the hatred and despair of the black nationalist. There is the more excellent way of love and nonviolent protest. I'm grateful to God that, through the Negro church, the dimension of nonviolence entered our struggle. If this philosophy had not emerged I am convinced that by now many streets of the South would be flowing with floods of blood. And I am further convinced that if our white brothers dismiss us as "rabble rousers" and "outside agitators"-- those of us who are working through the channels of nonviolent direct action – and refuse to support our nonviolent efforts, millions of Negroes, out of frustration and despair, will seek solace and security in black-nationalist ideologies, a development that will lead inevitably to a frightening racial nightmare.

Oppressed people cannot remain oppressed forever. The urge for freedom will eventually come. This is what has happened to the American Negro. Something within has reminded him of his birthright of freedom; something without has reminded him that he can gain it.

Consciously and unconsciously, he has been swept in by what the Germans call the Zeitgeist, and with his black brothers of Africa, and his brown and yellow brothers of Asia, South America, and the Caribbean, he is moving with a sense of cosmic urgency 12 toward the promised land of racial justice. Recognizing this vital urge that has engulfed the Negro community, one should readily understand public demonstrations.

The Negro has many pent-up resentments and latent frustrations. He has to get them out. So let him march sometime; let him have his prayer pilgrimages to the city hall; understand why he must have sit-ins and freedom rides. If his repressed emotions do not come out in these nonviolent ways, they will come out in ominous expressions of violence. This is not a threat; it is a fact of history. So I have not said to my people, "Get rid of your discontent." But I have tried to say that this normal and healthy discontent can be channeled through the creative outlet of nonviolent direct action. Now this approach is being dismissed as *extremist*. I must admit that I was initially disappointed in being so categorized. But as I continued to think about the matter I gradually gained a bit of satisfaction from being considered an extremist. Was not Jesus an extremist in love? "Love your enemies, bless them that curse you, pray for them that despitefully use you." Was not Amos an extremist for justice -- "Let justice roll down like waters and righteousness like a mighty stream." Was not Paul an extremist for the gospel of Jesus Christ -- "I bear in my body the marks of the Lord Jesus." Was not Martin Luther an extremist -- "Here I stand; I can do none other so help me God." Was not John Bunyan an extremist -- "I will stay in jail to the end of my days before I make a butchery of my conscience." Was not Abraham Lincoln an extremist -- "This nation cannot survive half slave and half free." Was not Thomas Jefferson an extremist -- "We hold these truths to be self-evident, that all men are created equal." So the question is not whether we will be extremist but what kind of extremist will we be. Will we be extremists for hate or will we be extremists for love? Will we be extremists for the preservation of injustice -- or will we be extremists for the cause of justice? In that dramatic scene on Calvary's hill three men were crucified. We must never forget that all three were crucified for the same crime -- the crime of extremism. Two were extremists for immorality, and thus fell below their environment. The other, Jesus Christ, was an extremist for love, truth, and goodness, and thereby rose above His environment. So, after all, maybe the South, the nation, and the world are in dire need of creative extremists.

I had hoped that the white moderate would see this. Maybe I was too optimistic. Maybe I expected too much. I guess I should have realized that few members of a race that has oppressed another race can understand or appreciate the deep groans and passionate yearnings of those that have been oppressed, and still fewer have the vision to see that injustice must be rooted out by strong, persistent, and determined action. I am thankful, however, that some of our white brothers have grasped the meaning of this social revolution and committed themselves to it. They are still all too small in quantity, but they are big in quality. Some like Ralph McGill, Lillian Smith, Harry Golden, and James Dabbs have written about our struggle in eloquent, prophetic, and understanding terms.

Others have marched with us down nameless streets of the South. They have languished in filthy, roach-infested jails, suffering the abuse and brutality of angry policemen who see them as "dirty nigger lovers." They, unlike so many of their moderate brothers and sisters, have recognized the urgency of the moment and sensed the need for powerful "action" antidotes to combat the disease of segregation.

Let me rush on to mention my other disappointment. I have been so greatly disappointed with the white Church and its leadership. Of course there are some notable exceptions. I am not unmindful of the fact that each of you has taken some significant stands on this issue. I commend you, Rev. Stallings, for your Christian stand on this past Sunday, in welcoming Negroes to your worship service on a non-segregated basis. I commend the Catholic leaders of this state for integrating Spring Hill College several years ago.

But despite these notable exceptions I must honestly reiterate that I have been disappointed with the Church. I do not say that as one of those negative critics who can always find something wrong with the Church. I say it as a minister of the gospel, who loves the Church; who was nurtured in its bosom; who has been sustained by its spiritual blessings and who will remain true to it as long as the cord of life shall lengthen.

I had the strange feeling when I was suddenly catapulted into the leadership of the bus protest in Montgomery several years ago that we would have the support of the white Church. I felt that the white ministers, priests, and rabbis of the South would be some of our strongest allies. Instead, some have been outright opponents, refusing to understand the freedom movement and misrepresenting its leaders; all too many others have been more cautious than courageous and have remained silent behind the *anesthetizing* security of the stained glass windows.

In spite of my shattered dreams of the past, I came to Birmingham with the hope that the white religious leadership of this community would see the justice of our cause and with deep moral concern, serve as the channel through which our just grievances could get to the power structure. I had hoped that each of you would understand. But again I have been disappointed.

I have heard numerous religious leaders of the South call upon their worshippers to comply with a desegregation decision because it is the law, but I have longed to hear white ministers say follow this decree because integration is morally right and the Negro is your brother. In the midst of blatant injustices inflicted upon the Negro, I have watched white churches stand on the sideline and merely mouth *pious* irrelevancies and *sanctimonious* trivialities. In the midst of a mighty struggle to rid our nation of racial and economic injustice, I have heard so many ministers say, "Those are social issues with which the gospel has no real concern," and I have watched so many churches commit themselves to a completely other-worldly religion which made a strange distinction between body and soul, the sacred and the secular. So here we are moving toward the exit of the twentieth century with a religious community largely adjusted to the status quo, standing as a tail-light behind other community agencies rather than a headlight leading men to higher levels of justice.

I have travelled the length and breadth of Alabama, Mississippi and all the other southern states. On *sweltering* summer days and crisp autumn mornings I have looked at her beautiful churches with their spires pointing heavenward. I have beheld the impressive outlay of her massive religious education buildings. Over and over again I have found myself asking: "Who worships here? Who is their God? Where were their voices when the lips of Governor Barnett dripped with words of *interposition* and *nullification*? Where were they when Governor Wallace gave the *clarion* call for defiance and hatred? Where were their voices of support when tired, bruised, and weary Negro men and women decided to rise from the dark dungeons of complacency to the bright hills of creative protest?"

Yes, these questions are still in my mind. In deep disappointment, I have wept over the *laxity* of the church. But be assured that my tears have been tears of love. There can be no deep disappointment where there is not deep love. Yes, I love the Church; I love her sacred walls. How could I do otherwise? I am in the rather unique position of being the son, the grandson, and the great-grandson of preachers. Yes, I see the Church as the body of Christ. But, oh! How we have blemished and scarred that body through social neglect and fear of being *nonconformist*.

There was a time when the Church was very powerful. It was during that period when the early Christians rejoiced when they were deemed worthy to suffer for what they believed. In those days the Church was not merely a thermometer that recorded the ideas and principles of popular opinion; it was a thermostat that transformed the mores of society.

Wherever the early Christians entered a town the power structure got disturbed and immediately sought to convict them for being "disturbers of the peace" and "outside agitators." But they went on with the conviction that they were "a colony of heaven" and had to obey God rather than man. They were small in number but big in commitment. They were too God-intoxicated to be "astronomically intimidated." They brought an end to such ancient evils as infanticide and gladiatorial contest.

Things are different now. The contemporary Church is so often a weak, ineffectual voice with an uncertain sound. It is so often the arch-supporter of the status quo. Far from being disturbed by the presence of the Church, the power structure of the average community is consoled by the Church's silent and often vocal sanction of things as they are. But the judgment of God is upon the Church as never before. If the Church of today does not recapture the sacrificial spirit of the early Church, it will lose its authentic ring, forfeit the loyalty of millions, and be dismissed as an irrelevant social club with no meaning for the twentieth century. I am meeting young people every day whose disappointment with the Church has risen to outright disgust.

Maybe again I have been too optimistic. Is organized religion too inextricably bound to the status quo to save our nation and the world? Maybe I must turn my faith to the inner spiritual Church, the church within the Church, as the true *ecclesia* and the hope of the world. But again I am thankful to God that some noble souls from the ranks of organized religion have broken loose from the paralyzing chains of conformity and joined us as active partners in the struggle for freedom. They have left their secure congregations and walked the streets of Albany, Georgia, with us. They have gone through the highways of the South on torturous rides for freedom. Yes, they have gone to jail with us. Some have been kicked out of their churches and lost the support of their bishops and fellow ministers. But they have gone with the faith that right defeated is stronger than evil triumphant. These men have been the leaven in the lump of the race. Their witness has been the spiritual salt that has preserved the true meaning of the Gospel in these troubled times. They have carved a tunnel of hope through the dark mountain of disappointment.

I hope the Church as a whole will meet the challenge of this decisive hour. But even if the Church does not come to the aid of justice, I have no despair about the future. I have no fear about the outcome of our struggle in Birmingham, even if our motives are presently misunderstood. We will reach the goal of freedom in Birmingham and all over the nation, because the goal of America is freedom. Abused and scorned though we may be, our destiny is tied up with the destiny of America. Before the pilgrims landed at Plymouth, we were here. Before the pen of Jefferson etched across the pages of history the majestic words of the Declaration of Independence, we were here. For more than two centuries our foreparents labored in this country without wages; they made cotton "king"; and they built the homes of their masters in the midst of brutal injustice and shameful humiliation -- and yet out of a bottomless vitality they continued to thrive and develop. If

the inexpressible cruelties of slavery could not stop us, the opposition we now face will surely fail. We will win our freedom because the sacred heritage of our nation and the eternal will of God are embodied in our echoing demands.

I must close now. But before closing I am impelled to mention one other point in your statement that troubled me profoundly. You warmly commend the Birmingham police force for keeping "order" and "preventing violence." I don't believe you would have so warmly commended the police force if you had seen its angry violent dogs literally biting six unarmed, nonviolent Negroes. I don't believe you would so quickly commend the policemen if you would observe their ugly and inhuman treatment of Negroes here in the city jail; if you would watch them push and curse old Negro women and young Negro girls; if you would see them slap and kick old Negro men and young Negro boys; if you will observe them, as they did on two occasions, refuse to give us food because we wanted to sing our grace together. I'm sorry that I can't join you in your praise for the police department.

It is true that they have been rather disciplined in their public handling of the demonstrators. In this sense they have been rather publicly "nonviolent." But for what purpose? To preserve the evil system of segregation. Over the last few years I have consistently preached that nonviolence demands the means we use must be as pure as the ends we seek. So I have tried to make it clear that it is wrong to use immoral means to attain moral ends. But now I must affirm that it is just as wrong or even more so to use moral means to preserve immoral ends. Maybe Mr. Connor and his policemen have been rather publicly nonviolent, as Chief Pritchett was in Albany, Georgia, but they have used the moral means of nonviolence to maintain the immoral end of flagrant injustice. T. S. Eliot has said that there is no greater treason than to do the right deed for the wrong reason.

I wish you had commended the Negro sit-inners and demonstrators of Birmingham for their *sublime* courage, their willingness to suffer, and their amazing discipline in the midst of the most *inhuman provocation*. One day the South will recognize its real heroes. They will be the James Merediths, courageously and with a majestic sense of purpose, facing jeering and hostile mobs and the agonizing loneliness that characterizes the life of the pioneer. They will be old, oppressed, battered Negro women, symbolized in a seventy-two year old woman of Montgomery, Alabama, who rose up with a sense of dignity and with her people decided not to ride the segregated buses, and responded to one who inquired about her tiredness with *ungrammatical profundity*: "My feets is tired, but my soul is rested." They will be the young high school and college students, young ministers of the gospel and a host of their elders courageously and nonviolently sitting-in at lunch counters and willingly going to jail for conscience sake. One day the South will know that when these disinherited children of God sat down at lunch counters they were in reality standing up for the best in the American dream and the most sacred values in

our Judeo-Christian heritage, and thus carrying our whole nation back to great wells of democracy which were dug deep by the founding fathers in the formulation of the Constitution and the Declaration of Independence.

Never before have I written a letter this long (or should I say a book?). I'm afraid it is much too long to take your precious time. I can assure you that it would have been much shorter if I had been writing from a comfortable desk, but what else is there to do when you are alone for days in the dull monotony of a narrow jail cell other than write long letters, think strange thoughts, and pray long prayers?

If I have said anything in this letter that is an *overstatement of the truth* and is indicative of an unreasonable impatience, I beg you to forgive me. If I have said anything in this letter that is an understatement of the truth and is indicative of my having a patience that makes me patient with anything less than brotherhood, I beg God to forgive me.

I hope this letter finds you strong in the faith. I also hope that circumstances will soon make it possible for me to meet each of you, not as an integrationist or a civil rights leader, but as a fellow clergyman and a Christian brother. Let us all hope that the dark clouds of racial prejudice will soon pass away and the deep fog of misunderstanding will be lifted from our fear-drenched communities and in some not too distant tomorrow the radiant stars of love and brotherhood will shine over our great nation with all their *scintillating* beauty.

Yours for the cause of Peace and Brotherhood,

Martin Luther King, Jr.

The Atlantic Monthly; August 1963; The Negro Is Your Brother; Volume 212, No. 2; pages 78 - 88.

Notes and Outline of "A Letter From a Birmingham Jail"

Write a summary of "A Letter From a Birmingham Jail".

Short Answer Questions – "A Letter From a Birmingham Jail"

1. What is King's definition of civil disobedience?

2. How does King emulate Gandhi's concept of satyagraha? In what ways is King's version different?

3. Discuss the conditions throughout the South that led to nonviolent civil disobedience. In particular, discuss the First Amendment issues that are relevant to King's protest actions.

4. In the fourth paragraph of "Letter From a Birmingham Jail", King states that, "Injustice anywhere is a threat to justice everywhere". What does the author mean by this statement?

5. According to King, what is the difference between a just and an unjust law, and how can we as citizens determine the difference between the two?

6. King distinguishes between negative and positive peace in his letter. What does he mean by these terms, and how does this terminology criticize tacit supporters of segregation?

Essay Topics

1. Do a "background check" on segregation in the South during the 1950's and 1960's. Discuss the conditions throughout the South that led to nonviolent civil disobedience. In particular, discuss the First Amendment issues that are relevant to King's protest actions.

2. What does King believe is the moral duty of all Christian people with respect to the African-American freedom movement? Provide specific examples from the text to support your claim.

3. How does King explain the purpose and effectiveness of nonviolent action? Discuss the ways in which King's views compare to those of Thoreau.

C H A R T

KNOW • WANT • LEARN

KWL

ALREADY KNOW	WANT TO KNOW	WHAT I LEARNED

Notes

On the Death of Martin Luther King, Jr.
Robert F. Kennedy
April 4, 1968
Indianapolis, Indiana

During an Indianapolis, Indiana rally for his presidential campaign, attended by a large number of African Americans, Robert F. Kennedy, despite suggestions he shouldn't appear at all, decided to proceed and announce the assassination of Martin Luther King, Jr., to a group unaware that the killing had taken place.

I have bad news for you, for all of our fellow citizens, and people who love peace all over the world, and that is that Martin Luther King was shot and killed tonight.

Martin Luther King dedicated his life to love and to justice for his fellow human beings, and he died because of that effort.

In this difficult day, in this difficult time for the United States, it is perhaps well to ask what kind of a nation we are and what direction we want to move in. For those of you who are black -- considering the evidence there evidently is that there were white people who were responsible -- you can be filled with bitterness, with hatred, and a desire for revenge. We can move in that direction as a country, in great polarization -- black people amongst black, white people amongst white, filled with hatred toward one another.

Or we can make an effort, as Martin Luther King did, to understand and to comprehend, and to replace that violence, that stain of bloodshed that has spread across our land, with an effort to understand with compassion and love.

For those of you who are black and are tempted to be filled with hatred and distrust at the injustice of such an act, against all white people, I can only say that I feel in my own heart the same kind of feeling. I had a member of my family killed, but he was killed by a white man. But we have to make an effort in the United States, we have to make an effort to understand, to go beyond these rather difficult times.

My favorite poet was Aeschylus. He wrote: "In our sleep, pain which cannot forget falls drop by drop upon the heart until, in our own despair, against our will, comes wisdom through the awful grace of God."

What we need in the United States is not division; what we need in the United States is not hatred; what we need in the United States is not violence or lawlessness; but love and wisdom, and compassion toward one another, and a feeling of justice toward those who still suffer within our country, whether they be white or they be black.

So I shall ask you tonight to return home, to say a prayer for the family of Martin Luther King, that's true, but more importantly to say a prayer for our own country, which all of us love -- a prayer for understanding and that compassion of which I spoke.

We can do well in this country. We will have difficult times; we've had difficult times in the past; we will have difficult times in the future. It is not the end of violence; it is not the end of lawlessness; it is not the end of disorder.

But the vast majority of white people and the vast majority of black people in this country want to live together, want to improve the quality of our life, and want justice for all human beings who abide in our land.

Let us dedicate ourselves to what the Greeks wrote so many years ago: to tame the savageness of man and make gentle the life of this world.

Let us dedicate ourselves to that, and say a prayer for our country and for our people.]

"American Rhetoric: Robert F. Kennedy -- Statement on the Assassination of Martin Luther King, Jr." N.p., n.d. Web. 07 Nov. 2014.   Audio available in the public domain.

Write a summary of "On the Death of Martin Luther King Jr."

Short Answer Questions:

1. What is Kennedy's tone throughout the speech? Provide evidence from the text to support your claim.

2. Why do you think Kennedy includes this quote in his speech? "My favorite poet was Aeschylus. He wrote: 'In our sleep, pain which cannot forget falls drop by drop upon the heart until, in our own despair, against our will, comes wisdom through the awful grace of God.'" What do you think it means and is it appropriate?

3. How does Kennedy's statement on King's stance on civil disobedience manifest itself in this speech? What quote(s) would qualify for evidence of Kennedy's support of King's nonviolent stance?

ENVISIONING AMERICAN POLICY

SELECTED PRESIDENTIAL INAUGURATION SPEECHES

John F. Kennedy

Lyndon B. Johnson

Richard Nixon

Ronald Reagan

George H. Bush

William H. Clinton

George W. Bush

Barack H. Obama

Notes

Chapter 6

Envisioning American Policy

Selected Presidential Inauguration Speeches

Public Policy from the Civil Rights

Movement to the Present

The custom of delivering an address on Inauguration Day started with the very first Inauguration—George Washington's—on April 30, 1789. After taking his oath of office on the balcony of Federal Hall in New York City, Washington proceeded to the Senate chamber where he read a speech before members of Congress and other dignitaries. His second Inauguration took place in Philadelphia on March 4, 1793, in the Senate chamber of Congress Hall. There, Washington gave the shortest Inaugural address on record—just 135 words—before repeating the oath of office.

Every President since Washington has delivered an Inaugural address. While many of the early Presidents read their addresses before taking the oath, current custom dictates that the Chief Justice of the Supreme Court administer the oath first, followed by the President's speech.

William Henry Harrison delivered the longest Inaugural address, at 8,445 words, on March 4, 1841—a bitterly cold, wet day. He died one month later of pneumonia, believed to have been brought on by prolonged exposure to the elements on his Inauguration Day. John Adams' Inaugural address, which totaled 2,308 words, contained the longest sentence, at 737 words. After Washington's second Inaugural address, the next shortest was Franklin D. Roosevelt's fourth address on January 20, 1945, at just 559 words. Roosevelt had chosen to have a simple Inauguration at the White House in light of the nation's involvement in World War II.

In 1921, Warren G. Harding became the first President to take his oath and deliver his Inaugural address through loud speakers. In 1925, Calvin Coolidge's Inaugural address was the first to be broadcast nationally by radio. And in 1949, Harry S. Truman became the first President to deliver his Inaugural address over television airwaves.

Most Presidents use their Inaugural address to present their vision of America and to set forth their goals for the nation. Some of the most eloquent and powerful speeches are still quoted today. In 1865, in the waning days of the Civil War, Abraham Lincoln stated, "With malice toward none, with charity for all, with firmness in the right as God gives us to see the right, let us strive on to finish the work we are in, to bind up the nation's wounds, to care for him who shall have borne the battle and for his widow and his orphan, to do all which may achieve and cherish a just and lasting peace among ourselves and with all nations." In 1933, Franklin D. Roosevelt avowed, "we have nothing to fear but fear itself." And in 1961, John F. Kennedy declared, "And so my fellow Americans: ask not what your country can do for you—ask what you can do for your country."

Today, Presidents deliver their Inaugural address on the west front of the Capitol, but this has not always been the case. Until Andrew Jackson's first Inauguration in 1829, most Presidents spoke in either the House or Senate chambers. Jackson became the first President to take his oath of office and deliver his address on the east front portico of the U.S. Capitol in 1829. With few exceptions, the next 37 Inaugurations took place there, until 1981, when Ronald Reagan's swearing-in ceremony and Inaugural address occurred on the west front terrace of the Capitol. The west front has been used ever since. (http://www.inaugural.senate.gov/days-events/days-event/inaugural-address)

In this chapter, we will explore the inauguration speeches of some of the most influential and controversial United States presidents since 1961. As you explore this chapter, as yourself the following questions:

- What does the inauguration speech tell us about the issues the president faces?
- What is the social situation of the United States globally?
- What does the president say about his vision for foreign policy?
- Where does the president stand on civil rights?
- How does the president suggest Americans establish racial unity?
- What is the role of government in the lives of American citizens?

These are the questions to explore as you read the next chapter.

INSTRUCTIONS

1. Complete the KWL chart to see what information you know about the stories you will read.
2. After completing the KWL chart, and doing a research on the story you about to read, write an introduction to introduce this text.
3. At the end of each section, you will complete an SQ3R exercise to study the texts in this chapter.

C H A R T

KNOW • WANT • LEARN

KW

ALREADY KNOW	WANT TO KNOW	WHAT I LEARNED

John F. Kennedy

On November 22, 1963, when he was hardly past his first thousand days in office, John Fitzgerald Kennedy was killed by an assassin's bullets as his motorcade wound through Dallas, Texas. Kennedy was the youngest man elected President; he was the youngest to die.

Of Irish descent, he was born in Brookline, Massachusetts, on May 29, 1917. Graduating from Harvard in 1940, he entered the Navy. In 1943, when his PT boat was rammed and sunk by a Japanese destroyer, Kennedy, despite grave injuries, led the survivors through perilous waters to safety.

Back from the war, he became a Democratic Congressman from the Boston area, advancing in 1953 to the Senate. He married Jacqueline Bouvier on September 12, 1953. In 1955, while recuperating from a back operation, he wrote Profiles in Courage, which won the Pulitzer Prize in history.

In 1956 Kennedy almost gained the Democratic nomination for Vice President, and four years later was a first-ballot nominee for President. Millions watched his television debates with the Republican candidate, Richard M. Nixon. Winning by a narrow margin in the popular vote, Kennedy became the first Roman Catholic President.

His Inaugural Address offered the memorable injunction: "Ask not what your country can do for you--ask what you can do for your country." As President, he set out to redeem his campaign pledge to get America moving again. His economic programs launched the country on its longest sustained expansion since World War II; before his death, he laid plans for a massive assault on persisting pockets of privation and poverty.

Responding to ever more urgent demands, he took vigorous action in the cause of equal rights, calling for new civil rights legislation. His vision of America extended to the quality of the national culture and the central role of the arts in a vital society.

He wished America to resume its old mission as the first nation dedicated to the revolution of human rights. With the Alliance for Progress and the Peace Corps, he brought American idealism to the aid of developing nations. But the hard reality of the Communist challenge remained.

Shortly after his inauguration, Kennedy permitted a band of Cuban exiles, already armed and trained, to invade their homeland. The attempt to overthrow the regime of Fidel Castro was a failure. Soon thereafter, the Soviet Union renewed its campaign against West Berlin. Kennedy replied by reinforcing the Berlin garrison and increasing the Nation's military strength, including new efforts in outer space. Confronted by this reaction, Moscow, after the erection of the Berlin Wall, relaxed its pressure in central Europe.

Instead, the Russians now sought to install nuclear missiles in Cuba. When this was discovered by air reconnaissance in October 1962, Kennedy imposed a quarantine on all offensive weapons bound for Cuba. While the world trembled on the brink of nuclear war, the Russians backed down and agreed to take the missiles away. The American response to the Cuban crisis evidently persuaded Moscow of the futility of nuclear blackmail.

Kennedy now contended that both sides had a vital interest in stopping the spread of nuclear weapons and slowing the arms race--a contention which led to the test ban treaty of 1963. The months after the Cuban crisis showed significant progress toward his goal of "a world of law and free choice, banishing the world of war and coercion." His administration thus saw the beginning of new hope for both the equal rights of Americans and the peace of the world.

The Presidential biographies on WhiteHouse.gov are from "The Presidents of the United States of America," by Frank Freidel and Hugh Sidey. Copyright 2006 by the White House Historical Association.

Notes

John F. Kennedy

"Ask Not What Your Country Can Do for You"

Inaugural Speech

Friday, January 20, 1961

Vice President Johnson, Mr. Speaker, Mr. Chief Justice, President Eisenhower, Vice President Nixon, President Truman, reverend clergy, fellow citizens, we observe today not a victory of party, but a celebration of freedom—symbolizing an end, as well as a beginning—signifying renewal, as well as change. For I have sworn before you and Almighty God the same solemn oath our forebears prescribed nearly a century and three quarters ago.

Revolution and Human Rights

The world is very different now. For man holds in his mortal hands the power to abolish all forms of human poverty and all forms of human life. And yet the same revolutionary beliefs for which our forebears fought are still at issue around the globe— the belief that the rights of man come not from the generosity of the state, but from the hand of God. We dare not forget today that we are the heirs of that first revolution. Let the word go forth from this time and place, to friend and foe alike, that the torch has been passed to a new generation of Americans—born in this century, tempered by war, disciplined by a hard and bitter peace, proud of our ancient heritage—and unwilling to witness or permit the slow undoing of those human rights to which this Nation has always been committed, and to which we are committed today at home and around the world.

Let every nation know, whether it wishes us well or ill, that we shall pay any price, bear any burden, meet any hardship, support any friend, oppose any foe, in order to assure the survival and the success of liberty. This much we pledge—and more. To those old **allies** whose cultural and spiritual origins we share, we pledge the loyalty of faithful friends. United, there is little we cannot do in a host of cooperative ventures. Divided, there is little we can do—for we dare not meet a powerful challenge at odds and split asunder. To those new States whom we welcome to the ranks of the free, we pledge our word that one form of colonial control shall not have passed away merely to be replaced by a far more iron tyranny. We shall not always expect to find them supporting our view. But we shall always hope to find them strongly supporting their own freedom—and to remember that, in the past, those who foolishly sought power by riding the back of the tiger ended up inside.

Foreign Policy

To those peoples in the huts and villages across the globe struggling to break the bonds of mass misery, we pledge our best efforts to help them help themselves,

Notes

for whatever period is required—not because the Communists may be doing it, not because we seek their votes, but because it is right. If a free society cannot help the many who are poor, it cannot save the few who are rich. To our sister republics south of our border, we offer a special pledge—to convert our good words into good deeds—in a new alliance for progress—to assist free men and free governments in casting off the chains of poverty. But this peaceful revolution of hope cannot become the prey of hostile powers. Let all our neighbors know that we shall join with them to oppose aggression or subversion anywhere in the Americas. And let every other power know that this **Hemisphere** intends to remain the master of its own house.

To that world assembly of sovereign states, the United Nations, our last best hope in an age where the instruments of war have far outpaced the instruments of peace, we renew our pledge of support—to prevent it from becoming merely a forum for invective—to strengthen its shield of the new and the weak—and to enlarge the area in which its writ may run.

Finally, to those nations who would make themselves our adversary, we offer not a pledge but a request: that both sides begin anew the quest for peace, before the dark powers of destruction unleashed by science engulf all humanity in planned or accidental self-destruction.

We dare not tempt them with weakness. For only when our arms are sufficient beyond doubt can we be certain beyond doubt that they will never be employed. But neither can two great and powerful groups of nations take comfort from our present course—both sides overburdened by the cost of modern weapons, both rightly alarmed by the steady spread of the deadly atom, yet both racing to alter that uncertain balance of terror that stays the hand of mankind's final war.

Civility, Unity and Peace

So let us begin anew—remembering on both sides that civility is not a sign of weakness, and sincerity is always subject to proof. Let us never negotiate out of fear. But let us never fear to negotiate. Let both sides explore what problems unite us instead of belaboring those problems which divide us. Let both sides, for the first time, formulate serious and precise proposals for the inspection and control of arms—and bring the absolute power to destroy other nations under the absolute control of all nations. Let both sides seek to **invoke** the wonders of science instead of its terrors. Together let us explore the stars, conquer the deserts, eradicate disease, tap the ocean depths, and encourage the arts and commerce. Let both sides unite to heed in all corners of the earth the command of Isaiah—to "undo the heavy burdens ... and to let the oppressed go free."

And if a **beachhead** of cooperation may push back the jungle of suspicion, let both sides join in creating a new endeavor, not a new balance of power, but a new world of law, where the strong are just and the weak secure and the peace preserved. All this will not be finished in the first 100 days. Nor will it be finished in the first 1,000 days, nor in the life of this Administration, nor even perhaps in our lifetime on this planet. But let us begin.

In your hands, my fellow citizens, more than in mine, will rest the final success or failure of our course. Since this country was founded, each generation of Americans has been summoned to give testimony to its national loyalty. The graves of young Americans who answered the call to service surround the globe.

Now the trumpet summons us again—not as a call to bear arms, though arms we need; not as a call to battle, though embattled we are—but a call to bear the burden of a long twilight struggle, year in and year out, "rejoicing in hope, patient in tribulation"—a struggle against the common enemies of man: **tyranny**, poverty, disease, and war itself. Can we forge against these enemies a grand and global alliance, North and South, East and West, that can assure a more fruitful life for all mankind? Will you join in that historic effort?

In the long history of the world, only a few generations have been granted the role of defending freedom in its hour of maximum danger. I do not shrink from this responsibility—I welcome it. I do not believe that any of us would exchange places with any other people or any other generation. The energy, the faith, the devotion which we bring to this endeavor will light our country and all who serve it—and the glow from that fire can truly light the world.

And so, my fellow Americans: ask not what your country can do for you—ask what you can do for your country. My fellow citizens of the world: ask not what America will do for you, but what together we can do for the freedom of man.

Finally, whether you are citizens of America or citizens of the world, ask of us the same high standards of strength and sacrifice which we ask of you. With a good conscience our only sure reward, with history the final judge of our deeds, let us go forth to lead the land we love, asking His blessing and His help, but knowing that here on earth God's work must truly be our own.

Complete the SQ3R Analysis. See Appendix.

Inaugural Address, January 20, 1961, United States Capitol, Washington, D.C. Date: January 20, 1961, Copyright: Public domain. Credit: John F. Kennedy Presidential Library & Museum, Boston, Massachusetts

Short Answer Questions – President John F. Kennedy

1. In President Kennedy's words, what are the common enemies of man?

2. Although it is never addressed directly, President Kennedy is referring to the Vietnam War. Why do you think he doesn't address it directly?

3. Identify one allusion to the war in President Kennedy's speech.

4. Why do you believe serving one's country was a key element in Kennedy's speech?

Essay Topics

1. Ask not what your country can do for you, but what together you can do for your country? Respond to both of these questions in a complete essay.

2. What do you believe was the purpose of President Kennedy's speech? Was it effective?

C H A R T

KNOW • WANT • LEARN

KW

ALREADY KNOW	WANT TO KNOW	WHAT I LEARNED

Lyndon B. Johnson

"A Great Society" for the American people and their fellow men elsewhere was the vision of Lyndon B. Johnson. In his first years of office he obtained passage of one of the most extensive legislative programs in the Nation's history. Maintaining collective security, he carried on the rapidly growing struggle to restrain Communist encroachment in Viet Nam.

Johnson was born on August 27, 1908, in central Texas, not far from Johnson City, which his family had helped settle. He felt the pinch of rural poverty as he grew up, working his way through Southwest Texas State Teachers College (now known as Texas State University-San Marcos); he learned compassion for the poverty of others when he taught students of Mexican descent.

In 1937 he campaigned successfully for the House of Representatives on a New Deal platform, effectively aided by his wife, the former Claudia "Lady Bird" Taylor, whom he had married in 1934.

During World War II he served briefly in the Navy as a lieutenant commander, winning a Silver Star in the South Pacific. After six terms in the House, Johnson was elected to the Senate in 1948. In 1953, he became the youngest Minority Leader in Senate history, and the following year, when the Democrats won control, Majority Leader. With rare skill he obtained passage of a number of key Eisenhower measures.

In the 1960 campaign, Johnson, as John F. Kennedy's running mate, was elected Vice President. On November 22, 1963, when Kennedy was assassinated, Johnson was sworn in as President.

First he obtained enactment of the measures President Kennedy had been urging at the time of his death--a new civil rights bill and a tax cut. Next he urged the Nation "to build a great society, a place where the meaning of man's life matches the marvels of man's labor." In 1964, Johnson won the Presidency with 61 percent of the vote and had the widest popular margin in American history--more than 15,000,000 votes.

The Great Society program became Johnson's agenda for Congress in January 1965: aid to education, attack on disease, Medicare, urban renewal, beautification, conservation, development of depressed regions, a wide-scale fight against poverty, control and prevention of crime and delinquency, removal of obstacles to the right to vote. Congress, at times augmenting or amending, rapidly enacted Johnson's recommendations. Millions of elderly people found succor through the 1965 Medicare amendment to the Social Security Act.

Under Johnson, the country made spectacular explorations of space in a program he had championed since its start. When three astronauts successfully orbited the moon in December 1968, Johnson congratulated them: "You've taken ... all of us, all over the world, into a new era. . . . "

Nevertheless, two overriding crises had been gaining momentum since 1965. Despite the beginning of new antipoverty and anti-discrimination programs, unrest and rioting in black ghettos troubled the Nation. President Johnson steadily exerted his influence against segregation and on behalf of law and order, but there was no early solution.

The other crisis arose from Viet Nam. Despite Johnson's efforts to end Communist aggression and achieve a settlement, fighting continued. Controversy over the war had become acute by the end of March 1968, when he limited the bombing of North Viet Nam in order to initiate negotiations. At the same time, he startled the world by withdrawing as a candidate for re-election so that he might devote his full efforts, un-impeded by politics, to the quest for peace.

When he left office, peace talks were under way; he did not live to see them success-ful, but died suddenly of a heart attack at his Texas ranch on January 22, 1973.

The Presidential biographies on WhiteHouse.gov are from "The Presidents of the United States of America," by Frank Freidel and Hugh Sidey. Copyright 2006 by the White House Historical Association.

Lyndon Baines Johnson

The American Covenant"

Inaugural Address

Wednesday, January 20, 1965

My fellow countrymen, on this occasion, the oath I have taken before you and before God is not mine alone, but ours together. We are one nation and one people. Our fate as a nation and our future as a people rest not upon one citizen, but upon all citizens. This is the majesty and the meaning of this moment. For every generation, there is a destiny. For some, history decides. For this generation, the choice must be our own.

Even now, a rocket moves toward Mars. It reminds us that the world will not be the same for our children, or even for ourselves in a short span of years. The next man to stand here will look out on a scene different from our own, because ours is a time of change—rapid and fantastic change bearing the secrets of nature, multiplying the nations, placing in uncertain hands new weapons for mastery and destruction, shaking old values, and uprooting old ways.

Our destiny in the midst of change will rest on the unchanged character of our people, and on their faith.

The American Covenant

They came here—the exile and the stranger, brave but frightened—to find a place where a man could be his own man. They made a covenant with this land. Conceived in justice, written in liberty, bound in union, it was meant one day to inspire the hopes of all mankind; and it binds us still. If we keep its terms, we shall flourish.

Justice and Change

First, justice was the promise that all who made the journey would share in the fruits of the land.

In a land of great wealth, families must not live in hopeless poverty. In a land rich in harvest, children just must not go hungry. In a land of healing miracles, neighbors must not suffer and die unattended. In a great land of learning and scholars, young people must be taught to read and write. For the more than 30 years that I have served this Nation, I have believed that this injustice to our people, this waste of our resources, was our real enemy. For 30 years or more, with the resources I have had, I have vigilantly fought against it. I have learned, and I know, that it will not surrender easily. But change has given us new weapons. Before this generation of Americans is finished, this enemy will not only retreat—it will be conquered. Justice requires us to remember that when any citizen denies his fellow, saying, "His color is not mine," or "His beliefs are strange and different," in that moment he betrays America, though his forebears created this Nation.

Notes

Liberty and Change

Liberty was the second article of our **covenant**. It was self-government. It was our Bill of Rights. But it was more. America would be a place where each man could be proud to be himself: stretching his talents, rejoicing in his work, important in the life of his neighbors and his nation. This has become more difficult in a world where change and growth seem to tower beyond the control and even the judgment of men. We must work to provide the knowledge and the surroundings which can enlarge the possibilities of every citizen. The American covenant called on us to help show the way for the liberation of man. And that is today our goal. Thus, if as a nation there is much outside our control, as a people no stranger is outside our hope. Change has brought new meaning to that old mission. We can never again stand aside, prideful in isolation. Terrific dangers and troubles that we once called "foreign" now constantly live among us. If American lives must end, and American treasure be spilled, in countries we barely know, that is the price that change has demanded of conviction and of our enduring covenant.

Think of our world as it looks from the rocket that is heading toward Mars. It is like a child's globe, hanging in space, the continents stuck to its side like colored maps. We are all fellow passengers on a dot of earth. And each of us, in the span of time, has really only a moment among our companions. How incredible it is that in this fragile existence, we should hate and destroy one another. There are possibilities enough for all who will abandon mastery over others to pursue mastery over nature. There is world enough for all to seek their happiness in their own way. Our nation's course is abundantly clear. We aspire to nothing that belongs to others. We seek no **dominion** over our fellow man, but man's dominion over **tyranny** and misery. But more is required. Men want to be a part of a common **enterprise**—a cause greater than themselves. Each of us must find a way to advance the purpose of the Nation, thus finding new purpose for ourselves. Without this, we shall become a nation of strangers.

Union and Change

The third article was union. To those who were small and few against the wilderness, the success of liberty demanded the strength of union. Two centuries of change have made this true again. No longer need capitalist and worker, farmer and clerk, city and countryside, struggle to divide our bounty. By working shoulder to shoulder, together we can increase the bounty of all. We have discovered that every child who learns, every man who finds work, every sick body that is made whole—like a candle added to an altar—brightens the hope of all the faithful. So let us reject any among us who seek to reopen old wounds and to rekindle old hatreds. They stand in the way of a seeking nation.

Let us now join reason to faith and action to experience, to transform our unity of interest into a unity of purpose. For the hour and the day and the time are here to achieve progress without strife, to achieve change without hatred—not without difference of opinion, but without the deep and abiding divisions which scar the union for generations.

The American Belief

Under this **covenant** of justice, liberty, and union we have become a nation—**prosperous**, great, and mighty. And we have kept our freedom. But we have no promise from God that our greatness will endure. We have been allowed by Him to seek greatness with the sweat of our hands and the strength of our spirit. I do not believe that the Great Society is the ordered, changeless, and sterile battalion of the ants. It is the excitement of becoming—always becoming, trying, probing, falling, resting, and trying again—but always trying and always gaining. In each generation, with toil and tears, we have had to earn our heritage again.

If we fail now, we shall have forgotten in abundance what we learned in hardship: that **democracy** rests on faith, that freedom asks more than it gives, and that the judgment of God is harshest on those who are most favored. If we succeed, it will not be because of what we have, but it will be because of what we are; not because of what we own, but, rather because of what we believe. For we are a nation of believers. Underneath the clamor of building and the rush of our day's pursuits, we are believers in justice and liberty and union, and in our own Union. We believe that every man must someday be free. And we believe in ourselves.

Our enemies have always made the same mistake. In my lifetime—in **depression** and in war—they have awaited our defeat. Each time, from the secret places of the American heart, came forth the faith they could not see or that they could not even imagine. It brought us victory. And it will again. For this is what America is all about. It is the uncrossed desert and the unclimbed ridge. It is the star that is not reached and the harvest sleeping in the unplowed ground.

Is our world gone? We say "Farewell." Is a new world coming? We welcome it—and we will bend it to the hopes of man. To these trusted public servants and to my family and those close friends of mine who have followed me down a long, winding road, and to all the people of this Union and the world, I will repeat today what I said on that sorrowful day in November 1963: "I will lead and I will do the best I can." But you must look within your own hearts to the old promises and to the old dream. They will lead you best of all. For myself, I ask only, in the words of an ancient leader: "Give me now wisdom and knowledge, that I may go out and come in before this people: for who can judge this thy people, that is so great?"

http://www.lbjlib.utexas.edu/johnson/inauguration/PDF/PresidentInaugural.pdf Public Domain

Complete the SQ3R Analysis. See Appendix.

Short Answer Questions

1. How did Lyndon B. Johnson become president of the United States? What does he say in his speech to reference the event?

2. How does the term "covenant" work in this speech? Who does it refer to, and what does it refer to?

Essay Topics

1. Johnson demonstrates his Judeo-Christian heritage by stating, "Under this covenant of justice, liberty, and union we have become a nation—prosperous, great, and mighty. And we have kept our freedom. But we have no promise from God that our greatness will endure. We have been allowed by Him to seek greatness with the sweat of our hands and the strength of our spirit." What are the religious images evoked in this statement? How do they reflect traditional American values? Explain.

2. The book Exodus in the Hebrew bible discusses the journey of the Children of Israel, or the people of God, from bondage and Egypt labor into a location of prosperity called the "Promised Land." What images evoke this idea in his Johnson's speech? Discuss the connection to America based upon what is going on in America during the 1960's.

C H A R T

KNOW • WANT • LEARN

KWL

ALREADY KNOW	WANT TO KNOW	WHAT I LEARNED

Richard M. Nixon

Reconciliation was the first goal set by President Richard M. Nixon. The Nation was painfully divided, with turbulence in the cities and war overseas. During his Presidency, Nixon succeeded in ending American fighting in Viet Nam and improving relations with the U.S.S.R. and China. But the Watergate scandal brought fresh divisions to the country and ultimately led to his resignation.

His election in 1968 had climaxed a career unusual on two counts: his early success and his comeback after being defeated for President in 1960 and for Governor of California in 1962.

Born in California in 1913, Nixon had a brilliant record at Whittier College and Duke University Law School before beginning the practice of law. In 1940, he married Patricia Ryan; they had two daughters, Patricia (Tricia) and Julie. During World War II, Nixon served as a Navy lieutenant commander in the Pacific.

On leaving the service, he was elected to Congress from his California district. In 1950, he won a Senate seat. Two years later, General Eisenhower selected Nixon, age 39, to be his running mate.

As Vice President, Nixon took on major duties in the Eisenhower Administration. Nominated for President by acclamation in 1960, he lost by a narrow margin to John F. Kennedy. In 1968, he again won his party's nomination, and went on to defeat Vice President Hubert H. Humphrey and third-party candidate George C. Wallace.

His accomplishments while in office included revenue sharing, the end of the draft, new anticrime laws, and a broad environmental program. As he had promised, he appointed Justices of conservative philosophy to the Supreme Court. One of the most dramatic events of his first term occurred in 1969, when American astronauts made the first moon landing.

Some of his most acclaimed achievements came in his quest for world stability. During visits in 1972 to Beijing and Moscow, he reduced tensions with China and the U.S.S.R. His summit meetings with Russian leader Leonid I. Brezhnev produced a treaty to limit strategic nuclear weapons. In January 1973, he announced an accord with North Viet Nam to end American involvement in Indochina. In 1974, his Secretary of State, Henry Kissinger, negotiated disengagement agreements between Israel and its opponents, Egypt and Syria.

In his 1972 bid for office, Nixon defeated Democratic candidate George McGovern by one of the widest margins on record.

Within a few months, his administration was embattled over the so-called "Watergate" scandal, stemming from a break-in at the offices of the Democratic National Committee during the 1972 campaign. The break-in was traced to officials of the Committee to Re-elect the President. A number of administration officials resigned; some were later convicted of offenses connected with efforts to cover up the affair. Nixon denied any personal involvement, but the courts forced him to yield tape recordings which indicated that he had, in fact, tried to divert the investigation.

As a result of unrelated scandals in Maryland, Vice President Spiro T. Agnew resigned in 1973. Nixon nominated, and Congress approved, House Minority Leader Gerald R. Ford as Vice President.

Faced with what seemed almost certain impeachment, Nixon announced on August 8, 1974, that he would resign the next day to begin "that process of healing which is so desperately needed in America."

In his last years, Nixon gained praise as an elder statesman. By the time of his death on April 22, 1994, he had written numerous books on his experiences in public life and on foreign policy.

The Presidential biographies on WhiteHouse.gov are from "The Presidents of the United States of America," by Frank Freidel and Hugh Sidey. Copyright 2006 by the White House Historical Association.

Richard M. Nixon

First Inaugural Address

Monday, January 20, 1969

Senator Dirksen, Mr. Chief Justice, Mr. Vice President, President Johnson, Vice President Humphrey, my fellow Americans—and my fellow citizens of the world community:

I ask you to share with me today the majesty of this moment. In the orderly transfer of power, we celebrate the unity that keeps us free. Each moment in history is a fleeting time, precious and unique. But some stand out as moments of beginning, in which courses are set that shape decades or centuries. This can be such a moment. Forces now are converging that make possible, for the first time, the hope that many of man's deepest aspirations can at last be realized. The spiraling pace of change allows us to **contemplate**, within our own lifetime, advances that once would have taken centuries. In throwing wide the horizons of space, we have discovered new horizons on earth. For the first time, because the people of the world want peace, and the leaders of the world are afraid of war, the times are on the side of peace. Eight years from now America will celebrate its 200th anniversary as a nation. Within the lifetime of most people now living, mankind will celebrate that great new year which comes only once in a thousand years—the beginning of the third millennium. What kind of nation we will be, what kind of world we will live in, whether we shape the future in the image of our hopes, is ours to determine by our actions and our choices.

Peacemakers

The greatest honor history can bestow is the title of peacemaker. This honor now beckons America—the chance to help lead the world at last out of the valley of turmoil, and onto that high ground of peace that man has dreamed of since the dawn of civilization. If we succeed, generations to come will say of us now living that we mastered our moment, that we helped make the world safe for mankind. This is our summons to greatness. I believe the American people are ready to answer this call. The second third of this century has been a time of proud achievement. We have made enormous strides in science and industry and agriculture. We have shared our wealth more broadly than ever. We have learned at last to manage a modern economy to assure its continued growth.

We have given freedom new reach, and we have begun to make its promise real for black as well as for white. We see the hope of tomorrow in the youth of today. I know America's youth. I believe in them. We can be proud that they are better educated, more committed, more passionately driven by conscience than any generation in our history. No people has ever been so close to the achievement of a just and abundant society, or so possessed of the will to achieve it. Because our strengths are so great, we can afford to appraise our weaknesses with candor and to approach them with hope.

Notes

Crisis of the Spirit

Standing in this same place a third of a century ago, Franklin Delano Roosevelt addressed a Nation ravaged by depression and gripped in fear. He could say in surveying the Nation's troubles: "They concern, thank God, only material things." Our crisis today is the reverse. We have found ourselves rich in goods, but ragged in spirit; reaching with magnificent precision for the moon, but falling into raucous discord on earth. We are caught in war, wanting peace. We are torn by division, wanting unity. We see around us empty lives, wanting fulfillment. We see tasks that need doing, waiting for hands to do them. To a crisis of the spirit, we need an answer of the spirit.   T o find that answer, we need only look within ourselves. When we listen to "the better angels of our nature," we find that they celebrate the simple things, the basic things— such as goodness, decency, love, kindness.

Trappings of Rhetoric

Greatness comes in simple trappings. The simple things are the ones most needed today if we are to surmount what divides us, and cement what unites us. To lower our voices would be a simple thing. In these difficult years, America has suffered from a fever of words; from inflated rhetoric that promises more than it can deliver; from angry rhetoric that fans discontents into hatreds; from bombastic rhetoric that postures instead of persuading.

We cannot learn from one another until we stop shouting at one another—until we speak quietly enough so that our words can be heard as well as our voices. For its part, government will listen. We will strive to listen in new ways—to the voices of quiet anguish, the voices that speak without words, the voices of the heart—to the injured voices, the anxious voices, the voices that have despaired of being heard. Those who have been left out, we will try to bring in. Those left behind, we will help to catch up.

For all of our people, we will set as our goal the decent order that makes progress possible and our lives secure. As we reach toward our hopes, our task is to build on what has gone before—not turning away from the old, but turning toward the new. In this past third of a century, government has passed more laws, spent more money, initiated more programs, than in all our previous history.

In pursuing our goals of full employment, better housing, excellence in education; in rebuilding our cities and improving our rural areas; in protecting our environment and enhancing the quality of life—in all these and more, we will and must press urgently forward. We shall plan now for the day when our wealth can be transferred from the destruction of war abroad to the urgent needs of our people at home.

Limitations of Government

The American dream does not come to those who fall asleep. But we are approaching the limits of what government alone can do. Our greatest need now is to reach beyond government, and to enlist the legions of the concerned and the committed. What has to be done, has to be done by government and people together or it will not be done at all. The lesson of past agony is that without the people we can do nothing; with the people we can do everything.

To match the magnitude of our tasks, we need the energies of our people—enlisted not only in grand enterprises, but more importantly in those small, splendid efforts that make headlines in the neighborhood newspaper instead of the national journal. With these, we can build a great cathedral of the spirit—each of us raising it one stone at a time, as he reaches out to his neighbor, helping, caring, doing.

I do not offer a life of uninspiring ease. I do not call for a life of grim sacrifice. I ask you to join in a high adventure—one as rich as humanity itself, and as exciting as the times we live in. The essence of freedom is that each of us shares in the shaping of his own destiny. Until he has been part of a cause larger than himself, no man is truly whole. The way to fulfillment is in the use of our talents; we achieve nobility in the spirit that inspires that use. As we measure what can be done, we shall promise only what we know we can produce, but as we chart our goals we shall be lifted by our dreams.

Racial Unity in America

No man can be fully free while his neighbor is not. To go forward at all is to go forward together. This means black and white together, as one nation, not two. The laws have caught up with our conscience. What remains is to give life to what is in the law: to ensure at last that as all are born equal in dignity before God, all are born equal in dignity before man. As we learn to go forward together at home, let us also seek to go forward together with all mankind. Let us take as our goal: where peace is unknown, make it welcome; where peace is fragile, make it strong; where peace is temporary, make it permanent.

Foreign Relations

After a period of confrontation, we are entering an era of negotiation. Let all nations know that during this administration our lines of communication will be open. We seek an open world—open to ideas, open to the exchange of goods and people—a world in which no people, great or small, will live in angry isolation. We cannot expect to make everyone our friend, but we can try to make no one our enemy. Those who would be our adversaries, we invite to a peaceful competition—not in conquering territory or extending dominion, but in enriching the life of man.

As we explore the reaches of space, let us go to the new worlds together—not as new worlds to be conquered, but as a new adventure to be shared. With those who are willing to join, let us cooperate to reduce the burden of arms, to strengthen the structure of peace, to lift up the poor and the hungry.

But to all those who would be tempted by weakness, let us leave no doubt that we will be as strong as we need to be for as long as we need to be. Over the past twenty years, since I first came to this Capital as a freshman Congressman, I have visited most of the nations of the world. I have come to know the leaders of the world, and the great forces, the hatreds, the fears that divide the world. I know that peace does not come through wishing for it—that there is no substitute for days and even years of patient and prolonged diplomacy.

America As a Beacon for the World

I also know the people of the world. I have seen the hunger of a homeless child, the pain of a man wounded in battle, the grief of a mother who has lost her son. I know these have no ideology, no race. I know America. I know the heart of America is good. I speak from my own heart, and the heart of my country, the deep concern we have for those who suffer, and those who sorrow.

I have taken an oath today in the presence of God and my countrymen to uphold and defend the Constitution of the United States. To that oath I now add this sacred commitment: I shall consecrate my office, my energies, and all the wisdom I can summon, to the cause of peace among nations.

Let this message be heard by strong and weak alike: The peace we seek to win is not victory over any other people, but the peace that comes "with healing in its wings"; with compassion for those who have suffered; with understanding for those who have opposed us; with the opportunity for all the peoples of this earth to choose their own destiny.

Only a few short weeks ago, we shared the glory of man's first sight of the world as God sees it, as a single sphere reflecting light in the darkness. As the Apollo astronauts flew over the moon's gray surface on Christmas Eve, they spoke to us of the beauty of earth—and in that voice so clear across the lunar distance, we heard them invoke God's blessing on its goodness.

In that moment, their view from the moon moved poet Archibald MacLeish to write: "To see the earth as it truly is, small and blue and beautiful in that eternal silence where it floats, is to see ourselves as riders on the earth together, brothers on that bright loveliness in the eternal cold—brothers who know now they are truly brothers."

In that moment of surpassing technological triumph, men turned their thoughts toward home and humanity—seeing in that far perspective that man's destiny on earth is not divisible; telling us that however far we reach into the cosmos, our destiny lies not in the stars but on Earth itself, in our own hands, in our own hearts. We have endured a long night of the American spirit. But as our eyes catch the dimness of the first rays of dawn, let us not curse the remaining dark. Let us gather the light.

Our destiny offers, not the cup of despair, but the **chalice** of opportunity. So let us seize it, not in fear, but in gladness—and, "riders on the earth together," let us go forward, firm in our faith, steadfast in our purpose, cautious of the dangers; but sustained by our confidence in the will of God and the promise of man.

Complete the SQ3R Analysis. See Appendix.

http://www.inaugural.senate.gov/swearing-in/address/address-by-richard-m-nixon-1969 Public Domain

Short Answer Questions – President Richard Nixon

1. How does President Nixon define "peacemaker"?

2. What does Nixon do to promote the idea of limited government?

3. President Nixon discusses rhetoric directly in his speech. What are his major points about rhetoric?

Essay Topics

1. What does President Nixon mean by this metaphor included in his speech.. "Our destiny offers, not the cup of despair, but the chalice of opportunity." Discuss its significance to you within the context of the American Dream.

2. President Nixon addresses "Racial Unity" in his essay. Do you think his words served as healing within a race torn country? Read "A Letter from a Birmingham Jail" by Dr. Martin Luther King to get an idea of race relations in the United States in the 1960's, then read Nixon's section on "Racial Unity" and evaluate it's effectiveness.

C H A R T

KNOW • WANT • LEARN

KWL

ALREADY KNOW	WANT TO KNOW	WHAT I LEARNED

Notes

Ronald Reagan

At the end of his two terms in office, Ronald Reagan viewed with satisfaction the achievements of his innovative program known as the Reagan Revolution, which aimed to reinvigorate the American people and reduce their reliance upon Government. He felt he had fulfilled his campaign pledge of 1980 to restore "the great, confident roar of American progress and growth and optimism."

On February 6, 1911, Ronald Wilson Reagan was born to Nelle and John Reagan in Tampico, Illinois. He attended high school in nearby Dixon and then worked his way through Eureka College. There, he studied economics and sociology, played on the football team, and acted in school plays. Upon graduation, he became a radio sports announcer. A screen test in 1937 won him a contract in Hollywood. During the next two decades he appeared in 53 films.

From his first marriage to actress Jane Wyman, he had two children, Maureen and Michael. Maureen passed away in 2001. In 1952 he married Nancy Davis, who was also an actress, and they had two children, Patricia Ann and Ronald Prescott.

As president of the Screen Actors Guild, Reagan became embroiled in disputes over the issue of Communism in the film industry; his political views shifted from liberal to conservative. He toured the country as a television host, becoming a spokesman for conservatism. In 1966 he was elected Governor of California by a margin of a million votes; he was re-elected in 1970.

Ronald Reagan won the Republican Presidential nomination in 1980 and chose as his running mate former Texas Congressman and United Nations Ambassador George Bush. Voters troubled by inflation and by the year-long confinement of Americans in Iran swept the Republican ticket into office. Reagan won 489 electoral votes to 49 for President Jimmy Carter.

On January 20, 1981, Reagan took office. Only 69 days later he was shot by a would-be assassin, but quickly recovered and returned to duty. His grace and wit during the dangerous incident caused his popularity to soar.

Dealing skillfully with Congress, Reagan obtained legislation to stimulate economic growth, curb inflation, increase employment, and strengthen national defense. He embarked upon a course of cutting taxes and Government expenditures, refusing to deviate from it when the strengthening of defense forces led to a large deficit.

A renewal of national self-confidence by 1984 helped Reagan and Bush win a second term with an unprecedented number of electoral votes. Their victory turned away Democratic challengers Walter F. Mondale and Geraldine Ferraro.

In 1986 Reagan obtained an overhaul of the income tax code, which eliminated many deductions and exempted millions of people with low incomes. At the end of his administration, the Nation was enjoying its longest recorded period of peacetime prosperity without recession or depression.

In foreign policy, Reagan sought to achieve "peace through strength." During his two terms he increased defense spending 35 percent, but sought to improve relations with the Soviet Union. In dramatic meetings with Soviet leader Mikhail Gorbachev, he negotiated a treaty that would eliminate intermediate-range nuclear missiles. Reagan declared war against international terrorism, sending American bombers against Libya after evidence came out that Libya was involved in an attack on American soldiers in a West Berlin nightclub.

By ordering naval escorts in the Persian Gulf, he maintained the free flow of oil during the Iran-Iraq war. In keeping with the Reagan Doctrine, he gave support to anti-Communist insurgencies in Central America, Asia, and Africa.

Overall, the Reagan years saw a restoration of prosperity, and the goal of peace through strength seemed to be within grasp.

The Presidential biographies on WhiteHouse.gov are from "The Presidents of the United States of America," by Frank Freidel and Hugh Sidey. Copyright 2006 by the White House Historical Association.

Ronald Reagan

"Government is Not the Answer"

First Inaugural Address

Tuesday, January 20, 1981

Senator Hatfield, Mr. Chief Justice, Mr. President, Vice President Bush, Vice President Mondale, Senator Baker, Speaker O'Neill, Reverend Moomaw, and my fellow citizens: To a few of us here today, this is a solemn and most momentous occasion; and yet, in the history of our Nation, it is a commonplace occurrence. The orderly transfer of authority as called for in the Constitution routinely takes place as it has for almost two centuries and few of us stop to think how unique we really are. In the eyes of many in the world, this every-4-year ceremony we accept as normal is nothing less than a miracle.

Mr. President, I want our fellow citizens to know how much you did to carry on this tradition. By your gracious cooperation in the transition process, you have shown a watching world that we are a united people pledged to maintaining a political system which guarantees individual liberty to a greater degree than any other, and I thank you and your people for all your help in maintaining the continuity which is the **bulwark** of our Republic.

Economic Responsibility

The business of our nation goes forward. These United States are confronted with an economic affliction of great proportions. We suffer from the longest and one of the worst **sustained inflations** in our national history. It **distorts** our economic decisions, penalizes thrift, and crushes the struggling young and the fixed-income elderly alike. It threatens to shatter the lives of millions of our people. Idle industries have cast workers into unemployment, causing human misery and personal indignity. Those who do work are denied a fair return for their labor by a tax system which penalizes successful achievement and keeps us from maintaining full productivity.

But great as our tax burden is, it has not kept pace with public spending. For decades, we have piled deficit upon deficit, mortgaging our future and our children's future for the temporary convenience of the present. To continue this long trend is to guarantee tremendous social, cultural, political, and economic upheavals. You and I, as individuals, can, by borrowing, live beyond our means, but for only a limited period of time. Why, then, should we think that collectively, as a nation, we are not bound by that same limitation? We must act today in order to preserve tomorrow. And let there be no misunderstanding—we are going to begin to act, beginning today. The economic ills we suffer have come upon us over several decades. They will not go away in days, weeks, or months, but they will go away. They will go away because we, as Americans, have the capacity now, as we have had in the past, to do whatever needs to be done to preserve this last and greatest bastion of freedom.

Government is Not the Answer

In this present crisis, government is not the solution to our problem. From time to time, we have been tempted to believe that society has become too complex to be managed by self-rule, that government by an elite group is superior to government for, by, and of the people. But if no one among us is capable of governing himself, then who among us has the capacity to govern someone else? All of us together, in and out of government, must bear the burden. The solutions we seek must be equitable, with no one group singled out to pay a higher price. We hear much of special interest groups. Our concern must be for a special interest group that has been too long neglected. It knows no sectional boundaries or ethnic and racial divisions, and it crosses political party lines. It is made up of men and women who raise our food, patrol our streets, man our mines and our factories, teach our children, keep our homes, and heal us when we are sick—professionals, industrialists, shopkeepers, clerks, cabbies, and truckdrivers. They are, in short, "We the people," this breed called Americans.

Well, this administration's objective will be a healthy, vigorous, growing economy that provides equal opportunity for all Americans, with no barriers born of bigotry or discrimination. Putting America back to work means putting all Americans back to work. Ending inflation means freeing all Americans from the terror of runaway living costs. All must share in the productive work of this "new beginning" and all must share in the bounty of a revived economy. With the idealism and fair play which are the core of our system and our strength, we can have a strong and prosperous America at peace with itself and the world.

Limit Federal Government Influence

So, as we begin, let us take inventory. We are a nation that has a government—not the other way around. And this makes us special among the nations of the Earth. Our Government has no power except that granted it by the people. It is time to check and reverse the growth of government which shows signs of having grown beyond the consent of the governed. It is my intention to curb the size and influence of the Federal establishment and to demand recognition of the distinction between the powers granted to the Federal Government and those reserved to the States or to the people. All of us need to be reminded that the Federal Government did not create the States; the States created the Federal Government. Now, so there will be no misunderstanding, it is not my intention to do away with government. It is, rather, to make it work—work with us, not over us; to stand by our side, not ride on our back. Government can and must provide opportunity, not smother it; foster productivity, not stifle it.

Individual Rights

If we look to the answer as to why, for so many years, we achieved so much, prospered as no other people on Earth, it was because here, in this land, we unleashed the energy and individual genius of man to a greater extent than has ever been done before. Freedom and the dignity of the individual have been more available and assured here than in any other place on Earth. The price for this freedom at times has been high, but we have never been unwilling to pay that price.

It is no coincidence that our present troubles parallel and are proportionate to the intervention and intrusion in our lives that result from unnecessary and excessive growth of government. It is time for us to realize that we are too great a nation to limit ourselves to small dreams. We are not, as some would have us believe, doomed to an inevitable decline. I do not believe in a fate that will fall on us no matter what we do. I do believe in a fate that will fall on us if we do nothing. So, with all the creative energy at our command, let us begin an era of national renewal. Let us renew our determination, our courage, and our strength. And let us renew our faith and our hope.

Everyday American Heroes

We have every right to dream heroic dreams. Those who say that we are in a time when there are no heroes just don't know where to look. You can see heroes every day going in and out of factory gates. Others, a handful in number, produce enough food to feed all of us and then the world beyond. You meet heroes across a counter— and they are on both sides of that counter. There are entrepreneurs with faith in themselves and faith in an idea who create new jobs, new wealth and opportunity. They are individuals and families whose taxes support the Government and whose voluntary gifts support church, charity, culture, art, and education. Their patriotism is quiet but deep. Their values sustain our national life. I have used the words "they" and "their" in speaking of these heroes. I could say "you" and "your" because I am addressing the heroes of whom I speak—you, the citizens of this blessed land. Your dreams, your hopes, your goals are going to be the dreams, the hopes, and the goals of this administration, so help me God.

We shall reflect the compassion that is so much a part of your makeup. How can we love our country and not love our countrymen, and loving them, reach out a hand when they fall, heal them when they are sick, and provide opportunities to make them self-sufficient so they will be equal in fact and not just in theory? Can we solve the problems confronting us? Well, the answer is an unequivocal and emphatic "yes." To paraphrase Winston Churchill, I did not take the oath I have just taken with the intention of presiding over the dissolution of the world's strongest economy.

In the days ahead I will propose removing the roadblocks that have slowed our economy and reduced productivity. Steps will be taken aimed at restoring the balance between the various levels of government. Progress may be slow—measured in inches and feet, not miles—but we will progress. Is it time to reawaken this industrial giant, to get government back within its means, and to lighten our punitive tax burden. And these will be our first priorities, and on these principles, there will be no compromise.

On the eve of our struggle for independence a man who might have been one of the greatest among the Founding Fathers, Dr. Joseph Warren, President of the Massachusetts Congress, said to his fellow Americans, "Our country is in danger, but not to be despaired of.... On you depend the fortunes of America. You are to decide the important questions upon which rests the happiness and the liberty of millions yet unborn. Act worthy of yourselves." Well, I believe we, the Americans of today, are ready to act worthy of ourselves, ready to do what must be done to ensure happiness and liberty for ourselves, our children and our children's children. And as we renew ourselves here in our own land, we will be seen as having greater strength throughout the world. We will again be the exemplar of freedom and a beacon of hope for those who do not now have freedom.

Foreign Affairs

To those neighbors and allies who share our freedom, we will strengthen our historic ties and assure them of our support and firm commitment. We will match loyalty with loyalty. We will strive for mutually beneficial relations. We will not use our friendship to impose on their sovereignty, for our own sovereignty is not for sale. As for the enemies of freedom, those who are potential **adversaries**, they will be reminded that peace is the highest aspiration of the American people. We will negotiate for it, sacrifice for it; we will not surrender for it—now or ever.

Our forbearance should never be misunderstood. Our reluctance for conflict should not be misjudged as a failure of will. When action is required to preserve our national security, we will act. We will maintain sufficient strength to prevail if need be, knowing that if we do so we have the best chance of never having to use that strength.

Above all, we must realize that no **arsenal**, or no weapon in the arsenals of the world, is so formidable as the will and moral courage of free men and women. It is a weapon our adversaries in today's world do not have. It is a weapon that we as Americans do have. Let that be understood by those who practice terrorism and prey upon their neighbors.

Honor and Occasion

I am told that tens of thousands of prayer meetings are being held on this day, and for that I am deeply grateful. We are a nation under God, and I believe God intended for us to be free. It would be fitting and good, I think, if on each Inauguration Day in future years it should be declared a day of prayer. This is the first time in history that this ceremony has been held, as you have been told, on this West Front of the Capitol. Standing here, one faces a magnificent vista, opening up on this city's special beauty and history. At the end of this open mall are those shrines to the giants on whose shoulders we stand.

Directly in front of me, the monument to a monumental man: George Washington, Father of our country. A man of humility who came to greatness reluctantly. He led America out of revolutionary victory into infant nationhood. Off to one side, the stately memorial to Thomas Jefferson. The Declaration of Independence flames with his eloquence. And then beyond the Reflecting Pool the dignified columns of the Lincoln Memorial. Whoever would understand in his heart the meaning of America will find it in the life of Abraham Lincoln.   Beyond those monuments to heroism is the Potomac River, and on the far shore the sloping hills of Arlington National Cemetery with its row on row of simple white markers bearing crosses or Stars of David. They add up to only a tiny fraction of the price that has been paid for our freedom. Each one of those markers is a monument to the kinds of hero I spoke of earlier.

Their lives ended in places called Belleau Wood, The Argonne, Omaha Beach, Salerno and halfway around the world on Guadalcanal, Tarawa, Pork Chop Hill, the

Notes

Chosin Reservoir, and in a hundred rice paddies and jungles of a place called Vietnam. Under one such marker lies a young man—Martin Treptow—who left his job in a small town barber shop in 1917 to go to France with the famed Rainbow Division. There, on the western front, he was killed trying to carry a message between **battalions** under heavy **artillery** fire. We are told that on his body was found a diary. On the flyleaf under the heading, "My Pledge," he had written these words: "America must win this war. Therefore, I will work, I will save, I will sacrifice, I will endure, I will fight cheerfully and do my utmost, as if the issue of the whole struggle depended on me alone."

The crisis we are facing today does not require of us the kind of sacrifice that Martin Treptow and so many thousands of others were called upon to make. It does require, however, our best effort, and our willingness to believe in ourselves and to believe in our capacity to perform great deeds; to believe that together, with God's help, we can and will resolve the problems which now confront us.   And, after all, why shouldn't we believe that? We are Americans. God bless you, and thank you.

Complete the SQ3R Analysis. See Appendix.

Ronald Reagan: "Inaugural Address," January 20, 1981. Online by Gerhard Peters and John T. Woolley, The American Presidency Project. http://www.presidency.ucsb.edu/ws/?pid=43130. Public Domain

Short Answer Questions – President Ronald Reagan

1. President Reagan starts his speech focusing on the function of government. What are three quotes he makes about government that clearly define his conservative ideology?

2. What is President Reagan's plan to move America forward in one sentence?

3. Describe President Reagan's economic policy?

4. Research and define the idea of rugged individualism. Can you find evidence of rugged individualism in this text? If so where?

Essay Topics

1. President Reagan is revered as one of America's greatest presidents. Identify three statements in his speech that you would consider as evidence of his greatness. Defend your claims.

2. Write an essay explaining how President Reagan formulates a strong stance using ideas relating to "heroism" and honor. How do you or how could you demonstrate these ideas today?

3. Based upon President Reagan's statement "We have every right to dream heroic dreams, " using his definition of "heroic dreams" write an essay discussing your "heroic dream and how you plan to fulfill it.

4. Write and essay where you Agree or disagree with the statement, "Our Government has no power except that granted it by the people. It is time to check and reverse the growth of government which shows signs of having grown beyond the consent of the governed."

C H A R T

KNOW • WANT • LEARN

KWL

ALREADY KNOW	WANT TO KNOW	WHAT I LEARNED

Notes

George H. W. Bush

George Bush brought to the White House a dedication to traditional American values and a determination to direct them toward making the United States "a kinder and gentler nation." In his Inaugural Address he pledged in "a moment rich with promise" to use American strength as "a force for good."

Coming from a family with a tradition of public service, George Herbert Walker Bush felt the responsibility to make his contribution both in time of war and in peace. Born in Milton, Massachusetts, on June 12, 1924, he became a student leader at Phillips Academy in Andover. On his 18th birthday he enlisted in the armed forces. The youngest pilot in the Navy when he received his wings, he flew 58 combat missions during World War II. On one mission over the Pacific as a torpedo bomber pilot he was shot down by Japanese antiaircraft fire and was rescued from the water by a U. S. submarine. He was awarded the Distinguished Flying Cross for bravery in action.

Bush next turned his energies toward completing his education and raising a family. In January 1945 he married Barbara Pierce. They had six children-- George, Robin (who died as a child), John (known as Jeb), Neil, Marvin, and Dorothy.

At Yale University he excelled both in sports and in his studies; he was captain of the baseball team and a member of Phi Beta Kappa. After graduation Bush embarked on a career in the oil industry of West Texas.

Like his father, Prescott Bush, who was elected a Senator from Connecticut in 1952, George became interested in public service and politics. He served two terms as a Representative to Congress from Texas. Twice he ran unsuccessfully for the Senate. Then he was appointed to a series of high-level positions: Ambassador to the United Nations, Chairman of the Republican National Committee, Chief of the U. S. Liaison Office in the People's Republic of China, and Director of the Central Intelligence Agency.

In 1980 Bush campaigned for the Republican nomination for President. He lost, but was chosen as a running mate by Ronald Reagan. As Vice President, Bush had responsibility in several domestic areas, including Federal deregulation and anti-drug programs, and visited scores of foreign countries. In 1988 Bush won the Republican nomination for President and, with Senator Dan Quayle of Indiana as his running mate, he defeated Massachusetts Governor Michael Dukakis in the general election.

Bush faced a dramatically changing world, as the Cold War ended after 40 bitter years, the Communist empire broke up, and the Berlin Wall fell. The Soviet Union ceased to exist; and reformist President Mikhail Gorbachev, whom Bush had supported, resigned. While Bush hailed the march of democracy, he insisted on restraint in U. S. policy toward the group of new nations.

In other areas of foreign policy, President Bush sent American troops into Panama to overthrow the corrupt regime of General Manuel Noriega, who was threatening the security of the canal and the Americans living there. Noriega was brought to the United States for trial as a drug trafficker.

Bush's greatest test came when Iraqi President Saddam Hussein invaded Kuwait, then threatened to move into Saudi Arabia. Vowing to free Kuwait, Bush rallied the United Nations, the U. S. people, and Congress and sent 425,000 American troops. They were joined by 118,000 troops from allied nations. After weeks of air and missile bombardment, the 100-hour land battle dubbed Desert Storm routed Iraq's million-man army.

Despite unprecedented popularity from this military and diplomatic triumph, Bush was unable to withstand discontent at home from a faltering economy, rising violence in inner cities, and continued high deficit spending. In 1992 he lost his bid for reelection to Democrat William Clinton.

The Presidential biographies on WhiteHouse.gov are from "The Presidents of the United States of America," by Frank Freidel and Hugh Sidey. Copyright 2006 by the White House Historical Association.

George H. Bush
"A New Engagement"
Inaugural Address

Friday, January 20, 1989

Mr. Chief Justice, Mr. President, Vice President Quayle, Senator Mitchell, Speaker Wright, Senator Dole, Congressman Michel, and fellow citizens, neighbors, and friends:

There is a man here who has earned a lasting place in our hearts and in our history. President Reagan, on behalf of our Nation, I thank you for the wonderful things that you have done for America.

I have just repeated word for word the oath taken by George Washington 200 years ago, and the Bible on which I placed my hand is the Bible on which he placed his. It is right that the memory of Washington be with us today, not only because this is our Bicentennial Inauguration, but because Washington remains the Father of our Country. And he would, I think, be gladdened by this day; for today is the concrete expression of a stunning fact: our continuity these 200 years since our government began.

We meet on democracy's front porch, a good place to talk as neighbors and as friends. For this is a day when our nation is made whole, when our differences, for a moment, are suspended.

Prayer

And my first act as President is a prayer. I ask you to bow your heads: Heavenly Father, we bow our heads and thank You for Your love. Accept our thanks for the peace that yields this day and the shared faith that makes its continuance likely. Make us strong to do Your work, willing to heed and hear Your will, and write on our hearts these words: "Use power to help people." For we are given power not to advance our own purposes, nor to make a great show in the world, nor a name. There is but one just use of power, and it is to serve people. Help us to remember it, Lord. Amen.

Presidential Promise

I come before you and assume the Presidency at a moment rich with promise. We live in a peaceful, prosperous time, but we can make it better. For a new breeze is blowing, and a world refreshed by freedom seems reborn; for in man's heart, if not in fact, the day of the dictator is over. The totalitarian era is passing, its old ideas blown away like leaves from an ancient, lifeless tree. A new breeze is blowing, and a nation refreshed by freedom stands ready to push on. There is new ground to be broken, and new action to be taken. There are times when the future seems thick as a fog; you sit and wait, hoping the mists will lift and reveal the right path. But this is a time when the future seems a door you can walk right through into a room called tomorrow. Great nations of the world are moving toward democracy through the door to freedom. Men and women of the world move toward free markets through the door to prosperity. The people of the world agitate for free expression and free thought through the door to the moral and intellectual satisfactions that only liberty allows.

Freedom and Free Will

We know what works: Freedom works. We know what's right: Freedom is right. We know how to secure a more just and prosperous life for man on Earth: through free markets, free speech, free elections, and the exercise of free will unhampered by the state. For the first time in this century, for the first time in perhaps all history, man does not have to invent a system by which to live. We don't have to talk late into the night about which form of government is better. We don't have to wrest justice from the kings. We only have to summon it from within ourselves. We must act on what we know. I take as my guide the hope of a saint: In crucial things, unity; in important things, diversity; in all things, generosity.

America today is a proud, free nation, decent and civil, a place we cannot help but love. We know in our hearts, not loudly and proudly, but as a simple fact, that this country has meaning beyond what we see, and that our strength is a force for good. But have we changed as a nation even in our time? Are we enthralled with **material** things, less appreciative of the nobility of work and sacrifice?

My friends, we are not the sum of our possessions. They are not the measure of our lives. In our hearts we know what matters. We cannot hope only to leave our children a bigger car, a bigger bank account. We must hope to give them a sense of what it means to be a loyal friend, a loving parent, a citizen who leaves his home, his neighborhood and town better than he found it. What do we want the men and women who work with us to say when we are no longer there? That we were more driven to succeed than anyone around us? Or that we stopped to ask if a sick child had gotten better, and stayed a moment there to trade a word of friendship?

The Moral Character of America

No President, no government, can teach us to remember what is best in what we are. But if the man you have chosen to lead this government can help make a difference; if he can celebrate the quieter, deeper successes that are made not of gold and silk, but of better hearts and finer souls; if he can do these things, then he must.

America is never wholly herself unless she is engaged in **high moral principle**. We as a people have such a purpose today. It is to make kinder the face of the Nation and gentler the face of the world. My friends, we have work to do. There are the homeless, lost and roaming. There are the children who have nothing, no love, no normalcy. There are those who cannot free themselves of enslavement to whatever addiction—drugs, welfare, the **demoralization** that rules the **slums**. There is crime to be conquered, the rough crime of the streets. There are young women to be helped who are about

Notes

to become mothers of children they can't care for and might not love. They need our care, our guidance, and our education, though we bless them for choosing life.

A New Engagement

The old solution, the old way, was to think that public money alone could end these problems. But we have learned that is not so. And in any case, our funds are low. We have a deficit to bring down. We have more will than wallet; but will is what we need. We will make the hard choices, looking at what we have and perhaps allocating it differently, making our decisions based on honest need and prudent safety. And then we will do the wisest thing of all: We will turn to the only resource we have that in times of need always grows—the goodness and the courage of the American people.

I am speaking of a new engagement in the lives of others, a new activism, hands-on and involved, that gets the job done. We must bring in the generations, **harnessing** the unused talent of the elderly and the unfocused energy of the young. For not only leadership is passed from generation to generation, but so is **stewardship**. And the generation born after the Second World War has come of age.

I have spoken of a thousand points of light, of all the community organizations that are spread like stars throughout the Nation, doing good. We will work hand in hand, encouraging, sometimes leading, sometimes being led, rewarding. We will work on this in the White House, in the **Cabinet** agencies. I will go to the people and the programs that are the brighter points of light, and I will ask every member of my government to become involved. The old ideas are new again because they are not old, they are timeless: duty, sacrifice, commitment, and a patriotism that finds its expression in taking part and pitching in.

Call to Congress

We need a new engagement, too, between the Executive and the Congress. The challenges before us will be thrashed out with the House and the Senate. We must bring the Federal budget into balance. And we must ensure that America stands before the world united, strong, at peace, and fiscally sound. But, of course, things may be difficult. We need compromise; we have had dissension. We need harmony; we have had a chorus of discordant voices.

For Congress, too, has changed in our time. There has grown a certain divisiveness. We have seen the hard looks and heard the statements in which not each other's ideas are challenged, but each other's motives. And our great parties have too often been far apart and untrusting of each other. It has been this way since Vietnam. That war cleaves us still. But, friends, that war began in earnest a quarter of a century ago; and surely the statute of limitations has been reached. This is a fact: The final lesson of Vietnam is that no great nation can long afford to be sundered by a memory. A new breeze is blowing, and the old bipartisanship must be made new again.

To my friends—and yes, I do mean friends—in the loyal opposition—and yes, I mean loyal: I put out my hand. I am putting out my hand to you, Mr. Speaker. I am putting out my hand to you, Mr. Majority Leader. For this is the thing: This is the age of the offered hand. We can't turn back clocks, and I don't want to. But when our fathers were young, Mr. Speaker, our differences ended at the water's edge. And we don't wish to turn back time, but when our mothers were young, Mr. Majority Leader, the Congress and the Executive were capable of working together to produce a budget on which this nation could live. Let us negotiate soon and hard. But in the end, let us produce. The American people await action. They didn't send us here to bicker. They ask us to rise above the merely partisan. "In crucial things, unity"—and this, my friends, is crucial.

Foreign Policy

To the world, too, we offer new engagement and a renewed vow: We will stay strong to protect the peace. The "offered hand" is a reluctant fist; but once made, strong, and can be used with great effect. There are today Americans who are held against their will in foreign lands, and Americans who are unaccounted for. Assistance can be shown here, and will be long remembered. Good will begets good will. Good faith can be a spiral that endlessly moves on.

Great nations like great men must keep their word. When America says something, America means it, whether a treaty or an agreement or a vow made on marble steps. We will always try to speak clearly, for candor is a compliment, but subtlety, too, is good and has its place. While keeping our alliances and friendships around the world strong, ever strong, we will continue the new closeness with the Soviet Union, consistent both with our security and with progress. One might say that our new relationship in part reflects the triumph of hope and strength over experience. But hope is good, and so are strength and vigilance.

Here today are tens of thousands of our citizens who feel the understandable satisfaction of those who have taken part in democracy and seen their hopes fulfilled. But my thoughts have been turning the past few days to those who would be watching at home, to an older fellow who will throw a salute by himself when the flag goes by, and the women who will tell her sons the words of the battle hymns. I don't mean this to be sentimental. I mean that on days like this, we remember that we are all part of a continuum, inescapably connected by the ties that bind.

Our children are watching in schools throughout our great land. And to them I say, thank you for watching democracy's big day. For democracy belongs to us all, and freedom is like a beautiful kite that can go higher and higher with the breeze. And to all I say: No matter what your circumstances or where you are, you are part of this day, you are part of the life of our great nation.

War on Drugs

A President is neither prince nor pope, and I don't seek a window on men's souls. In fact, I yearn for a greater tolerance, an easy-goingness about each other's attitudes and way of life. There are few clear areas in which we as a society must rise up united and express our intolerance. The most obvious now is drugs. And when that first cocaine was smuggled in on a ship, it may as well have been a deadly bacteria, so much has it hurt the body, the soul of our country. And there is much to be done and to be said, but take my word for it: This scourge will stop.

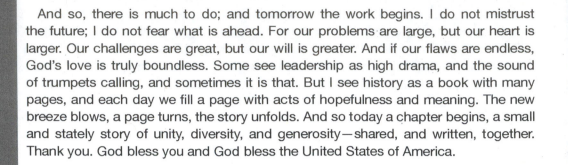

And so, there is much to do; and tomorrow the work begins. I do not mistrust the future; I do not fear what is ahead. For our problems are large, but our heart is larger. Our challenges are great, but our will is greater. And if our flaws are endless, God's love is truly boundless. Some see leadership as high drama, and the sound of trumpets calling, and sometimes it is that. But I see history as a book with many pages, and each day we fill a page with acts of hopefulness and meaning. The new breeze blows, a page turns, the story unfolds. And so today a chapter begins, a small and stately story of unity, diversity, and generosity—shared, and written, together. Thank you. God bless you and God bless the United States of America.

Complete the SQ3R Analysis. See Appendix.

http://www.inaugural.senate.gov/swearing-in/event/george-h-w-bush-1989 - Pubic Domain

Short Answer Questions – President George H. Bush

1. This speech opens with a prayer. Analyze the prayer as an opening for his speech. Does it foreshadow any of the major points he later addresses in his speech? If so how?

2. How does President Bush handle the ideas of "freedom" and "free will"? What does he want the listener to do as a result of his statements?

3. President Bush does not directly condemn the United States congress. Using you're the tool of inference, determine what problems exist within the United States Congress.

4. What is President Bush's position on "materialism"?

5. What is meant by the phrase "high moral principle"?

Essay Topics

1. President Bush ends his speech with a discussion of drugs. Compare his words with the Nancy Reagan's in her famous "Just Say No" speech. What connections can you make as it relates to their message.

2. President Bush uses figurative language throughout his speech. Identify and analyze three more elements of figurative language. Discuss the type and function of the language as well as its potential effect on the listener.

3. In an essay, discuss Bush's idea of materialism and its potential impact on America. Do you agree or disagree with his statements.

CHART

KNOW • WANT • LEARN

KWL

ALREADY KNOW	WANT TO KNOW	WHAT I LEARNED

Notes

William J. Clinton

During the administration of William Jefferson Clinton, the U.S. enjoyed more peace and economic well being than at any time in its history. He was the first Democratic president since Franklin D. Roosevelt to win a second term. He could point to the lowest unemployment rate in modern times, the lowest inflation in 30 years, the highest home ownership in the country's history, dropping crime rates in many places, and reduced welfare rolls. He proposed the first balanced budget in decades and achieved a budget surplus. As part of a plan to celebrate the millennium in 2000, Clinton called for a great national initiative to end racial discrimination.

After the failure in his second year of a huge program of health care reform, Clinton shifted emphasis, declaring "the era of big government is over." He sought legislation to upgrade education, to protect jobs of parents who must care for sick children, to restrict handgun sales, and to strengthen environmental rules.

President Clinton was born William Jefferson Blythe III on August 19, 1946, in Hope, Arkansas, three months after his father died in a traffic accident. When he was four years old, his mother wed Roger Clinton, of Hot Springs, Arkansas. In high school, he took the family name.

He excelled as a student and as a saxophone player and once considered becoming a professional musician. As a delegate to Boys Nation while in high school, he met President John Kennedy in the White House Rose Garden. The encounter led him to enter a life of public service.

Clinton was graduated from Georgetown University and in 1968 won a Rhodes Scholarship to Oxford University. He received a law degree from Yale University in 1973, and entered politics in Arkansas.

He was defeated in his campaign for Congress in Arkansas's Third District in 1974. The next year he married Hillary Rodham, a graduate of Wellesley College and Yale Law School. In 1980, Chelsea, their only child, was born.

Clinton was elected Arkansas Attorney General in 1976, and won the governorship in 1978. After losing a bid for a second term, he regained the office four years later, and served until he defeated incumbent George Bush and third party candidate Ross Perot in the 1992 presidential race.

Clinton and his running mate, Tennessee's Senator Albert Gore Jr., then 44, represented a new generation in American political leadership. For the first time in 12 years both the White House and Congress were held by the same party. But that political edge was brief; the Republicans won both houses of Congress in 1994.

In 1998, as a result of issues surrounding personal indiscretions with a young woman White House intern, Clinton was the second U.S. president to be impeached by the House of Representatives. He was tried in the Senate and found not guilty of the charges brought against him. He apologized to the nation for his actions and continued to have unprecedented popular approval ratings for his job as president.

In the world, he successfully dispatched peace keeping forces to war-torn Bosnia and bombed Iraq when Saddam Hussein stopped United Nations inspections for evidence of nuclear, chemical, and biological weapons. He became a global proponent for an expanded NATO, more open international trade, and a worldwide campaign against drug trafficking. He drew huge crowds when he traveled through South America, Europe, Russia, Africa, and China, advocating U.S. style freedom.

The Presidential biographies on WhiteHouse.gov are from "The Presidents of the United States of America," by Frank Freidel and Hugh Sidey. Copyright 2006 by the White House Historical Association.

William H. Clinton

"American Renewal"

Inaugural Address

January 21, 1993

My fellow citizens:

Today we celebrate the mystery of American renewal.

This ceremony is held in the depth of winter. But, by the words we speak and the faces we show the world, we force the spring. A spring reborn in the world's oldest democracy, that brings forth the vision and courage to reinvent America. When our founders boldly declared America's independence to the world and our purposes to the Almighty, they knew that America, to endure, would have to change. Not change for change's sake, but change to preserve America's ideals—life, liberty, the pursuit of happiness. Though we march to the music of our time, our mission is timeless.

New Generation of Americans

Each generation of Americans must define what it means to be an American. On behalf of our nation, I salute my predecessor, President Bush, for his half-century of service to America. And I thank the millions of men and women whose steadfastness and sacrifice triumphed over Depression, fascism and Communism. Today, a generation raised in the shadows of the Cold War assumes new responsibilities in a world warmed by the sunshine of freedom but threatened still by ancient hatreds and new plagues. Raised in unrivaled prosperity, we inherit an economy that is still the world's strongest, but is weakened by business failures, stagnant wages, increasing inequality, and deep divisions among our people.

When George Washington first took the oath I have just sworn to uphold, news traveled slowly across the land by horseback and across the ocean by boat. Now, the sights and sounds of this ceremony are broadcast instantaneously to billions around the world. Communications and commerce are global; investment is mobile; technology is almost magical; and ambition for a better life is now universal. We earn our livelihood in peaceful competition with people all across the earth.

Changing the Guard

Profound and powerful forces are shaking and remaking our world, and the urgent question of our time is whether we can make change our friend and not our enemy. This new world has already enriched the lives of millions of Americans who are able to compete and win in it. But when most people are working harder for less; when others cannot work at all; when the cost of health care devastates families and threatens to bankrupt many of our enterprises, great and small; when fear of crime robs law-abiding citizens of their freedom; and when millions of poor children cannot even imagine the lives we are calling them to lead—we have not made change our friend.

We know we have to face hard truths and take strong steps. But we have not done so. Instead, we have drifted, and that drifting has eroded our resources, fractured our economy, and shaken our confidence. Though our challenges are fearsome, so are our strengths. And Americans have ever been a restless, questing, hopeful people. We must bring to our task today the vision and will of those who came before us. From our revolution, the Civil War, to the Great Depression to the civil rights movement, our people have always mustered the determination to construct from these crises the pillars of our history. Thomas Jefferson believed that to preserve the very foundations of our nation, we would need dramatic change from time to time. Well, my fellow citizens, this is our time. Let us embrace it.

American Renewal

Our democracy must be not only the envy of the world but the engine of our own renewal. There is nothing wrong with America that cannot be cured by what is right with America. And so today, we pledge an end to the era of deadlock and drift—a new season of American renewal has begun.

To renew America, we must be bold. We must do what no generation has had to do before. We must invest more in our own people, in their jobs, in their future, and at the same time cut our massive debt. And we must do so in a world in which we must compete for every opportunity. It will not be easy; it will require sacrifice. But it can be done, and done fairly, not choosing sacrifice for its own sake, but for our own sake. We must provide for our nation the way a family provides for its children.

Our Founders saw themselves in the light of posterity. We can do no less. Anyone who has ever watched a child's eyes wander into sleep knows what posterity is. Posterity is the world to come—the world for whom we hold our ideals, from whom we have borrowed our planet, and to whom we bear sacred responsibility.

We must do what America does best: offer more opportunity to all and demand responsibility from all. It is time to break the bad habit of expecting something for nothing, from our government or from each other. Let us all take more responsibility, not only for ourselves and our families but for our communities and our country.

To renew America, we must revitalize our democracy. This beautiful capital, like every capital since the dawn of civilization, is often a place of intrigue and calculation. Powerful people maneuver for position and worry endlessly about who is in and who is out, who is up and who is down, forgetting those people whose toil and sweat sends us here and pays our way.

Renewal in Congress

Americans deserve better, and in this city today, there are people who want to do better. And so I say to all of us here, let us resolve to reform our politics, so that power and privilege no longer shout down the voice of the people. Let us put aside personal

Notes

advantage so that we can feel the pain and see the promise of America. Let us resolve to make our government a place for what Franklin Roosevelt called "bold, persistent experimentation," a government for our tomorrows, not our yesterdays. Let us give this capital back to the people to whom it belongs. To renew America, we must meet challenges abroad as well at home. There is no longer division between what is foreign and what is domestic—the world economy, the world environment, the world AIDS crisis, the world arms race—they affect us all.

American Identity Abroad

Today, as an old order passes, the new world is more free but less stable. Communism's collapse has called forth old animosities and new dangers. Clearly America must continue to lead the world we did so much to make. While America rebuilds at home, we will not shrink from the challenges, nor fail to seize the opportunities, of this new world. Together with our friends and allies, we will work to shape change, lest it engulf us.

When our vital interests are challenged, or the will and conscience of the international community is defied, we will act—with peaceful diplomacy whenever possible, with force when necessary. The brave Americans serving our nation today in the Persian Gulf, in Somalia, and wherever else they stand are testament to our resolve. But our greatest strength is the power of our ideas, which are still new in many lands. Across the world, we see them embraced—and we rejoice. Our hopes, our hearts, our hands, are with those on every continent who are building democracy and freedom. Their cause is America's cause.

America's Call to Renewal

The American people have summoned the change we celebrate today. You have raised your voices in an unmistakable chorus. You have cast your votes in historic numbers. And you have changed the face of Congress, the presidency and the political process itself. Yes, you, my fellow Americans have forced the spring. Now, we must do the work the season demands. To that work I now turn, with all the authority of my office. I ask the Congress to join with me. But no president, no Congress, no government, can undertake this mission alone. My fellow Americans, you, too, must play your part in our renewal. I challenge a new generation of young Americans to a season of service—to act on your idealism by helping troubled children, keeping company with those in need, reconnecting our torn communities. There is so much to be done—enough indeed for millions of others who are still young in spirit to give of themselves in service, too. In serving, we recognize a simple but powerful truth— we need each other. And we must care for one another. Today, we do more than celebrate America; we rededicate ourselves to the very idea of America. An idea born in revolution and renewed through two centuries of challenge. An idea tempered by the knowledge that, but for fate, we—the fortunate and the unfortunate—might have been each other. An idea ennobled by the faith that our nation can summon from its myriad diversity the deepest measure of unity. An idea infused with the conviction that America's long heroic journey must go forever upward.

And so, my fellow Americans, at the edge of the 21st century, let us begin with energy and hope, with faith and discipline, and let us work until our work is done. The scripture says, "And let us not be weary in well-doing, for in due season, we shall reap, if we faint not." From this joyful mountaintop of celebration, we hear a call to service in the valley. We have heard the trumpets. We have changed the guard. And now, each in our way, and with God's help, we must answer the call. Thank you and God bless you all.

Complete the SQ3R Analysis. See Appendix.

http://www.inaugural.senate.gov/swearing-in/address/address-by-bill-clinton-1993 Public Domain

Short Answer Questions – President William H. Clinton

1. President Clinton seems to write his address to arouse a certain group of Americans. Who does his speech appeal to and why?

2. How does President Clinton discuss his ideas on foreign policy? What are his major points?

3. What is President Clinton's main idea? What is the main point he wants to communicate to the listener?

Essay Topics

4. In the section on "America's Renewal" he says, "Yes, you, my fellow Americans have forced the spring. Now, we must do the work the season demands." What does spring represent, and how is the symbol a part of the larger point he is making in his speech?

5. President Clinton calls America to renewal. In an essay, discuss how you and your generation can fulfill President Clinton's call for American renewal?

CHART

KNOW • WANT • LEARN

KWL

ALREADY KNOW	WANT TO KNOW	WHAT I LEARNED

George W. Bush

The airborne terrorist attacks on the World Trade Center, the Pentagon, and the thwarted flight against the White House or Capitol on September 11, 2001, in which nearly 3,000 Americans were killed, transformed George W. Bush into a wartime president. The attacks put on hold many of Bush's hopes and plans, and Bush's father, George Bush, the 41st president, declared that his son "faced the greatest challenge of any president since Abraham Lincoln."

In response, Bush formed a new cabinet-level Department of Homeland Security, sent American forces into Afghanistan to break up the Taliban, a movement under Osama bin Laden that trained financed and exported terrorist teams. The Taliban was successfully disrupted but Bin Laden was not captured and was still on the loose as Bush began his second term. Following the attacks, the president also recast the nation's intelligence gathering and analysis services, and ordered reform of the military forces to meet the new enemy. At the same time he delivered major tax cuts which had been a campaign pledge. His most controversial act was the invasion of Iraq on the belief that Iraqi President Saddam Hussein posed a grave threat to the United States. Saddam was captured, but the disruption of Iraq and the killing of American servicemen and friendly Iraqis by insurgents became the challenge of Bush's government as he began his second term. President Bush pledged during his 2005 State of the Union Address that the United States would help the Iraqi people establish a fully democratic government because the victory of freedom in Iraq would strengthen a new ally in the war on terror, bring hope to a troubled region, and lift a threat from the lives of future generations.

Bush was born in New Haven, Connecticut while his father was attending Yale University after service in World War II. The family moved to Midland, Texas, where the senior Bush entered the oil exploration business. The son spent formative years there, attended Midland public schools, and formed friendships that stayed with him into the White House. Bush graduated from Yale, received a business degree from Harvard, and then returned to Midland where he too got into the oil business. In Midland he met and married Laura Welch, a teacher and librarian. They had twin daughters, Jenna and Barbara, now out of college and pursuing careers.

When George W. Bush, at the age of 54, became the 43rd president of the United States, it was only the second time in American history that a president's son went on to the White House. John Quincy Adams, elected the sixth president in 1824, was the son of John Adams, the second president. While John Adams had groomed his son to be president, George Bush, the 41st president, insisted he was surprised when the eldest of his six children became interested in politics, became governor of Texas, and then went on to the White House.

During the early part of the 2000 campaign for the White House, Bush enjoyed a double-digit lead in the polls over his opponent Vice President Al Gore Jr. But the gap closed as the election approached and though Gore finally won the popular vote by 543,895 votes, victory or loss of the presidency hinged on Florida's electoral votes. That struggle through recounts and lawsuits worked its way to the Supreme Court. In the end Bush won the electoral count 271 to 266. His new administration was focused on "compassionate conservatism," which embraced excellence in education, tax relief and volunteerism among faith-based and community organizations.

Bush was challenged in his re-election bid in 2004 by Massachusetts Democratic Senator John Kerry. The election was a good contest, but Bush's contention that the invasion of Iraq had made the world more secure against terrorism won the national political debate. Bush was re-elected with 51 percent to 48 percent.

On the inaugural stand, George W. Bush set the theme for his second term: "At this second gathering, our duties are defined not by the words I use, but by the history we have seen together. For half a century, America defended our own freedom by standing watch on distant borders. After the shipwreck of communism came years of relative quiet- and then there came a day of fire. There is only one force of history that can break the reign of hatred and resentment, and expose the pretensions of tyrants, and reward the hopes of the decent and tolerant, and that is the force of human freedom – tested but not weary… we are ready for the greatest achievements in the history of freedom."

The Presidential biographies on WhiteHouse.gov are from "The Presidents of the United States of America," by Frank Freidel and Hugh Sidey. Copyright 2006 by the White House Historical Association.

George W. Bush

"The American Story"

Inaugural Address

Saturday, January 20, 2001

President Clinton, distinguished guests and my fellow citizens, the peaceful transfer of authority is rare in history, yet common in our country. With a simple oath, we affirm old traditions and make new beginnings. As I begin, I thank President Clinton for his service to our nation. And I thank Vice President Gore for a contest conducted with spirit and ended with grace. I am honored and humbled to stand here, where so many of America's leaders have come before me, and so many will follow.

We have a place, all of us, in a long story—a story we continue, but whose end we will not see. It is the story of a new world that became a friend and liberator of the old, a story of a slave-holding society that became a servant of freedom, the story of a power that went into the world to protect but not possess, to defend but not to conquer. It is the American story—a story of flawed and fallible people, united across the generations by grand and enduring ideals. The grandest of these ideals is an unfolding American promise that everyone belongs, that everyone deserves a chance, that no insignificant person was ever born. Americans are called to enact this promise in our lives and in our laws. And though our nation has sometimes halted, and sometimes delayed, we must follow no other course.

Faith in America

Through much of the last century, America's faith in freedom and democracy was a rock in a raging sea. Now it is a seed upon the wind, taking root in many nations. Our democratic faith is more than the creed of our country, it is the inborn hope of our humanity, an ideal we carry but do not own, a trust we bear and pass along. And even after nearly 225 years, we have a long way yet to travel. While many of our citizens prosper, others doubt the promise, even the justice, of our own country. The ambitions of some Americans are limited by failing schools and hidden prejudice and the circumstances of their birth. And sometimes our differences run so deep, it seems we share a continent, but not a country. We do not accept this, and we will not allow it. Our unity, our union, is the serious work of leaders and citizens in every generation. And this is my solemn pledge: I will work to build a single nation of justice and opportunity.

I know this is in our reach because we are guided by a power larger than ourselves who creates us equal in His image. And we are confident in principles that unite and lead us onward. America has never been united by blood or birth or soil. We are bound by ideals that move us beyond our backgrounds, lift us above our interests and teach us what it means to be citizens. Every child must be taught these principles. Every citizen must uphold them. And every immigrant, by embracing these ideals, makes our country more, not less, American.

Notes

Civility and Freedom

Today, we affirm a new commitment to live out our nation's promise through civility, courage, compassion and character. America, at its best, matches a commitment to principle with a concern for civility. A civil society demands from each of us good will and respect, fair dealing and forgiveness.

Some seem to believe that our politics can afford to be petty because, in a time of peace, the stakes of our debates appear small. But the stakes for America are never small. If our country does not lead the cause of freedom, it will not be led. If we do not turn the hearts of children toward knowledge and character, we will lose their gifts and undermine their idealism. If we permit our economy to drift and decline, the vulnerable will suffer most. We must live up to the calling we share. Civility is not a tactic or a sentiment. It is the determined choice of trust over cynicism, of community over chaos. And this commitment, if we keep it, is a way to shared accomplishment.

Courage to Reform

America, at its best, is also courageous. Our national courage has been clear in times of depression and war, when defending common dangers defined our common good. Now we must choose if the example of our fathers and mothers will inspire us or condemn us. We must show courage in a time of blessing by confronting problems instead of passing them on to future generations. Together, we will reclaim America's schools, before ignorance and apathy claim more young lives. We will reform Social Security and Medicare, sparing our children from struggles we have the power to prevent. And we will reduce taxes, to recover the momentum of our economy and reward the effort and enterprise of working Americans. We will build our defenses beyond challenge, lest weakness invite challenge. We will confront weapons of mass destruction, so that a new century is spared new horrors.

The enemies of liberty and our country should make no mistake: America remains engaged in the world by history and by choice, shaping a balance of power that favors freedom. We will defend our allies and our interests. We will show purpose without arrogance. We will meet aggression and bad faith with resolve and strength. And to all nations, we will speak for the values that gave our nation birth.

American Compassion

America, at its best, is compassionate. In the quiet of American conscience, we know that deep, persistent poverty is unworthy of our nation's promise. And whatever our views of its cause, we can agree that children at risk are not at fault. Abandonment and abuse are not acts of God, they are failures of love. And the proliferation of prisons, however necessary, is no substitute for hope and order in our souls Where there is suffering, there is duty. Americans in need are not strangers, they are citizens, not problems, but priorities. And all of us are diminished when any are hopeless.

Government has great responsibilities for public safety and public health, for civil rights and common schools. Yet compassion is the work of a nation, not just a government. And some needs and hurts are so deep they will only respond to a mentor's touch or a pastor's prayer. Church and charity, synagogue and mosque lend our communities their humanity, and they will have an honored place in our plans and in our laws.

Social Responsibility

Many in our country do not know the pain of poverty, but we can listen to those who do. And I can pledge our nation to a goal: When we see that wounded traveler on the road to Jericho, we will not pass to the other side. America, at its best, is a place where personal responsibility is valued and expected. Encouraging responsibility is not a search for scapegoats, it is a call to conscience. And though it requires sacrifice, it brings a deeper fulfillment. We find the fullness of life not only in options, but in commitments. And we find that children and community are the commitments that set us free. Our public interest depends on private character, on civic duty and family bonds and basic fairness, on uncounted, unhonored acts of decency which give direction to our freedom. Sometimes in life we are called to do great things. But as a saint of our times has said, every day we are called to do small things with great love. The most important tasks of a democracy are done by everyone. I will live and lead by these principles: to advance my convictions with civility, to pursue the public interest with courage, to speak for greater justice and compassion, to call for responsibility and try to live it as well.

Service to Others

In all these ways, I will bring the values of our history to the care of our time. What you do is as important as anything government does. I ask you to seek a common good beyond your comfort; to defend needed reforms against easy attacks; to serve your nation, beginning with your neighbor. I ask you to be citizens: citizens, not spectators; citizens, not subjects; responsible citizens, building communities of service and a nation of character. Americans are generous and strong and decent, not because we believe in ourselves, but because we hold beliefs beyond ourselves. When this spirit of citizenship is missing, no government program can replace it. When this spirit is present, no wrong can stand against it.

After the Declaration of Independence was signed, Virginia statesman John Page wrote to Thomas Jefferson: "We know the race is not to the swift nor the battle to the strong. Do you not think an angel rides in the whirlwind and directs this storm? "Much time has passed since Jefferson arrived for his inauguration. The years and changes accumulate. But the themes of this day he would know: our nation's grand story of courage and its simple dream of dignity.

We are not this story's author, who fills time and eternity with his purpose. Yet his purpose is achieved in our duty, and our duty is fulfilled in service to one another. Never tiring, never yielding, never finishing, we renew that purpose today, to make our country more just and generous, to affirm the dignity of our lives and every life. This work continues. This story goes on. And an angel still rides in the whirlwind and directs this storm.

God bless you all, and God bless America.

Complete the SQ3R Analysis. See Appendix.

http://www.presidency.ucsb.edu/ws/?pid=25853 Public Domain

Short Answer Questions – President George W. Bush

1. How does President Bush address the idea of social responsibility?

2. Define the term "civility". What do you believe the term means to President Bush? List various ways he uses the term civility.

3. What is the main idea of the section "Courage to Reform"?

4. In discussing the 20th century, President Bush suggests that American faith in Democracy has been like "a rock in a raging sea". Discuss this image and how it could represent challenges in the 20th century. Provide examples.

Essay Topics

5. According to President Bush, compassion is one of America's strongest assets. Do you believe that America has overstepped its bounds based upon the compassion it feels for democracy in regards to foreign affairs.

6. In an essay, predict how you feel President George W. Bush would respond to the statement Cain makes in the "Biblical Account of Cain and Abel" (Chapter 3): "Am I my brother's keeper?" Use evidence from his speech to discuss Bush's views on social responsibility.

7. Bush speaks a lot of duty. How would you define duty? Do you agree with President Bush's ideas regarding duty and service to the United States?

C H A R T

KNOW • WANT • LEARN

KWL

ALREADY KNOW	WANT TO KNOW	WHAT I LEARNED

Barack Obama

Barack H. Obama is the 44th President of the United States.

His story is the American story — values from the heartland, a middle-class upbringing in a strong family, hard work and education as the means of getting ahead, and the conviction that a life so blessed should be lived in service to others.

With a father from Kenya and a mother from Kansas, President Obama was born in Hawaii on August 4, 1961. He was raised with help from his grandfather, who served in Patton's army, and his grandmother, who worked her way up from the secretarial pool to middle management at a bank.

After working his way through college with the help of scholarships and student loans, President Obama moved to Chicago, where he worked with a group of churches to help rebuild communities devastated by the closure of local steel plants.

He went on to attend law school, where he became the first African—American president of the Harvard Law Review. Upon graduation, he returned to Chicago to help lead a voter registration drive, teach constitutional law at the University of Chicago, and remain active in his community.

President Obama's years of public service are based around his unwavering belief in the ability to unite people around a politics of purpose. In the Illinois State Senate, he passed the first major ethics reform in 25 years, cut taxes for working families, and expanded health care for children and their parents. As a United States Senator, he reached across the aisle to pass groundbreaking lobbying reform, lock up the world's most dangerous weapons, and bring transparency to government by putting federal spending online.

He was elected the 44th President of the United States on November 4, 2008, and sworn in on January 20, 2009. He and his wife, Michelle, are the proud parents of two daughters, Malia, 14, and Sasha, 11.

http://www.whitehouse.gov/administration/president-obama Public Domain

Barack Obama

"Remaking America"

Inaugural Address

Tuesday, January 20, 2009

My fellow citizens:

I stand here today humbled by the task before us, grateful for the trust you have bestowed, mindful of the sacrifices borne by our ancestors. I thank President Bush for his service to our nation, as well as the generosity and cooperation he has shown throughout this transition.

Forty-four Americans have now taken the presidential oath. The words have been spoken during rising tides of prosperity and the still waters of peace. Yet, every so often the oath is taken amidst gathering clouds and raging storms. At these moments, America has carried on not simply because of the skill or vision of those in high office, but because We the People have remained faithful to the ideals of our forbearers, and true to our founding documents. So it has been. So it must be with this generation of Americans.

Indications of Crisis

That we are in the midst of crisis is now well understood. Our nation is at war, against a far-reaching network of violence and hatred. Our economy is badly weakened, a consequence of greed and irresponsibility on the part of some, but also our collective failure to make hard choices and prepare the nation for a new age. Homes have been lost; jobs shed; businesses shuttered. Our health care is too costly; our schools fail too many; and each day brings further evidence that the ways we use energy strengthen our adversaries and threaten our planet. These are the indicators of crisis, subject to data and statistics. Less measurable but no less profound is a sapping of confidence across our land—a nagging fear that America's decline is inevitable, that the next generation must lower its sights.

Today I say to you that the challenges we face are real. They are serious and they are many. They will not be met easily or in a short span of time. But know this, America— they will be met. On this day, we gather because we have chosen hope over fear, unity of purpose over conflict and discord. On this day, we come to proclaim an end to the petty grievances and false promises, the recriminations and worn-out dogmas that for far too long have strangled our politics.

We remain a young nation, but in the words of Scripture, the time has come to set aside childish things. The time has come to reaffirm our enduring spirit; to choose our better history; to carry forward that precious gift, that noble idea, passed on from generation to generation: the God-given promise that all are equal, all are free, and all deserve a chance to pursue their full measure of happiness.

The Work of Remaking America

In reaffirming the greatness of our nation, we understand that greatness is never a given. It must be earned. Our journey has never been one of shortcuts or settling for less. It has not been the path for the faint-hearted—for those who prefer leisure over work, or seek only the pleasures of riches and fame. Rather, it has been the risk-takers, the doers, the makers of things—some celebrated but more often men and women obscure in their labor, who have carried us up the long, rugged path towards prosperity and freedom. For us, they packed up their few worldly possessions and traveled across oceans in search of a new life. For us, they toiled in sweatshops and settled the West; endured the lash of the whip and plowed the hard earth. For us, they fought and died, in places like Concord and Gettysburg; Normandy and Khe Sahn.

Time and again these men and women struggled and sacrificed and worked till their hands were raw so that we might live a better life. They saw America as bigger than the sum of our individual ambitions; greater than all the differences of birth or wealth or faction. This is the journey we continue today. We remain the most prosperous, powerful nation on Earth. Our workers are no less productive than when this crisis began. Our minds are no less inventive, our goods and services no less needed than they were last week or last month or last year. Our capacity remains undiminished. But our time of standing pat, of protecting narrow interests and putting off unpleasant decisions—that time has surely passed. Starting today, we must pick ourselves up, dust ourselves off, and begin again the work of remaking America.

American Ambition

For everywhere we look, there is work to be done. The state of our economy calls for action, bold and swift, and we will act—not only to create new jobs, but to lay a new foundation for growth. We will build the roads and bridges, the electric grids and digital lines that feed our commerce and bind us together. We will restore science to its rightful place, and wield technology's wonders to raise health care's quality and lower its cost. We will harness the sun and the winds and the soil to fuel our cars and run our factories. And we will transform our schools and colleges and universities to meet the demands of a new age. All this we can do. All this we will do.

Now, there are some who question the scale of our ambitions—who suggest that our system cannot tolerate too many big plans. Their memories are short. For they have forgotten what this country has already done; what free men and women can achieve when imagination is joined to common purpose, and necessity to courage.

The Function of Government

What the cynics fail to understand is that the ground has shifted beneath them—that the stale political arguments that have consumed us for so long no longer apply.

The question we ask today is not whether our government is too big or too small, but whether it works—whether it helps families find jobs at a decent wage, care they can afford, a retirement that is dignified. Where the answer is yes, we intend to move forward. Where the answer is no, programs will end. And those of us who manage the public's dollars will be held to account—to spend wisely, reform bad habits, and do our business in the light of day—because only then can we restore the vital trust between a people and their government.

American Economy

Nor is the question before us whether the market is a force for good or ill. Its power to generate wealth and expand freedom is unmatched, but this crisis has reminded us that without a watchful eye, the market can spin out of control—the nation cannot prosper long when it favors only the prosperous. The success of our economy has always depended not just on the size of our Gross Domestic Product, but on the reach of our prosperity; on the ability to extend opportunity to every willing heart—not out of charity, but because it is the surest route to our common good.

Foreign Policy

As for our common defense, we reject as false the choice between our safety and our ideals. Our Founding Fathers, faced with perils that we can scarcely imagine, drafted a charter to assure the rule of law and the rights of man, a charter expanded by the blood of generations. Those ideals still light the world, and we will not give them up for expedience's sake. And so to all the other peoples and governments who are watching today, from the grandest capitals to the small village where my father was born: know that America is a friend of each nation and every man, woman, and child who seeks a future of peace and dignity, and we are ready to lead once more.

Recall that earlier generations faced down fascism and communism not just with missiles and tanks, but with the sturdy alliances and enduring convictions. They understood that our power alone cannot protect us, nor does it entitle us to do as we please. Instead, they knew that our power grows through its prudent use; our security emanates from the justness of our cause, the force of our example, the tempering qualities of humility and restraint.

We are the keepers of this legacy. Guided by these principles once more, we can meet those new threats that demand even greater effort—even greater cooperation and understanding between nations. We will begin to responsibly leave Iraq to its people, and forge a hard-earned peace in Afghanistan. With old friends and former foes, we will work tirelessly to lessen the nuclear threat, and roll back the specter of a warming planet. We will not apologize for our way of life, nor will we waver in its defense, and for those who seek to advance their aims by inducing terror and slaughtering the innocent, we say to you now that our spirit is stronger and cannot be broken; you cannot outlast us, and we will defeat you.

Diversity is Strength

For we know that our patchwork heritage is a strength, not a weakness. We are a nation of Christians and Muslims, Jews and Hindus—and non-believers. We are shaped by every language and culture, drawn from every end of this Earth; and because we have tasted the bitter swill of civil war and segregation, and emerged from that dark chapter stronger and more united, we cannot help but believe that the old hatreds shall someday pass; that the lines of tribe shall soon dissolve; that as the world grows smaller, our common humanity shall reveal itself; and that America must play its role in ushering in a new era of peace.

To the Muslim world, we seek a new way forward, based on mutual interest and mutual respect. To those leaders around the globe who seek to sow conflict, or blame their society's ills on the West—know that your people will judge you on what you can build, not what you destroy. To those who cling to power through corruption and deceit and the silencing of dissent, know that you are on the wrong side of history; but that we will extend a hand if you are willing to unclench your fist.

Social Responsibility

To the people of poor nations, we pledge to work alongside you to make your farms flourish and let clean waters flow; to nourish starved bodies and feed hungry minds. And to those nations like ours that enjoy relative plenty, we say we can no longer afford indifference to the suffering outside our borders; nor can we consume the world's resources without regard to effect. For the world has changed, and we must change with it.

As we consider the road that unfolds before us, we remember with humble gratitude those brave Americans who, at this very hour, patrol far-off deserts and distant mountains. They have something to tell us, just as the fallen heroes who lie in Arlington whisper through the ages. We honor them not only because they are the guardians of our liberty, but because they embody the spirit of service; a willingness to find meaning in something greater than themselves. And yet, at this moment—a moment that will define a generation—it is precisely this spirit that must inhabit us all.

For as much as government can do and must do, it is ultimately the faith and determination of the American people upon which this nation relies. It is the kindness to take in a stranger when the levees break, the selflessness of workers who would rather cut their hours than see a friend lose their job which sees us through our darkest hours. It is the firefighter's courage to storm a stairway filled with smoke, but also a parent's willingness to nurture a child, that finally decides our fate.

New Challenges

Our challenges may be new. The instruments with which we meet them may be new. But those values upon which our success depends—honesty and hard work, courage and fair play, tolerance and curiosity, loyalty and patriotism—these things are old. These things are true. They have been the quiet force of progress throughout our history. What is demanded then is a return to these truths. What is required of us now is a new era of responsibility—a recognition, on the part of every American, that we have duties to ourselves, our nation, and the world, duties that we do not grudgingly accept but rather seize gladly, firm in the knowledge that there is nothing so satisfying to the spirit, so defining of our character, than giving our all to a difficult task.

This is the price and the promise of citizenship. This is the source of our confidence—the knowledge that God calls on us to shape an uncertain destiny. This is the meaning of our liberty and our creed—why men and women and children of every race and every faith can join in celebration across this magnificent mall, and why a man whose father less than sixty years ago might not have been served at a local restaurant can now stand before you to take a most sacred oath.

So let us mark this day with remembrance, of who we are and how far we have traveled. In the year of America's birth, in the coldest of months, a small band of patriots huddled by dying campfires on the shores of an icy river. The capital was abandoned. The enemy was advancing. The snow was stained with blood. At a moment when the outcome of our revolution was most in doubt, the father of our nation ordered these words be read to the people: "Let it be told to the future world ... that in the depth of winter, when nothing but hope and virtue could survive ... that the city and the country, alarmed at one common danger, came forth to meet ... it."

America! In the face of our common dangers, in this winter of our hardship, let us remember these timeless words. With hope and virtue, let us brave once more the icy currents, and endure what storms may come. Let it be said by our children's children that when we were tested we refused to let this journey end, that we did not turn back nor did we falter; and with eyes fixed on the horizon and God's grace upon us, we carried forth that great gift of freedom and delivered it safely to future generations.

Thank you. God bless you. And God bless the United States of America.

Complete the SQ3R Analysis. See Appendix.

http://www.whitehouse.gov/blog/inaugural-address/ Public Domain

Short Answer Questions – President Barack Obama

1. President Obama's speech starts with addressing various forms of crisis in America. What can you infer are the issues America faces at the time when he delivers this speech? List them.

2. According to his speech, how does Obama view American creativity? How does he predict it will function on the road to American renewal.

3. What images of diversity and unity does Obama present in his speech.

4. How does President Obama address the new challenges ahead? What is his tone?

Essay Topics

1. President Obama provides vivid images of hard work and the American spirit. Write a narrative essay where you connect to the spirit of American hard work. Consider the images Obama provides as you write your personal narrative.

2. Write an essay where you agree or disagree with President Obama's ideas regarding social responsibility. How could you implement one of his platforms?

3. Although President Obama is the first African-American president in United States history, his inauguration speech does not highlight the uniqueness of his achievement although African Americans voted in record numbers to aid his success. Would you agree with those who felt that he did not do African American culture justice because he did not celebrate the accomplishment for the African Americans as a people?

4. Compare and contrast Obama's acceptance speech for the Democratic nomination in 2008 to his inauguration speech in 2009. Discuss the strengths and weaknesses as you defend the stronger of the two speeches from your point of view.

CHAPTER 7

THE FIRST LADIES OF THE UNITED STATES
SPEECHES FOR AMERICA
ON SOCIAL ISSUES

OUTLINE/NOTES

Chapter 7

The First Ladies of the United States

Speeches for America on Social Issues

The Feminine Prospective

The role of the first lady in any capacity is not defined. In many ways, the first lady, whether it is a political or religious "first lady," functions essentially the same way. Generally, she is a social diplomat in the community, state or nation. If she speaks, she usually speaks to social issues while her husband may speak to either political or religious issues. She serves as a counterpart to her husband by addressing issues women, children or families face. She focuses on things that involve the social development of a body of people, usually in concert with her husband's political or religious vision for the people they lead.

In this chapter, you will meet Eleanor Roosevelt, one of the most vocal first ladies in American history, and the wife of President Franklin D. Roosevelt. Also, included in the chapter is Hillary Rodham Clinton, President Bill Clinton's wife. Hillary Clinton served as the United States Secretary of State and ran against Michelle Obama's husband, President Barack Obama, for the democratic nomination for the position of the President of the United States. Both Hillary Clinton and Michelle Obama are educationally trained as attorneys, and they have been instrumental in influencing their husbands' political agendas through their social endeavors.

Notes

Nancy Reagan, President Ronald Reagan's wife, uttered the words that started the nationwide march against drugs in her "Just Say No" speech, which was instrumental in moving America's "War on Drugs" to tiny foot soldiers. Her Just Say No campaign penetrated the hallways of K-12 schools throughout the country as children took a stance against drugs in the 1980's. These women have been powerful and influential while serving at their husbands' sides.

In this chapter, you will explore the speeches of American first ladies. As you read ask yourself the following questions:

- How does each first lady's speech compliment their husband's vision for the United States? What conflicts are present?
- How did the social agendas of the first ladies of the United States impact social policy and human rights during their husband's years in the Whitehouse and beyond?
- Which of the messages are still areas of concern today?
- How does Aristotle's three appeals work in their speeches? What evidence can you find of pathos, ethos and logos?

These are the questions to explore as you read the next chapter.

INSTRUCTIONS

1. Complete the KWL chart to see what information you know about the stories you will read.
2. After completing the KWL chart, and doing a research on the story you about to read, write an introduction to introduce this text.
3. At the end of each section, you will complete an outlining notetaking exercise to help you study texts in this chapter. Afterwards, you will write a chapter summary.

C H A R T

KNOW • WANT • LEARN

KWL

ALREADY KNOW	WANT TO KNOW	WHAT I LEARNED

Anna Eleanor Roosevelt

A shy, awkward child, starved for recognition and love, Eleanor Roosevelt grew into a woman with great sensitivity to the underprivileged of all creeds, races, and nations. Her constant work to improve their lot made her one of the most loved--and for some years one of the most revered--women of her generation.

She was born in New York City on October 11, 1884, daughter of lovely Anna Hall and Elliott Roosevelt, younger brother of Theodore. When her mother died in 1892, the children went to live with Grandmother Hall; her adored father died only two years later. Attending a distinguished school in England gave her, at 15, her first chance to develop self-confidence among other girls.

Tall, slender, graceful of figure but apprehensive at the thought of being a wallflower, she returned for a debut that she dreaded. In her circle of friends was a distant cousin, handsome young Franklin Delano Roosevelt. They became engaged in 1903 and were married in 1905, with her uncle the President giving the bride away. Within eleven years Eleanor bore six children; one son died in infancy. "I suppose I was fitting pretty well into the pattern of a fairly conventional, quiet, young society matron," she wrote later in her autobiography.

In Albany, where Franklin served in the state Senate from 1910 to 1913, Eleanor started her long career as political helpmate. She gained a knowledge of Washington and its ways while he served as Assistant Secretary of the Navy. When he was stricken with poliomyelitis in 1921, she tended him devotedly. She became active in the women's division of the State Democratic Committee to keep his interest in politics alive. From his successful campaign for governor in 1928 to the day of his death, she dedicated her life to his purposes. She became eyes and ears for him, a trusted and tireless reporter.

When Mrs. Roosevelt came to the White House in 1933, she understood social conditions better than any of her predecessors and she transformed the role of First Lady accordingly. She never shirked official entertaining; she greeted thousands with charming friendliness. She also broke precedent to hold press conferences, travel to all parts of the country, give lectures and radio broadcasts, and express her opinions candidly in a daily syndicated newspaper column, "My Day."

This made her a tempting target for political enemies but her integrity, her graciousness, and her sincerity of purpose endeared her personally to many--from heads of state to servicemen she visited abroad during World War II. As she had written wistfully at 14: "...no matter how plain a woman may be if truth & loyalty are stamped upon her face all will be attracted to her...."

After the President's death in 1945 she returned to a cottage at his Hyde Park estate; she told reporters: "the story is over." Within a year, however, she began her service as American spokesman in the United Nations. She continued a vigorous career until her strength began to wane in 1962. She died in New York City that November, and was buried at Hyde Park beside her husband.

The biographies of the First Ladies on WhiteHouse.gov are from "The First Ladies of the United States of America," by Allida Black. Copyright 2009 by the White House Historical Association.

Notes

"Adoption of the Declaration of Human Rights"

Eleanor Roosevelt
1948

Mr. President, fellow delegates:

The long and meticulous study and debate of which this Universal Declaration of Human Rights is the product means that it reflects the composite views of the many men and governments who have contributed to its formulation. Not every man nor every government can have what he wants in a document of this kind. There are of course particular provisions in the declaration before us with which we are not fully satisfied. I have no doubt this is true of other delegations, and it would still be true if we continued our labors over many years. Taken as a whole the Delegation of the United States believes that this a good document -- even a great document -- and we propose to give it our full support. The position of the United States on the various parts of the declaration is a matter of record in the Third Committee. I shall not burden the Assembly, and particularly my colleagues of the Third Committee, with a restatement of that position here.

Provisions

Certain provisions of the declaration are stated in such broad terms as to be acceptable only because of the limitations in article 29 providing for limitation on the exercise of the rights for the purpose of meeting the requirements of morality, public order, and the general welfare. An example of this is the provision that everyone has the right of equal access to the public service in his country. The basic principle of equality and of nondiscrimination as to public employment is sound, but it cannot be accepted without limitations. My government, for example, would consider that this is unquestionably subject to limitation in the interest of public order and the general welfare. It would not consider that the exclusion from public employment of persons holding **subversive** political beliefs and not loyal to the basic principles and practices of the constitution and laws of the country would in any way **infringe** upon this right.

Likewise, my Government has made it clear in the course of the development of the declaration that it does not consider that the economic and social and cultural rights stated in the declaration imply an obligation on governmental action. This was made quite clear in the Human Rights Commission text of article 23 which served as a so-called "umbrella" article to the articles on economic and social rights. We consider that the principle has not been affected by the fact that this article no longer contains a reference to the articles which follow it. This in no way affects our whole-hearted support for the basic principles of economic, social, and cultural rights set forth in these articles.

Declaration Defined

In giving our approval to the declaration today it is of primary importance that we keep clearly in mind the basic character of the document. It is not a treaty; it is not an international agreement. It is not and does not **purport** to be a statement of basic principles of law or legal obligation. It is a declaration of basic principles of human rights and freedoms, to be stamped with the approval of the General Assembly by formal vote of its members, and to serve as a common standard of achievement for all peoples of all nations.

We stand today at the **threshold** of a great event both in the life of the United Nations and in the life of mankind, that is the approval by the General Assembly of the Universal Declaration of Human Rights recommended by the Third Committee. This declaration may well become the international **Magna Carta** of all men everywhere. We hope its proclamation by the General Assembly will be an event comparable to the proclamation of the Declaration of the Rights of the Man by the French people in 1789, the adoption of the Bill of Rights by the people of the United States, and the adoption of comparable declarations at different times in other countries.

At a time when there are so many issues on which we find it difficult to reach a common basis of agreement, it is a significant fact that 58 states have found such a large measure of agreement in the complex field of human rights. This must be taken as testimony of our common aspiration first voiced in the Charter of the United Nations to lift men everywhere to a higher standard of life and to a greater enjoyment of freedom. Man's desire for peace lies behind this declaration. The realization that the fragrant violation of human rights by **Nazi** and **Fascist** countries sowed the seeds of the last world war has supplied the impetus for the work which brings us to the moment of achievement here today.

Gladstone Murray

In a recent speech in Canada, Gladstone Murray said:

The central fact is that man is fundamentally a moral being, that the light we have is imperfect does not matter so long as we are always trying to improve it … we are equal in sharing the moral freedom that distinguishes us as men. Man's status makes each individual an end in himself. No man is by nature simply the servant of the state or of another man … the ideal and fact of freedom -- and not technology -- are the true distinguishing marks of our civilization. This declaration is based upon the spiritual fact that man must have freedom in which to develop his full stature and through common effort to raise the level of human dignity. We have much to do to fully achieve and to assure the rights set forth in this declaration. But having them put before us with the moral backing of 58 nations will be a great step forward.

As we here bring to fruition our labors on this Declaration of Human Rights, we must at the same time rededicate ourselves to the unfinished task which lies before us. We can now move on with new courage and inspiration to the completion of an international covenant on human rights and of measures for the implementation of human rights.

In conclusion I feel that I cannot do better than to repeat the call to action by Secretary Marshall in his opening statement to this Assembly: Let this third regular session of the General Assembly approve by an overwhelming majority the Declaration of Human Rights as a statement of conduct for all; and let us, as Members of the United Nations, conscious of our own short-comings and imperfections, join our effort in all faith to live up to this high standard.

"American Rhetoric: Eleanor Roosevelt -- "The Struggle for Human Rights"" American Rhetoric:. Web. 04 Nov. 2014. Audio in Public Domain

Practice the Outline Note Taking Skill Here. Then write a summary of Eleanor Roosevelt's, "Adoption of the Declaration of Human Rights"

OUTLINE / NOTES

Write a summary of *"Adoption of the Declaration of Human Rights"* by Eleanor Roosevelt

Short Answer Questions – Eleanor Roosevelt

1. Who or what is Eleanor Roosevelt referring to when talks about Human Rights?

2. What do you think Eleanor Roosevelt means by "universal rights"?

3. Paraphrase the final sentence of the quotation. What does it say about individual responsibility for human rights? What do you think Eleanor Roosevelt means by "concerned citizen action to uphold" rights close to home?

_____

_____

_____

_____

_____

_____

_____

_____

_____

_____

_____

_____

_____

Essay Topics

1. Some people feel that universal values or standards of behavior are impossible. What do you think?

2. Some people in the world have only what is necessary to survive while others have luxury and convenience. Is this situation just? Is it a human rights violation?

3. Eleanor Roosevelt mentions that, "Man's desire for peace lies behind this declaration. The realization that the fragrant violation of human rights by Nazi and Fascist countries sowed the seeds of the last world war has supplied the impetus for the work which brings us to the moment of achievement here today." Discuss the violation of Human Rights generally, and then compare and contrast the violation of human rights in Nazi and Fascist countries as well as in the United States during the 1950's.

C H A R T

KNOW • WANT • LEARN

KWL

ALREADY KNOW	WANT TO KNOW	WHAT I LEARNED

Nancy Davis Reagan

"My life really began when I married my husband," says Nancy Reagan, who in the 1950's happily gave up an acting career for a permanent role as the wife of Ronald Reagan and mother to their children. Her story actually begins in New York City, her birthplace. She was born on July 6, 1921.

When the future First Lady was six, her mother, Edith--a stage actress--married Dr. Loyal Davis, a neurosurgeon. Dr. Davis adopted Nancy, and she grew up in Chicago. It was a happy time: summer camp, tennis, swimming, dancing. She received her formal education at Girls' Latin School and at Smith College in Massachusetts, where she majored in theater.

Soon after graduation she became a professional actress. She toured with a road company, then landed a role on Broadway in the hit musical Lute Song. More parts followed. One performance drew an offer from Hollywood. Billed as Nancy Davis, she performed in 11 films from 1949 to 1956. Her first screen role was in Shadow on the Wall. Other releases included The Next Voice Your Hear and East Side, West Side. In her last movie, Hellcats of the Navy, she played opposite her husband.

She had met Ronald Reagan in 1951, when he was president of the Screen Actors Guild. The following year they were married in a simple ceremony in Los Angeles in the Little Brown Church in the Valley. Mrs. Reagan soon retired from making movies so she "could be the wife I wanted to be...A woman's real happiness and real fulfillment come from within the home with her husband and children," she says. President and Mrs. Reagan have a daughter, Patricia Ann, and a son, Ronald Prescott.

While her husband was Governor of California from 1967 to 1975, she worked with numerous charitable groups. She spent many hours visiting veterans, the elderly, and the emotionally and physically handicapped. These people continued to interest her as First Lady. She gave her support to the Foster Grandparent Program, the subject of her 1982 book, To Love A Child. Increasingly, she has concentrated on the fight against drug and alcohol abuse among young people. She visited prevention and rehabilitation centers, and in 1985 she held a conference at the White House for First Ladies of 17 countries to focus international attention on this problem.

Mrs. Reagan shared her lifelong interest in the arts with the nation by using the Executive Mansion as a showcase for talented young performers in the PBS television series "In Performance at the White House." In her first year in the mansion she directed a major renovation of the second- and third-floor quarters.

Now living in retirement in California, she continues to work on her campaign to teach children to "just say no" to drugs. In her book My Turn, published in 1989, she gives her own account of her life in the White House. Through the joys and sorrows of those days, including the assassination attempt on her husband, Nancy Reagan held fast to her belief in love, honesty, and selflessness. "The ideals have endured because they are right and are no less right today than yesterday."

The biographies of the First Ladies on WhiteHouse.gov are from "The First Ladies of the United States of America," by Allida Black. Copyright 2009 by the White House Historical Association.

Address to the Nation

Nancy Reagan

September 14, 1986

As a mother, I've always thought of September as a special month, a time when we bundled our children off to school, to the warmth of an environment in which they could fulfill the promise and hope in those restless minds. But so much has happened over these last years, so much to shake the foundations of all that we know and all that we believe in. Today there's a drug and alcohol abuse epidemic in this country, and no one is safe from it - not you, not me, and certainly not our children, because this epidemic has their names written on it. Many of you may be thinking: "Well, drugs don't concern me." But it does concern you. It concerns us all because of the way it tears at our lives and because it's aimed at destroying the brightness and life of the sons and daughters of the United States.

Drugs Effect Everyone

For five years I've been traveling across the country - learning and listening. And one of the most hopeful signs I've seen is the building of an essential, new awareness of how terrible and threatening drug abuse is to our society. This was one of the main purposes when I started, so of course it makes me happy that that's been accomplished. But each time I meet with someone new or receive another letter from a troubled person on drugs, I yearn to find a way to help share the message that cries out from them. As a parent, I'm especially concerned about what drugs are doing to young mothers and their newborn children. Listen to this news account from a hospital in Florida of a child born to a mother with a cocaine habit: "Nearby, a baby named Paul lies motionless in an incubator, feeding tubes riddling his tiny body. He needs a respirator to breathe and a daily spinal tap to relieve fluid buildup on his brain. Only 1 month old, he's already suffered 2 strokes."

Drugs Steal

Now you can see why drug abuse concerns every one of us-all the American family. Drugs steal away so much. They take and take, until finally every time a drug goes into a child, something else is forced out - like love and hope and trust and confidence. Drugs take away the dream from every child's heart and replace it with a nightmare, and it's time we in America stand up and replace those dreams. Each of us has to put our principles and consciences on the line, whether in social settings or in the workplace, to set forth solid standards and stick to them. There's no **moral middle ground**. Indifference is not an option. We want you to help us create an outspoken intolerance for drug use. For the sake of our children, I implore each of you to be unyielding and inflexible in your opposition to drugs.

Children are Activist Against Drugs

Our young people are helping us lead the way. Not long ago, in Oakland, California, I was asked by a group of children what to do if they were offered drugs, and I answered, "Just say no." Soon after that, those children in Oakland formed a Just Say No club, and now there are over 10,000 such clubs all over the country. Well, their participation and their courage in saying no needs our encouragement. We can help by using every opportunity to force the issue of not using drugs to the point of making others uncomfortable, even if it means making ourselves unpopular.

Drug Dealers are Relentless

Our job is never easy because drug criminals are ingenious. They work everyday to plot a new and better way to steal our children's lives, just as they've done by developing this new drug, crack. For every door that we close, they open a new door to death. They prosper on our unwillingness to act. So, we must be smarter and stronger and tougher than they are. It's up to us to change attitudes and just simply dry up their markets.

Personal Appeal

And finally, to young people watching or listening, I have a very personal message for you: There's a big, wonderful world out there for you. It belongs to you. It's exciting and stimulating and rewarding. Don't cheat yourselves out of this promise. Our country needs you, but it needs you to be clear-eyed and clear-minded. I recently read one teenager's story. She's now determined to stay clean but was once strung out on several drugs. What she remembered most clearly about her recovery was that during the time she was on drugs everything appeared to her in shades of black and gray and after her treatment she was able to see colors again.

So, to my young friends out there: Life can be great, but not when you can't see it. So, open your eyes to life: to see it in the vivid colors that God gave us as a precious gift to His children, to enjoy life to the fullest, and to make it count. Say yes to your life. And when it comes to drugs and alcohol just say no.

Speech transcribed from http://www.cnn.com/SPECIALS/2004/reagan/stories/speech.archive/just.say. no.html Public Domain

Practice the Outline Note taking skill Here. Then write a summary of Nancy Reagan's speech "Just Say No"

OUTLINE AND NOTES

Write a summary of "Just Say No" by Nancy Reagan

Short Answer Questions – Nancy Reagan

1. Aristotle's three appeals are pathos - the appeal to emotions, ethos – the appeal to character and logos – the appeal to reason. Which of the appeals does Nancy Reagan use appeal to her audience in the paragraph "Drugs Effect Everyone"?

2. What is Mrs. Reagan's dominant pattern of organization in her speech over all? How do you know?

3. Is the paragraph structure for the section "Drug Dealers are Relentless" an example of inductive or deductive reasoning?

Essay Topics

1. Was Nancy Reagans "Just Say No" speech persuasive enough to discourage her audience to say no to drugs?

2. Write a personal narrative or memoir where you discuss peer pressure and its positive or negative effect on your life.

C H A R T

KNOW • WANT • LEARN

KWL

ALREADY KNOW	WANT TO KNOW	WHAT I LEARNED

Notes

Hillary Rodham Clinton

During the 1992 presidential campaign, Hillary Rodham Clinton observed, "Our lives are a mixture of different roles. Most of us are doing the best we can to find whatever the right balance is . . . For me, that balance is family, work, and service."

Hillary Diane Rodham, Dorothy and Hugh Rodham's first child, was born on October 26, 1947. Two brothers, Hugh and Tony, soon followed. Hillary's childhood in Park Ridge, Illinois, was happy and disciplined. She loved sports and her church, and was a member of the National Honor Society, and a student leader. Her parents encouraged her to study hard and to pursue any career that interested her.

As an undergraduate at Wellesley College, Hillary mixed academic excellence with school government. Speaking at graduation, she said, "The challenge now is to practice politics as the art of making what appears to be impossible, possible."

In 1969, Hillary entered Yale Law School, where she served on the Board of Editors of Yale Law Review and Social Action, interned with children's advocate Marian Wright Edelman, and met Bill Clinton. The President often recalls how they met in the library when she strode up to him and said, "If you're going to keep staring at me, I might as well introduce myself." The two were soon inseparable--partners in moot court, political campaigns, and matters of the heart.

After graduation, Hillary advised the Children's Defense Fund in Cambridge and joined the impeachment inquiry staff advising the Judiciary Committee of the House of Representatives. After completing those responsibilities, she "followed her heart to Arkansas," where Bill had begun his political career.

They married in 1975. She joined the faculty of the University of Arkansas Law School in 1975 and the Rose Law Firm in 1976. In 1978, President Jimmy Carter appointed her to the board of the Legal Services Corporation, and Bill Clinton became governor of Arkansas. Their daughter, Chelsea, was born in 1980.

Hillary served as Arkansas's First Lady for 12 years, balancing family, law, and public service. She chaired the Arkansas Educational Standards Committee, co-founded the Arkansas Advocates for Children and Families, and served on the boards of the Arkansas Children's Hospital, Legal Services, and the Children's Defense Fund.

As the nation's First Lady, Hillary continued to balance public service with private life. Her active role began in 1993 when the President asked her to chair the Task Force on National Health Care Reform. She continued to be a leading advocate for expanding health insurance coverage, ensuring children are properly immunized, and raising public awareness of health issues. She wrote a weekly newspaper column entitled "Talking It Over," which focused on her experiences as First Lady and her observations of women, children, and families she has met around the world. Her 1996 book It Takes a Village and Other Lessons Children Teach Us was a best seller, and she received a Grammy Award for her recording of it.

As First Lady, her public involvement with many activities sometimes led to controversy. Undeterred by critics, Hillary won many admirers for her staunch support for women around the world and her commitment to children's issues.

Hillary Clinton was elected United States Senator from New York on November 7, 2000. She is the first First Lady elected to the United States Senate and the first woman elected statewide in New York.

The biographies of the First Ladies on WhiteHouse.gov are from "The First Ladies of the United States of America," by Allida Black. Copyright 2009 by the White House Historical Association.

Notes

Women's Rights Are Human Rights

By Hillary Rodham Clinton
1995

This speech was given during the United Nations Fourth World Conference on Women.

Thank you very much Gertrude Mongella, for your dedicated work that has brought us to this point.

Distinguished delegates and guests, I would like to thank the Secretary General of the United Nations for inviting me to be part of this important United Nations Fourth World Conference on Women. This is truly a celebration -- a celebration of the contributions women make in every aspect of life: in the home, on the job, in the community, as mothers, wives, sisters, daughters, learners, workers, citizens and leaders.

Common Bond Amongst Women Globally

It is also a coming together, much the way women come together every day in every country. We come together in fields and in factories. In village markets and supermarkets. In living rooms and board rooms. Whether it is while playing with our children in the park, or washing clothes in a river, or taking a break at the office water cooler, we come together and talk about our aspirations and concerns. And time and again, our talk turns to our children and our families. However different we may appear, there is far more that unites us than divides us. We share a common future. And we are here to find common ground so that we may help bring new dignity and respect to women and girls all over the world -- and in so doing, bring new strength and stability to families as well.

The Importance of the United Nations World Conference on Women

By gathering in Beijing, we are focusing world attention on issues that matter most in the lives of women and their families: access to education, health care, jobs, and credit, the chance to enjoy basic legal and human rights and to participate fully in the political life of their countries. There are some who question the reason for this conference. Let them listen to the voices of women in their homes, neighborhoods, and workplaces. There are some who wonder whether the lives of women and girls matter to economic and political progress around the globe. ... Let them look at the women gathered here and at Hairou.... the homemakers, nurses, teachers, lawyers, policymakers, and women who run their own businesses. It is conferences like this that compel governments and peoples everywhere to listen, look and face the world's most pressing problems.

Wasn't it after the women's conference in Nairobi ten years ago that the world focused for the first time on the crisis of domestic violence? Earlier today, I participated in a World Health Organization forum. In that forum we talked about ways that where government officials, NGOs, and individual citizens are working on ways to address the health problems of women and girls. Tomorrow, I will attend a gathering of the

United Nations Development Fund for Women. There, the discussion will focus on local -- and highly successful -- programs that give hardworking women access to credit so they can improve their own lives and the lives of their families.

What we are learning around the world is that, if women are healthy and educated, their families will flourish. If women are free from violence, their families will flourish. If women have a chance to work and earn as full and equal partners in society, their families will flourish. And when families flourish, communities and nations will flourish.

The Conference Empowers More Than Just Women

That is why every woman, every man, every child, every family, and every nation on our planet does have a stake in the discussion that takes place here.

Over the past 25 years, I have worked persistently on issues relating to women, children and families. Over the past two-and-a-half years, I have had the opportunity to learn more about the challenges facing women in my own country and around the world. I have met new mothers in Indonesia, who come together regularly in their village to discuss nutrition, family planning, and baby care. I have met working parents in Denmark who talk about the comfort they feel in knowing that their children can be cared for in creative, safe, and nurturing afterschool centers. I have met women in South Africa who helped lead the struggle to end apartheid and are now helping build a new democracy. I have met with the leading women of my own hemisphere who are working every day to promote literacy and better health care for the children in their countries. I have met women in India and Bangladesh who are taking out small loans to buy milk cows, rickshaws, thread and other materials to create a livelihood for themselves and their families. I have met doctors and nurses in Belarus and Ukraine who are trying to keep children alive in the aftermath of Chernobyl.

Women Who Can Speak Must Speak for Those Who Can't

The great challenge of this conference is to give voice to women everywhere whose experiences go unnoticed, whose words go unheard. Women comprise more than half the world's population. Women are 70% percent of the world's poor, and two-thirds of those who are not taught to read and write. Women are the primary caretakers for most of the world's children and elderly. Yet much of the work we do is not valued -- not by economists, not by historians, not by popular culture, not by government leaders. At this very moment, as we sit here, women around the world are giving birth, raising children, cooking meals, washing clothes, cleaning houses, planting crops, working on assembly lines, running companies, and running countries.

Women also are dying from diseases that should have been prevented or treated; they are watching their children succumb to malnutrition caused by poverty and economic deprivation; they are being denied the right to go to school by their own fathers and brothers; they are being forced into prostitution, and they are being barred from the bank lending office and banned from the ballot box. Those of us who have the opportunity to be here have the responsibility to speak for those who could not.

Challenges for American Women

As an American, I want to speak up for women in my own country -- women who are raising children on the minimum wage, women who can't afford health care or child care, women whose lives are threatened by violence, including violence in their own homes.

I want to speak up for mothers who are fighting for good schools, safe neighborhoods, clean air and clean airwaves... for older women, some of them widows, who have raised their families and now find that their skills and life experiences are not valued in the workplace... for women who are working all night as nurses, hotel clerks, and fast food chefs so that they can be at home during the day with their kids... and for women everywhere who simply don't have time to do everything they are called upon to do each day.

Speaking to you today, I speak for them, just as each of us speaks for women around the world who are denied the chance to go to school, or see a doctor, or own property, or have a say about the direction of their lives, simply because they are women.

The truth is that most women around the world work both inside and outside the home, usually by necessity. We need to understand that there is no one formula for how women should lead their lives.

That is why we must respect the choices that each woman makes for herself and her family. Every woman deserves the chance to realize her God-given potential. We also must recognize that women will never gain full dignity until their human rights are respected and protected.

Stronger Protection for Women Globally

Our goals for this conference, to strengthen families and societies by empowering women to take greater control over their own destinies, cannot be fully achieved unless all governments -- here and around the world -- accept their responsibility to protect and promote internationally recognized human rights.

The international community has long acknowledged -- and recently affirmed at Vienna -- that both women and men are entitled to a range of protections and personal freedoms, from the right of personal security to the right to determine freely the number and spacing of the children they bear.

No one should be forced to remain silent for fear of religious or political persecution, arrest, abuse or torture. Tragically, women are most often the ones whose human rights are violated. Even in the late 20th century, the rape of women continues to be used as an instrument of armed conflict. Women and children make up a large majority of the world's refugees. And when women are excluded from the political process, they become even more vulnerable to abuse.

Call to Action

I believe that, on the eve of a new millennium, it is time to break our silence. It is time for us to say here in Beijing, and the world to hear, that it is no longer acceptable to discuss women's rights as separate from human rights. These abuses have continued because, for too long, the history of women has been a history of silence. Even today, there are those who are trying to silence our words.

The voices of this conference and of the women at Hairou must be heard loud and clear:

It is a violation of human rights when babies are denied food, or drowned, or suffocated, or their spines broken, simply because they are born girls.

It is a violation of human rights when women and girls are sold into the slavery of prostitution.

It is a violation of human rights when women are doused with gasoline, set on fire and burned to death because their marriage dowries are deemed too small.

It is a violation of human rights when individual women are raped in their own communities and when thousands of women are subjected to rape as a tactic or prize of war.

It is a violation of human rights when a leading cause of death worldwide among women ages 14 to 44 is the violence they are subjected to in their own homes by their own relatives.

It is a violation of human rights when young girls are brutalized by the painful and degrading practice of genital mutilation.

It is a violation of human rights when women are denied the right to plan their own families, and that includes being forced to have abortions or being sterilized against their will.

If there is one message that echoes forth from this conference, let it be that human rights are women's rights.... And women's rights are human rights, once and for all.

Let us not forget that among those rights are the right to speak freely. And the right to be heard.

Women must enjoy the right to participate fully in the social and political lives of their countries if we want freedom and democracy to thrive and endure.

It is indefensible that many women in non-governmental organizations who wished to participate in this conference have not been able to attend -- or have been prohibited from fully taking part.

Let me be clear. Freedom means the right of people to assemble, organize, and debate openly. It means respecting the views of those who may disagree with the views of their governments.

Practice the Outline Note Taking Skill Here. Then write a summary of Hillary Clinton's Women's Rights are Human Rights

OUTLINE AND NOTES

Write a summary of "Women's Rights are Human Rights" by Hillary Clinton

Short Answer Questions – Hillary Clinton

1. Hillary Clinton ends her speech with the repetition of the words "It's a violation…" How does this impact the audience as she moves to the close of her speech?

2. Who is Clinton's primary audience? How do you know who they are?

3. What is the occasion for Clinton's speech?

4. What are the issues American Women face according to her speech? Does she express bias toward working women or stay at home moms?

_____

_____

_____

_____

_____

_____

_____

_____

_____

_____

_____

_____

_____

_____

_____

_____

_____

Essay Topics

1. Write and essay where you discuss Hillary Clinton and social responsibility globally.

2. Write an essay where you affirm the statement "Am I my sister's keeper?" Discuss what you would do in your community to become an advocate for women and women's issues?

C H A R T

KNOW • WANT • LEARN

KWL

ALREADY KNOW	WANT TO KNOW	WHAT I LEARNED

Michelle Obama

First Lady Michelle Obama When people ask First Lady Michelle Obama to describe herself, she doesn't hesitate to say that first and foremost, she is Malia and Sasha's mom.

But before she was a mother -- or a wife, lawyer or public servant -- she was Fraser and Marian Robinson's daughter.

The Robinsons lived in a brick bungalow on the South Side of Chicago. Fraser was a pump operator for the Chicago Water Department, and despite being diagnosed with multiple sclerosis at a young age, he hardly ever missed a day of work. Marian stayed home to raise Michelle and her older brother Craig, skillfully managing a busy household filled with love, laughter, and important life lessons.

A product of Chicago public schools, Mrs. Obama studied sociology and African-American studies at Princeton University. After graduating from Harvard Law School in 1988, she joined the Chicago law firm Sidley & Austin, where she later met the man who would become the love of her life.

After a few years, Mrs. Obama decided her true calling was working with people to serve their communities and their neighbors. She served as assistant commissioner of planning and development in Chicago's City Hall before becoming the founding executive director of the Chicago chapter of Public Allies, an AmeriCorps program that prepares youth for public service.

In 1996, Mrs. Obama joined the University of Chicago with a vision of bringing campus and community together. As Associate Dean of Student Services, she developed the university's first community service program, and under her leadership as Vice President of Community and External Affairs for the University of Chicago Medical Center, volunteerism skyrocketed.

Promoting Service and working with young people has remained a staple of her career and her interest. Continuing this effort now as First Lady, Mrs. Obama recently launched the Let's Move! campaign to bring together community leaders, teachers, doctors, nurses, moms and dads in a nationwide effort to tackle the challenge of childhood obesity. Let's Move! has an ambitious but important goal: to solve the epidemic of childhood obesity within a generation.

Let's Move! will give parents the support they need, provide healthier food in schools, help our kids to be more physically active, and make healthy, affordable food available in every part of our country.

In 2011, Mrs. Obama and Dr. Jill Biden together launched Joining Forces, a nationwide initiative that mobilizes all sectors of society to give our service members and their families the opportunities and support they have earned, and to raise awareness of military families' unique needs as pertains to employment, education and wellness. Joining Forces has been working hand in hand with American businesses who are committed to answering the President's challenge to hire or train 100,000 unemployed veterans and military spouses by 2013.

As First Lady, Mrs. Obama looks forward to continuing her work on the issues close to her heart — supporting military families, helping working women balance career and family, encouraging national service, promoting the arts and arts education, and fostering healthy eating and healthy living for children and families across the country.

Michelle and Barack Obama have two daughters: Malia, 14, and Sasha, 11. Like their mother, the girls were born on the South Side of Chicago.

Michelle Obama

"The Power of Education"

Bell Multicultural High School
Washington, D.C.
2014

Let me tell you, I'm thrilled to be back here at the Columbia Heights Education Campus. How many of you guys were here when the President and I were here the last time? (Applause.) Yes, show -- applause are good. That will help me out. That's good. So you guys have made some good progress, and now we're back because we are so proud of what you all have been doing here, and we thought that this was the best place to begin this conversation. So let me start by thanking Menbere for that very kind introduction. She is a proud representative of what this school can do, and her story is one that we want you all to emulate. I also want to recognize Mayor Gray, as well as Kaya Henderson, the Chancellor of the D.C. Public Schools. And of course, I want to recognize your principal, Principal Tukeva, and all of the faculty and staff here at Bell Multicultural High School. Thank you for hosting us.

Of course, I want to thank Secretary Duncan for joining me today, as well as Jeff and Keshia and everyone from 106 & Park for helping to facilitate today's discussion. Let's give them all a big round of applause. (Applause.) But most of all, I want to recognize all of the young people who are here with us, the sophomores here at CHEC. And I wanted to come here today because you guys and students like you across America are at the heart of one of my husband's most important goals as President.

Obama's Vision for Students

See, when Barack came into office, one of the very first things he did was to set what he calls a North Star goal for the entire country -- that by the year 2020, the year that all of you will be graduating from college, that this country will have the highest proportion of college graduates in the world. Now, Barack set this goal because as a -- a generation ago, we were number one in college graduates. But over the past couple of decades, this country has slipped all the way to 12th. We've slipped. And that's unacceptable, and we've all got a lot of work to do to turn that around and get back on top.

The Goal of Higher Education

But Barack didn't just set that goal because it's good for our country. He did it because he knows how important higher education is to all of you as individuals. Because when the year 2020 rolls around, nearly two-thirds of all jobs in this country are going to require some form of training beyond high school. That means whether it's a vocational program, community college, a four-year university, you all are going to need some form of higher education in order to build the kind of lives that you want for yourselves, good careers, to be able to provide for your family.

And that's why the President and Secretary Duncan have been doing everything they can to make sure that kids like you get the best education possible and that you have everything you need to continue your education after high school. They've been fighting to strengthen your schools and to support your teachers. They've been working hard to make college more affordable for all young people in this country no matter where you come from or how much money your parents have. They've been working with parents, teachers, administrators, community leaders all across this country just to help you succeed.

Taking Individual Responsibility

But here's the thing -- and I want you to listen to this -- at the end of the day, no matter what the President does, no matter what your teachers and principals do or whatever is going on in your home or in your neighborhood, the person with the biggest impact on your education is you. It's that simple. It is you, the student. And more than anything else, meeting that 2020 goal is going to take young people like all of you across this country stepping up and taking control of your education.

And that's what we're going to talk about today. We're going to talk about the power that each of you has to commit to your education. We're going to talk about the power that you have to fulfill your potential and unlock opportunities that you can't even begin to imagine for yourselves right now. And when I talk about students needing to take responsibility for their education, I want you all to know that I'm speaking from my own personal life experience.

Like Menbere, growing up, I considered myself pretty lucky. Even though my parents didn't have a lot of money, they never went to college themselves, they had an unwavering belief in the power of education. So they always pushed me and my brother to do whatever it took to succeed in school. So when it came time for me to go to high school, they encouraged me to enroll in one of the best schools in Chicago. It was a school a lot like this one.

And listening to Menbere's story, it was so similar, because my school was way across the other side of the city from where I lived. So at 6:00 a.m. every morning, I had to get on a city bus and ride for an hour, sometimes more, just to get to school. And I was willing to do that because I was willing to do whatever it took for me to go to college.

I set my sights high. I decided I was going to Princeton. But I quickly realized that for me, a kid like me, getting into Princeton wasn't just going to happen on its own. See I went to a great school, but at my school we had so many kids, so few guidance counselors, they were dealing with hundreds of students so they didn't always have much time to help me personally get my applications together. Plus, I knew I couldn't afford to go on a bunch of college visits. I couldn't hire a personal tutor. I couldn't enroll in SAT prep classes. We didn't have the money.

And then -- get this -- some of my teachers straight up told me that I was setting my sights too high. They told me I was never going to get into a school like Princeton. I still hear that doubt ringing in my head. So it was clear to me that nobody was going

Notes

to take my hand and lead me to where I needed to go. nstead, it was going to be up to me to reach my goal. I would have to chart my own course. And I knew that the first thing I needed to do was have the strongest academic record possible.

So I worked hard to get the best grades I could in all of my classes. I got involved in leadership opportunities in school where I developed close relationships with some of my teachers and administrators. I knew I needed to present very solid and thoughtful college applications, so I stayed up late, got up early in the morning to work on my essays and personal statements. I knew my parents would not be able to pay for all of my tuition, so I made sure that I applied for financial aid on time. That FAFSA form was my best friend. I knew the deadlines, everything.

Most importantly, when I encountered doubters, when people told me I wasn't going to cut it, I didn't let that stop me -- in fact, I did the opposite. I used that negativity to fuel me, to keep me going. And at the end, I got into Princeton, and that was one of the proudest days of my life.

But getting into Princeton was only the beginning. Graduating from Princeton was my ultimate goal. So I had to start all over again, developing and executing a plan that would lead me to my goal. And of course, I struggled a little bit. I had to work hard, again, to find a base of friends and build a community of support for myself in this Ivy League University.

I remember as a freshman I mistakenly rolled into a class that was meant for juniors and seniors. And there were times when I felt like I could barely keep my head above water. But through it all, I kept that college diploma as my **North Star**. And four years later, I reached that goal, and then I went on to build a life I never could have imagined for myself.

I went to law school, became a lawyer. I've been a vice president for a hospital. I've been the head of a nonprofit organization. And I am here today because I want you to know that my story can be your story. The details might be a little different, but let me tell you, so many of the challenges and the triumphs will be just the same.

You might be dreaming of becoming a doctor or a teacher; maybe a mechanic or a software designer. Or you might not know what you want to do right now -- and that's fine. But no matter what path you choose, no matter what dreams you have, you have got to do whatever it takes to continue your education after high school -- again, whether that's going to community college, getting a technical certificate, or completing a training opportunity, or going off to a four-year college.

And once you've completed your education, you will have the foundation you need to build a successful life. That's how me, that's how Menbere, that's how so many other students have overcome adversities to reach our goals.

Roger Sanchez

There's another young man, Roger Sanchez. He is another example of a CHEC alum who is working toward his North Star goal.

Notes

In fifth grade, Roger came to the United States from the Dominican Republic to live with his mother. When Roger arrived in America, he could barely speak a word of English. He often couldn't understand anything his teachers were saying, so he decided to put a piece of paper in his pocket so he could jot down all the new words he heard, and then he'd ask his friends and teachers to translate for him.

He went to the library and poured through books and videos and cassettes to help teach himself English. And after all those hours of studying and practicing, Roger arrived here at Bell ready to thrive. And every day, he put the same effort into his classes that he put into learning English. He joined the baseball, the football teams. He helped found your Global Kids Club so that students could discuss world issues. And last spring, he graduated with nearly a 4.0 GPA.

And today, Roger is a freshman at American University. He's majoring in international relations, and he also volunteers as a mentor. He's paying it forward. He's helping high school students just like all of you with their college applications and essays. And I had a chance to meet Roger, who's here today, and I'd like to -- Roger, can you stand up if you're in the audience so we can give you a round of applause? We're so proud of you. There Roger is. (Applause.) Congratulations.

Your Attitude Defines Your Future

So every day, students like Menbere and Roger and all of you are proving that it is not your circumstance that define your future -- it's your attitude. It's your commitment. You decide how high you set your goals. You decide how hard you're going to work for those goals. You decide how you're going to respond when something doesn't go your way.

And here's the thing: Studies show that those kinds of skills -- skills like grit, determination, skills like optimism and resilience -- those skills can be just as important as your test scores or your grade scores -- or your grades. And so many of you already have those skills because of everything you've already overcome in your lives.

Maybe you've had problems at home and you've had to step up, take on extra responsibilities for your family. Maybe you come from a tough neighborhood, and you've been surrounded by things like violence and drugs. Maybe one of your parents has lost a job and you've had to struggle just to make it here today.

One of the most important things you all must understand about yourselves is that those experiences are not weaknesses. They're not something to be ashamed of. Experiences like those can make you stronger and more determined. They can teach you all kinds of skills that you could never learn in a classroom -- the skills that will lead you to success anywhere in life. But first, you've got to apply those skills toward getting an education.

Believe in Yourself and Study Hard Regardless of Obstacles

So what does that mean? That means, first and foremost, believing in yourselves no matter what obstacles you face. It means going to class every single day -- that's what I did -- not just showing up, but actually paying attention, taking some notes, asking questions.

It means doing your homework every single night -- I did -- studying hard for every test, even if it's not your favorite subject. It means reaching out to your teachers and counselors and coaches and asking for help whenever you need it. And when you stumble and fall — and I guarantee you, you will, because we all do -- it means picking yourself up and trying again and again and again.

All of that is on you. You've got to own that part of it. You've got to step up as individuals. Because here's the key: If you step up, if you choose to own your future and commit to your education, and if you don't let anything stand in your way until you complete it, then you will not only lead our country to that North Star goal, but you will lead yourselves to whatever future you dream of.

Educational Programs and Opportunities for Students

That is my message for all of you today. And over these next few years, I'm going to continue sharing that message all across the country and all across the world to students just like you. We, with the help of Arne and the President and everyone in this administration, we're going to do everything we can to help connect you to all the resources that are available to help you on your journey -- many resources that weren't around when I was your age.

For example, we're going to tell students about our College Navigator and College Scorecard that can help you find affordable programs that fit your interests, your goals. We also want to make sure that you know about websites like StudentAid.gov, which helps you apply for grants and loans, and also provides you with a year-by-year checklist so you know what you need to be doing to get you to college, or whatever program you need to get to.

But I also believe that this conversation -- it's got to be a two-way conversation. I know that you all have important things to say, you have important questions that you deserve answers to, and that that's why I want to make sure that I continue to hear your stories as well as talking to you. I want to hear about your dreams. I want to hear about the things you're worried about. I want folks like me and my husband and your teachers and parents, I want you to tell us what we can do to help you get to college and fulfill your dreams.

So that's what we're going to do next. I'm going to step away from the podium, and Secretary Duncan, Menbere, Jeff, and Keshia are going to come back out, and we're going to talk. We're going to ask you some questions, you're going to ask you some questions. We'll listen. I don't want you go be shy, I want you to be relaxed, okay? And we'll talk more about how do we get you to your goals, okay? And hopefully, this conversation here will help students around the country.

http://www.whitehouse.gov/photos-and-video/video/2013/11/12/first-lady-michelle-obama-speaks-power-education Public Domain

Practice the Outline Note Taking Skill Here. Then write a summary of Michelle Obama's The Power of Education Speech

OUTLINE /NOTES

Write a summary of "The Power of Education" by Michelle Obama

Short Answer Questions – Michelle Obama

1. Who is the general audience for this speech? Who did she name as people in the audience to help you predict who is listening to the speech?

2. What is the symbol of the North Star in this speech? Why does Michelle Obama use this symbol for this audience?

3. How does Mrs. Obama use statistics in her speech? Which of Aristotle's three appeals is she employing by using statistics to support her claim in the section "Obama's Vision for Education"

4. Which of the Aristotle's three appeals does Michelle Obama use most in the section "Roger Sanchez"?

Essay Topics

1. Complete a rhetorical analysis of Michelle Obama's speech by dissecting it for Aristotle's three appeals. How does she use pathos, ethos, and logos to persuade her audience to think seriously about education? Where does her speech succeed or fail according to her rhetorical choices.

2. How does Michelle Obama's speech reflect social responsibility? "What would her response be to "Am I my brother's keeper?"

3. President Obama and Mrs. Obama are celebrated for the rhetorical abilities when it comes to winning audiences through speeches. Compare President Barack Obama's 2008 Fathers Day Speech to determine if you see ideas similar to those in Michelle Obama's speech. Go to this link to find Obama's Father's Day Address. http://www.politico.com/news/stories/0608/11094.html.